URBAN VILLAGE

STEPHANIE GRAUMAN WOLF

URBAN
VILLAGE

Population, Community, and

Family Structure in

Germantown, Pennsylvania

1683-1800

PRINCETON UNIVERSITY PRESS

Copyright © 1976 by Princeton University Press
Published by Princeton University Press, Princeton, New Jersey
In the United Kingdom:
Princeton University Press, Guildford, Surrey

ALL RIGHTS RESERVED

Library of Congress Cataloging in Publication Data will
be found on the last printed page of this book

Publication of this book has been aided by the
Andrew W. Mellon Foundation

This book has been composed in Linotype Janson

Printed in the United States of America
by Princeton University Press, Princeton, New Jersey

*For a twentieth-century
Germantown family*

CONTENTS

FIGURES

TABLES

ACKNOWLEDGMENTS

THERE ARE many people to whom I owe a sincere debt of gratitude for aid and encouragement generously offered during the seemingly endless time it has taken to bring this project to fruition. Among these are Mary Dunn, a stimulating teacher and friend, who provided germinal ideas and suggested directions without ever trying to override my own instincts or insights; Caroline Robbins, my first friend and kindest critic in the Bryn Mawr history department; and Philip Greven, Jr., who read the original manuscript and provided valuable constructive criticism. Also much appreciation is due the staffs of the numerous libraries and record repositories throughout the Philadelphia area: Margaret Tinkcom and her staff at the Historical Commission of Philadelphia helped point me in the right direction and cheerfully opened their files and memories; John Daly and Ward Childs at the Philadelphia Archives in City Hall; Dr. Henry Scherer and Dorothy B. Hildenbrand at the Lutheran Theological Seminary in Mount Airy; Marion McLeskey at St. Michael's Lutheran Church in Germantown; Miss Mabel Irle, librarian of the Germantown Historical Society; Laura Reid at the Friends' Department of Records; and the staffs of the Pennsylvania Historical Society, the Presbyterian Historical Society in Philadelphia, the Rare Book Room of the Van Pelt Library at the University of Pennsylvania, and the Friends' Free Library in Germantown. The pictures used are through the courtesy of the Germantown Historical Society.

On a more personal level, thanks to Ann Lunne and Evelyn Major for help with some sticky mathematical points, and to Dagmar Davis and Lotte Porter for help on questions of translation. Nancy W. Hess and Ruth L. Gales offered friendship, kindly criticism, and sensitive suggestions which helped to pinpoint problems and make solutions achievable. My mother, Doris Grauman, was very generous in helping to organize some of the early data. Finally, my husband,

Acknowledgments

Ted, and my children—Deborah, Martha, Jim, Dan, and Becky—proved through their unfailing patience and support how pleasant it could be to be a member of a Germantown family. In addition, Ted and Becky were particularly helpful in the final preparation of the manuscript.

ABBREVIATIONS

AbMMRec.	Records of the Abington Monthly Meeting of Friends
EHR	*Economic History Review*, 2nd Series
FrDR	Friends' Department of Records, Philadelphia
Gen.Mag.	*Magazine of the Pennsylvania Genealogical Society*
GHS	Germantown Historical Society
HSP	Historical Society of Pennsylvania
Pa.Berichte	*Pennsylvanische Berichte*, Christopher Saur's newspaper
Pa.Gaz.	*Pennsylvania Gazette*, an eighteenth-century newspaper
Pa.Ger.	*Proceedings and Addresses of the Pennsylvania German Society*
PHC	Philadelphia Historical Commission, City Hall
Phila.Arch.	Philadelphia Archives, City Hall
PMHB	*Pennsylvania Magazine of History and Biography*
QS Rec.	Records of the Court of Quarter Sessions, Philadelphia Archives
Ref.Ch.Consis. Rec.	Consistory Records of the Reformed Church of Germantown, 1750-1829
Ref.Ch.Rec.	Records of the Reformed Church of Germantown, Market Square
St.M.Rec.	Records of St. Michael's Lutheran Church, Germantown
WB	Will Books, Department of Wills, Philadelphia City Hall
WMQ	*William and Mary Quarterly*, 3rd Series

URBAN VILLAGE

INTRODUCTION

In 1954 a group of scholars comprising a Committee on Historiography issued a provocative report for the Social Science Research Council. Bulletin #64, as it is known, began by defining history as one of the social sciences, but one that must maintain a particularly flexible set of goals, since "the problems that historians recognize and regard as 'basic' vary from generation to generation."[1] It then suggested that the relevant questions to be asked of the past by historians of the second half of the twentieth century might be those of the other social sciences—anthropology, sociology, demography, and social psychology, as well as the more familiar (to historians) disciplines of political science and economics.

Bulletin #64 sidestepped the grand philosophical problems of positivism and relativism, and rejected large sweeping explanations of historic change in favor of monographic studies of particular aspects of human behavior and interrelationships in time. Among the concepts developed within the social sciences that the Committee thought might prove most fruitful for historians were those of the sociologist. The focus on roles, institutions, and social structure, the study of human ecology, population, and urbanology could surely "help the historian to ask more pertinent questions of his data,"[2] and at the same time furnish historical perspective for the understanding of the problems of the present.

In addition to adopting much of the conceptual framework of the other social disciplines, the Committee recommended the adoption of much of their methodology as well. It was suggested that the historian choose an hypothesis and test it by seeking appropriate documentation, rather than follow the more traditional method of starting with a

[1] *The Social Sciences in Historical Study: A Report of the Committee on Historiography*, Bulletin #64, New York, 1954, p. 23.
[2] Ibid., p. 107.

3

collection of sources and seeing where they led. The skills required for handling materials and for testing working hypotheses included mathematical calculation and techniques of statistical verification. The technique of sampling, familiar to the social scientist, was found to have much to offer the historical investigator since he is involuntarily forced to work with material that is never more than a sample.

Finally, the members of the Committee on Historiography regretted that "in the field of American history . . . the past fifty years of rapid progress in the development of social science methods and hypotheses have had surprisingly little effect on historical interests, content, or forms of synthesis."[3] They looked forward to the time when periodization would be recognized as purely arbitrary if it dealt only with "historic events" rather than underlying social factors.

Actually, the use of the statistical methods as an additional tool for the historian was already being applied to the solving of traditional problems, especially in such well-established fields as political history.[4] But the concepts of the social disciplines were not as easily assimilated. The framework that subordinated or ignored the great events of the time in favor of studying the internal forces that held people together or pulled them apart; the bypassing of the great man in order to study how the average individual lived and felt; the demotion of studying philosophies of education in favor of discovering what percentage of which population could actually read or write—it took over a decade of gradual familiarization with other fields before historians were comfortable with the new approach and at ease in

---

[3] Ibid., p. 157.

[4] See, for example, the use of statistics in the service of political history by Robert E. Brown in *Middle Class Democracy and the Revolution in Massachusetts, 1691-1780*, Ithaca, N.Y., 1955, and the criticism of his technique by a younger historian as the use of statistics became surer—John Cary, "Statistical Method and the Brown Thesis on Colonial Democracy," *WMQ*, 20 (1963).

handling the scientific methods involved.[5] Perhaps the growing availability of the computer (a scarcely considered experimental research tool at the time the Bulletin was written) and its fascination for the children of the age of electronic technology have made the transition easier. Perhaps it is the growing desire (even on the part of those who live in the "ivory tower") to understand the crises of modern mass society—overpopulation, the breakdown of the family, the deterioration of the city and the environment, the loneliness of the individual—that is making almost a fad of the new approach. There may even be in it an element of scholarly greed, for in the style of the seventies where the framework is sociological and the method largely statistical, whole new worlds of source material are opened for the historian. Once the property of genealogists and antiquarians, the church registers, contributor lists, tombstone inscriptions, and family trees become code-numbered data for the statistician, with or without computer.

Studies of past societies that seek to explore the internal structure and mechanisms of individual, family, and community life are the newest example of history as a social science, relying heavily on modern sociological monographs for form and on demographic records for source material.[6] The most complete illustration of this kind of work in the study of colonial America is *Four Generations* by Philip Greven. In his preface Greven sets forth the common convictions of the new generation of historians in regard to local history: "historians must seek to explore the basic structure and character of society through close, detailed

[5] Sumner C. Powell, *Puritan Village: The Formation of a New England Town*, rpt. New York, 1965, gathered the material but failed to analyze it in modern terms.

[6] This new development, coming to be known as cliometrics (unfortunately for the elegance of the English language), has created the opportunity for a great deal of controversial revision, particularly in the field of nineteenth-century American history. The most notable example to date is probably *Time on The Cross*, 2 vols., Boston, 1974, by Robert Fogel and Stanley Engerman.

examinations of the experiences of individuals, families and groups in particular communities and localities."[7] He makes use of the family reconstitution forms of the Cambridge group of demographers to build complete genealogical histories of twenty-eight colonial families for a century and a half.[8] Using this material, together with the more general vital statistics for aggregate work,[9] and combining these with probate records, deeds, and other town holdings, Greven studies, among other things, the effects of birth, marriage, and death on the individual family and the community, the relationship of families to the land, and the control exercised by one generation over another. Kenneth Lockridge uses similar source material, but examines the first hundred years of Dedham, Massachusetts from the point of view of a political scientist, emphasizing community, rather than family, structure.[10]

Other studies of New England towns in these new veins are continuing to appear in books and journals and contribute to a deeper and better understanding of the whole region.[11] In part, the history of this area is adaptable to such

[7] Philip J. Greven, Jr., *Four Generations: Population, Land and Family in Colonial Andover, Massachusetts*, Ithaca, N.Y., 1970, p. viii.

[8] For an explanation of the Cambridge Group for the History of Population and Social Structure, see E. A. Wrigley, ed., *An Introduction to English Historical Demography: From the Sixteenth to the Nineteenth Century*, London, 1966. Family reconstitution is discussed by Wrigley in chapter 4, pp. 96-159. (Hereafter cited as *EHD*.)

[9] Ibid., especially chapter 3, "Exploitation of Anglican Parish Registers by Aggregative Analysis," by D.E.C. Eversley. See also Philip J. Greven, Jr., "Family Structure in Seventeenth Century Andover, Massachusetts," *WMQ*, 23 (1966), pp. 234-256.

[10] Kenneth A. Lockridge, *A New England Town, The First Hundred Years: Dedham, Massachusetts, 1636-1736*, New York, 1970. Journal articles using the social science approach to history include Richard Dunn, "The Barbados Census of 1680: Profile of the Richest Colony in English America," *WMQ*, 26 (1969) and Robert Gough, "Notes on the Pennsylvania Revolutionaries of 1776," *PMHB*, 96 (1972).

[11] Charles S. Grant, *Democracy in the Connecticut Frontier Town of Kent*, New York, 1961; Michael Zuckerman, *Peaceable Kingdoms:*

studies because of its early settlement and its consequent isolation during formative generations, the homogeneity of its population, which makes more secure generalization possible, and the excellent records and vital statistics kept by many of the towns. Anyone engaged in this kind of research cannot help but envy Greven his "full vital statistics" for Andover from 1650 to 1800.

The multiplicity of ethnic backgrounds and community models found in the Middle Colonies makes generalization a risky business. The closest attempt to date is James Lemon's historical geography, *Best Poor Man's Country*, which probes the relationship and attachment of man to land in early southeastern Pennsylvania.[12] Many, many local studies must be put together before meaningful patterns can be traced. Yet the very heterogeneity and unplanned development of the area speak directly to the later growth of the country at large. Twentieth-century urban America with its polyglot population, with the breakdown of family and community social patterns bears little resemblance to the carefully ordered, homogeneous towns of seventeenth- and eighteenth-century Massachusetts. The roots of today's problems are usually traced no further back than the nineteenth-century twin bursts of industrialization and large-

---

New England Towns in the Eighteenth Century, New York, 1970; J. M. Bumsted and James Lemon, "New Approaches in Early American Studies: The Local Community in New England," *Social History* II (1968); John Demos, "Families in Colonial Bristol, Rhode Island: An Exercise in Historical Demography," *WMQ*, 25 (1968); and John Demos, *A Little Commonwealth: Family Life in Plymouth Colony*, New York, 1970. This last is interesting for its relation to the field of social psychology, although unfortunately it does not make quantitative use of its data.

[12] James T. Lemon, *The Best Poor Man's Country: A Geographical Study of Early Southeastern Pennsylvania*, Baltimore, 1972. Lemon's professional orientation is as a geographer rather than a historian, but his work is tremendously useful for its exploration of social concepts related to the land, particularly since it is a pioneer study for Pennsylvania.

scale immigration, but it may be that enough careful exploration of the social structure of Middle Colony town and family culture in the eighteenth century will isolate some colonial origins of these social processes.[13]

To make a start in this direction, Germantown, Pennsylvania has been selected to serve as a case in point. The choice was neither random nor arbitrary, for this is a town around which a particularly inaccurate and tenacious myth of eighteenth-century life has grown. In addition, Germantown's reputation as one of the better-known battlefields of the Revolution has given the false picture a greater celebrity than it might otherwise possess. The myth seems to be based partially on nineteenth-century observations of rural Pennsylvania Dutch life-styles and a superimposition of them onto the history of Germantown; and partially on grandmother and grandfather reminiscences of a time that seemed stable and close knit, in comparison to the vastly different way of life brought about by the introduction of the railroad and the factory system. The myth perpetuated a notion of a "quaint old Germantown," a place which "after more than a century of growth and development . . . remained a straggling village of a few Hundred inhabitants, most of them still German in language and characteristics."[14] It also described a bucolic family life of long-settled residence in one place and attachment to the land by large, extended family groups. Lockridge has said that it is almost hopeless and probably pointless for the historian to try to shatter popular American myths of this nature, and perhaps he is

[13] In a somewhat different context, Sam Bass Warner, Jr., *The Private City: Philadelphia in Three Periods of its Growth*, Philadelphia, 1968, has used the social government of Philadelphia colonial life as the starting point of his analysis of American urban crises. His methods are quantitative.

[14] Naaman Keyser et al., *History of Old Germantown: With a Description of Its Settlement and Some Account of Its Important Persons, Buildings and Places Connected With Its Development*, Germantown, 1907, p. 20.

right.[15] But it is the multitude of little myths, repeated over and over, that gives credence to the myth on a grand scale of a colonial Eden of selfless individuals, convivial families, helpful neighbors, and friendly villages. If enough of the individual myths are reexamined with the techniques of the modern social sciences (which allow for quantifiable results more acceptable to the science-oriented mind of the twentieth century), it may be possible to expose a more accurate vision of the past and, therefore, a more useful tool with which to shape the future.

Looking beyond the mythological description of Germantown, one finds at once an active, industrious community, possessed of many attributes that make it especially useful for exploring the roots of urban society. The character of the town was determined from the very beginning by a highly heterogeneous population of great mobility, which was not primarily engaged in agriculture. There were five active religious groups—Quakers, Lutherans, Reformed, Mennonites, and Dunkards—to say nothing of free thinkers, Separatists, Schwenkfelders, the Hermits of the Wissahickon, and a substantial minority who were totally unchurched. There was considerable representation of at least three different nationalities—German, Dutch, and English—in addition to a sprinkling of Huguenots, Swiss, Swedes, Irish, and Blacks. The term "German" is in itself misleading, since it masks a wide divergence of backgrounds, beliefs, and practices among the settlers from the dozens of semi-autonomous little German-speaking states of seventeenth-century Europe. Mobility was fostered not only by this lack of central tendency but also by the lack of isolation, physical or psychological, of its residents. Proximity to Philadelphia and connections with up-country relatives both played a role in the cosmopolitan air of Germantown.

The earliest documents show that the bent of the community was industrial rather than agricultural; a letter writ-

---

[15] Lockridge, *A New England Town*, p. xi.

ten in 1684 describes the people of Germantown a year after its founding as "mostly linen weavers . . . not too well skilled in the culture of the ground."[16] One of the first land rental agreements, made in June 1683, included with fifty acres of land the promise "to lend him a Linnen weaving stool with three combs, and he shall have said weaving stool for two years . . . and for this Jan Lensen shall teach my son Leonard in one year the art of weaving, and Leonard shall be bound to weave faithfully during said year."[17] Throughout the eighteenth century, Germantown was the only area in Philadelphia County, beyond the City proper and its adjacent districts of Northern Liberties (east) and Southwark, that listed people by occupation; at no time did the number of those involved in agriculture make up a majority of the Germantown population.

The size of Germantown and the amount of surviving data pertaining to it are other factors that make it a good choice for a sociological study of this sort. There is abundant source material although it is marred by frustrating gaps in basic demographic data. Statistical material must frequently be excavated from rather indirect evidence, since systematic records were not kept for this area until the nineteenth century. For example, no provision was made for registering births in Philadelphia and vicinity until 1819, and the act passed at that time did not include German-

[16] Julius Friedrich Sachse, *Letters Relating to the Settlement of Germantown, in Pennsylvania, 1683-4, From the Könneken Manuscript in the Ministerial-Archiv of Lübeck*, limited edition of 25 copies, privately printed by the author: Philadelphia, 1903. This volume contains translations of four letters out of twelve in the original collection. Available at the Friends' Free Library, Germantown, pp. 15-16.

[17] Samuel W. Pennypacker, "The Settlement of Germantown, Pennsylvania and the Beginning of German Immigration to North America," *Pennsylvania: The German Influence in its Settlement and Development: A Narrative and Critical History*, Part IV; *Pa.Ger.*, IX (1898), pp. 56-57. Early Crefeld agreement between Jan Streepers and Jan Lensen.

town.[18] While the minutes of the Germantown Council provide that a vital statistics record be kept (in English) from 1695, no record ever appears to have been kept in any language.[19] Still, a good proportion of eighteenth-century births as well as marriages and burials can be recovered from church registers, family genealogies, and the like. Deeds and tax lists provide much useful information, despite gaping holes in the latter around the middle of the century. Minutes, accounts, and contributor lists for the various religious and civic organizations within the community are abundant after 1750 and become even more so following the Revolution. Newspapers, especially in their advertising notices, contain much information about Germantown.

Least satisfactory are colony and county records (with the exception of tax returns) since, for the most part, these do not list Germantown separately but only as part of Philadelphia County. Wills, inventories, and accounts can be separated because they regularly included the place of the writer's residence, but much of the court material is useless for general purposes. Only those Germantowners with unique names or problems that were already known to the historian can be extracted from them. For the same reason, it is also difficult to determine political participation of Germantowners in the affairs of the colony from election returns or other material in the Pennsylvania Archives.

Still, the historian has an advantage over the social scientist in that he can lengthen his time span to make up for specific shortcomings in any period of his material. In fact, the focus of interest in a historical study should be "the

[18] C. S. Miller, *A Digest of the Ordinances of the Corporation of the City of Phila[d] and of the Acts of Assembly Relating Thereto,* Philadelphia, 1828, Act of Assembly, March 27, 1819.

[19] The Generall Court Book of the Corporation of Germantown oder Raths-Buch der Germantownischen Gemeinde angefangen den 2ten tag des 4ten monats Anno 1691, January 25, 1694/5. This manuscript is located at the HSP, Philadelphia. (Hereafter cited as Raths-Buch.)

analysis of change over time"[20] rather than the static description of an unchanging culture at a given moment. From a group of 13 families and a total population of 33 persons in 1683,[21] Germantown had grown to a community of 556 families containing almost 3,000 individuals by 1790.[22] While this is a large number of people to deal with over the century, it helped to insure that, despite the haphazard nature of record taking and record preserving in Pennsylvania, a large enough sample was obtained to allow for a statistical approach that was not skewed too far by error or incompleteness. On the other hand, it was small enough to be fairly representative and not to fall into the special category of "metropolis," where every example—Philadelphia, New York, Boston—is a case unto itself.[23]

Germantown seemed throughout the eighteenth century on the brink of becoming an important little city in its own right. It had been founded in 1683 by Francis Daniel Pastorius, legal representative of the German-based Frankfort Land Company, and by a group of Dutch Quakers who had also bought land from William Penn.[24] Because of confusion

[20] Bulletin #64, p. 22.

[21] Keyser, *Germantown*, p. 29.

[22] *Heads of Families: At the First Census of the United States Taken in the Year 1790*, Washington, D.C., 1908, Volume for Pennsylvania, pp. 195-197.

[23] For classification of towns by size and function, see James T. Lemon, "Urbanization and the Development of Eighteenth Century South East Pennsylvania and Adjacent Delaware," *WMQ*, 24 (1967), pp. 504-506.

[24] There are several secondary sources that detail the history of Germantown from the time of its founding to the twentieth century, and some that deal specifically with the colonial period. Keyser, *Germantown*, in fact, begins with the development of the Germanic tribes in the Rhine valley and the Roman invasion. He also includes copies of original source material that seems to be available nowhere else. The most modern and best of the local histories is also the briefest: Harry M. and Margaret B. Tinkcom and Grant Miles Simon, *Historic Germantown: From the Founding to the Early Part of the Nineteenth Century: A Survey of the German Township*, Philadelphia, 1955.

in the terms of sale, instead of each group receiving 25,000 acres, the two claimants together received 5,700 acres of what became the Germantownship, with a promise of the rest to be laid out later, further up-country. In addition, Pastorius, who was influential as a friend of Thomas Lloyd and of the proprietor himself, acquired, on behalf of the Frankfort Company, three lots in the City between Front and 4th streets and 300 acres in the Liberties.

The earliest and most prominent of the heavily German settlements of Pennsylvania, Germantown received contemporary fame and reputation as the scene of many important novelties. The first non-English Quaker meeting was established there, with Pastorius as its leader;[25] in 1688 it issued the first protest against slavery to originate in the colonies. In 1691 William Penn granted Germantown a charter for a closed corporation borough with the power to make ordinances, impose fines, admit citizens, and hold a court and market. In 1707 this brief experiment in government came to an end as the Queen's Attorney permanently adjourned the local Court of Record, and Germantown became a township within the county of Philadelphia. As a manufacturing center, Germantown was the site of the first paper mill in the colonies and the first grist mill in Philadelphia. The first American Bible was printed in Germantown (in German) by Christopher Saur, and the contemporary reputation of the town's importance was probably exaggerated among Germans in Europe and in the colonies because it was the location of Saur's German newspaper.

After the middle of the century, the outside world had

[25] There was some controversy in the late nineteenth century over whether the early settlers of Germantown were Mennonites or Quakers. See Daniel Cassel, *History of the Mennonites*, Philadelphia, 1888. Scholars, even Mennonite ones, no longer accept this, as is shown in the article by H. S. Bender, "Germantown (Pennsylvania) Mennonite Settlement," *The Mennonite Encyclopedia: A Comprehensive Reference Work on the Anabaptist-Mennonite Movement*, Scottdale, Pa., 1956, II, 482-483.

increasing impact on the style and development of Germantown. The size of the town, as measured by the number of its houses, more than tripled between 1745 and 1758, jumping from 100 to 350,[26] reflecting not only the enormous upsurge of German immigration during this period,[27] but also the growing popularity of Germantown as a summer residence for city folk. This latter circumstance was to have a profound effect on the civic and social structure of the town, and in the end, perhaps, on its very survival as an independent community. For several decades, beginning in the 1740s, civic life blossomed—churches, schools, and a market were built; library and fire companies were organized; numerous taverns opened; and regular stages ran to Philadelphia and to Bethlehem. As more strangers passed through and stopped over in Germantown, some of them, alas, eternally, a potter's field had to be provided.

The yellow fever epidemic that swept Philadelphia in 1793 marked the beginning of yet another boom in Germantown. Governor Mifflin of Pennsylvania and President Washington of the United States both moved there to be

[26] These numbers are largely traditional, but appear probable enough. They are quoted in all the secondary sources, their basis appearing to be: for the first, a quotation from Zimmermann, the surveyor (Keyser, *Germantown*, p. 110) and for the second, a letter from the Reverend Israel Acrelius, provost of the Swedish churches, quoted by Edward W. Hocker, *Germantown, 1683-1933: The Record that a Pennsylvania Community had Achieved in the Course of 250 Years: Being a History of the People of Germantown, Mount Airy and Chestnut Hill*, Germantown, 1933, p. 78.

[27] Daniel I. Rupp, *A Collection of Upwards of 30,000 Names of German, Swiss, Dutch, French and Other Immigrants in Pennsylvania From 1727 to 1776*, Philadelphia, 1876. Comparative work done on these lists of ships and passengers shows that between 1749 and 1756, when immigration was halted for a time because of the French and English wars, an average of seventeen immigrant ships, carrying over 1,000 males over sixteen, and more than twice that many in total passengers, landed per year in Philadelphia. With the exceptions of 1732, 1738, 1764, and 1773, no other period saw as many as ten ships per year, nor did the average number of males and passengers even approach these figures.

on healthy, high ground, and state and national business was conducted on Market Square. The town became so crowded that Thomas Jefferson and James Madison could scarcely find accommodations.[28] There was even a movement by local boosters to have Germantown designated the permanent capital of the young nation, although, of course, nothing came of it. Many who found the town pleasant, however, continued to return summer after summer, and as a result, when yellow fever again plagued Philadelphia in the summer and fall of the years 1797, 1798, and 1799, city businesses moved to Germantown to set up branches, many of which began as temporary shops but evolved into year-round establishments.[29] Former summer people began to list Germantown as their permanent address, commuting to the city almost daily to transact their business. Then, in 1798, this wealthy group of "newcomers" engineered the passage of a turnpike bill in the state legislature, which turned the whole community irrevocably into a suburb of its large, metropolitan neighbor.[30] While industrialization and population continued to increase, community structure, never strong, quietly passed away.

For the purpose of extracting as much material as possible

[28] Thomas Jefferson in a letter to James Madison, November 1, 1793. Charles F. Jenkins, *The Guide Book to Historic Germantown: Prepared for the Site and Relic Society*, Germantown, 1904, p. 49.

[29] No less than sixty-one businesses and public offices advertised their removal to Germantown during these years. Based on a count from the *Pa.Gaz.*, the *U.S. Gazette, Claypoole's Advertiser*, and the *Aurora and General Advertiser*, all Pennsylvania newspapers of the period. Most of the studies of newspaper items found here have come from an invaluable, though unsorted, typescript collection at the GHS. Charles F. Jenkins, "Newspaper Items Relating to Germantown: Historical and Genealogical," unpublished typescript, 1934. (Hereafter cited as Jenkins, "News.")

[30] See the *Pa.Gaz.* during 1797 and early 1798 for reports of Germantown agitation over the turnpike: on March 28, 1798 the passage of the bill was reported; on April 5, 1798, its enactment; on April 18, 1798, the opening of the subscription books and the names of the commissioners.

from the surviving data, and with the hope of serving as some kind of model for methods of exploiting it, the scope of this investigation has not been narrowed by the presentation of a limited thesis or tightly reasoned argument in any predetermined direction. Rather, there is an attempt to consider from as many angles as possible, and as fully as possible, the nature and dynamics of an eighteenth-century Middle Colony township and the families that inhabit it. The constant influences, which seem to affect Germantown in all aspects of its development, are those of the mobility and heterogeneity of its population; diversity and fluidity run like a bright red thread throughout the narrative, even to the extent of regulating the nature and availability of the source material. The hand of the past is never really dead! In addition, there are three yardsticks that have been used to place the Germantown experience within the larger sociological framework: the continuum along which a society advances from rural to urban; the line along which the community's institutions are measured in terms of traditional and communal, or associational and legalistic; and the scale on which family structures can be seen to be nuclear, extended, or somewhere in between. It is to these measures, and to the relationship between them, that one must look to begin to discover the essential nature of social life in an eighteenth-century community.

PART I

THE URBAN VILLAGE

"Village," "town," "city"—all words that define gatherings of human individuals and families into communities. In pragmatic terms they form a kind of continuum from the simplest rural settlement, a few houses gathered at a crossroad, to the largest, most sophisticated urban complex of highly developed specialists and intricately structured institutions. It is easy enough to place specific communities at either end of the continuum—no one doubts, for instance, that New York is a city. In between, it is more difficult to determine at what point a village becomes a town, or a town a city. There is not even any general agreement among urbanologists on a complete list of criteria to mark the "urbanity" of a community.[1]

To begin at the rural end of the scale. Mumford defines the village in poetic terms as "a small cluster of families, from half a dozen to threescore. . . . Speaking the same tongue, meeting together under the same tree or in the shadow of the same upstanding stone, walking along the footway trodden by their cattle, each family follows the same way of life and participates in the same labors. If there is any division of labor, it is of the most rudimentary kind, determined more by age and strength than vocational aptitude."[2] Here then are the basic criteria: a small, homogene-

---

[1] For a technical, sociological discussion of this topic, see Paul K. Hatt and Albert J. Reiss, Jr., eds., *Cities and Society: The Revised Reader in Urban Sociology*, Glencoe, Ill., 1959. One point of view is presented by Horace Miner, "Folk-Urban Continuum," pp. 22-34. A contrasting opinion appears in Owen Dudley Duncan, "Community Size and the Rural-Urban Continuum," pp. 35-45, where the whole idea of a continuum is questioned.

[2] Lewis Mumford, *The City in History: Its Origins, Its Transformations, and Its Prospects*, New York, 1961, p. 18.

ous, agricultural community, lacking any real divisions of class or occupation and ruled by a traditional hierarchy made up of the village elders. As a modern example of this form, the village of Ashworthy, in England, is a good choice.[3] With a population of 520, spread largely in isolated farms over a fourteen-square-mile area, Ashworthy centers on a Nonconformist chapel. There are two general stores, a butcher shop, a bakery, an inn, a post office, a draper's shop, and two garages. Resident craftsmen include a cobbler, a smith, two tailors, four carpenters, and a wheelwright. For transportation, there are a hauling company for produce, a bus, and a taxi. To serve the people, there are two churches and ministers and a village school with two teachers for 50 children up to eleven years old. There is a village hall for social organizations to meet in. Ashworthy has no doctors, no barbers, no lawyers, and no bank. Forty-seven percent of the population have their homes and livelihoods completely on the farm while another 34 percent are farm workers and craftsmen or tradesmen who supply services to farmers.

It is obvious that it takes more than mere numbers to change a village into a city; density, as related to the location of the community in time and space is one factor, but by no means the only one. A city is really the opposite of a village in many ways—large, heterogeneous, divorced from the soil, characterized by division of labor and class, and often ruled by the young (or at least not the most elderly), nontraditionally oriented members of the upper class.[4] It offers a permanent meeting place for a variety of

---

[3] W. M. Williams, *A West County Village, Ashworthy: Family, Kinship, and Land*, Darlington Hall Studies in Rural Sociology, London, 1963. This study is an excellent model for applying sociological concepts to specific examples. Many of his insights are useful in a historical context, and many of his methods are admirably adaptable to the historian and the kinds of materials he has available.

[4] A full discussion of the criteria for judging what makes a city, with an historiographical essay on the subject, may be found in

Dear
Book Reviewer:

We are happy to send you this book for review. Two copies of any mention of it which appears in your publication will be appreciated.

publication date: 1977

price: 19.50

Cordially,

Marcia E. Brubeck

Publicity Manager

Princeton University Press

Princeton, New Jersey 08540

races and cultures; it provides openings for strangers and outsiders. The development of writing and arithmetic is encouraged as the transference of culture in the urban setting requires a written record. The segregated economic functions and social roles in a community where occupational specialization is the rule, lead to segregated living patterns and simultaneous division between rich and poor.[5] Government tends to be legalistic and formalized, based on current social situations rather than on personal and traditional factors. Lemon summarizes these variables of social and economic change, which contribute to urbanization, as population growth, public administration, an increasing degree of economic elaboration especially in the commercial sector, the desire of people to live "where the action is," and a changing standard of living.[6]

For the purposes of the colonial historian, a further distinction must be made within the urban framework. The kind of rationalized economic functions relating to large-scale manufacturing found in the modern industrial city certainly form no part of the early American experience. But there are many preindustrial cities still existing in the twentieth century, and their characteristic manner of functioning may be used as a guidepost to the past.[7] These cities have in common an emphasis on exchange and trade, with the market at the center. Manufacturing does exist, but it is confined to the craft level (goods made to order rather than for stock). Furthermore, it is scattered throughout the community and is associated with the residence of the worker rather than being segregated in a separate business district. This being so, the finer houses belonging to more important and higher-class craftsmen are centrally located, while the

---

Emrys Jones, *Towns and Cities*, rpt. New York, 1970, chapter 1, "What is a Town?"

[5] Mumford, pp. 94-114, sets forth many of the sociological consequences of urban development in relation to ancient cities.

[6] Lemon, "Urbanization," *WMQ* (1967), p. 501.

[7] Jones, *Towns*, pp. 39-40.

poorer members of the community are found on the periphery.

Towns are those communities that fall between the two extremes. They share with cities the fact of being basically nonagricultural but lack the mystic "non-material aspects of civilization, together with their manifestation in institutions and monumental architecture."[8] In this sense, eighteenth-century Germantown was probably a town, although it possessed many specific urban attributes to a very high degree; for example, heterogeneity, mobility, and an economic system that included an impressive degree of occupational specialization. In other ways, it hardly seemed more than a village: as will be seen, local government was almost nonexistent, and legislation was largely confined to worries about free-running cows and pigs.[9]

While this odd combination of highly urban and purely village traits in the same community is not a familiar model in western civilization, Jones finds it common in the large town-like centers of precolonial and colonial Africa. He concludes that "although these often had more of the characteristics of a large village, they cannot be denied urban status."[10] There is a common denominator between these African "cities" and the towns of colonial America, in that both are artificial population centers in the midst of very thinly settled areas, bearing little organic connection to their surroundings. It may be, therefore, that this pattern of a community that exhibits tendencies from both ends of the urban-rural continuum, rather than from some midpoint along the line, as westerners are conditioned to think of it, is more characteristic of colonial settlements than has generally been recognized. A study of the structure of German-

---

[8] Ibid., p. 5.

[9] Pennypacker, *Pa.Ger.*, IX, pp. 319-339. While these ordinances were early, stray cows were still a major item of Germantown news as late as the 1790s. For example, *Pa.Gaz.*, November 4, 1795; May 21, 1797.

[10] Jones, *Towns*, p. 34.

town and its patterns of growth could help to provide a general model for small city development in frontier situations in which European conditions cannot be expected to be present, despite the origin of the settlers. The bases for traditional communities are lacking; the influential factors are heterogeneity, mobility, and a need for the trade and manufacturing facilities of an urban area. However the inhabitants see themselves, they are creating an urban atmosphere and not the village situation of their backgrounds. To the European eyes of eighteenth-century Pennsylvanians, Germantown was a village, despite Pastorius's vision of a city in the wilderness and his attempt to popularize the name "Germanopolis" for the community.[11] Certainly in comparison to nearby Philadelphia, Germantown lacked both density and a sophisticated life-style. Yet, much of its sociology was, indeed, distinctly urban, and its inhabitants unconsciously underscored this character when they erected and maintained for generations a market building that was not really needed or used.[12] Although never successful and frequently abandoned, the Germantown market stood as an ancient urban symbol of a community's ability to accumulate a surplus.[13]

[11] Keyser, *Germantown*, p. 43.

[12] Margaret Tinkcom, "Germantown's Market Square," Report for Colonial Germantown, Inc., unpublished, 1966.

[13] Jones, *Towns*, pp. 19-20.

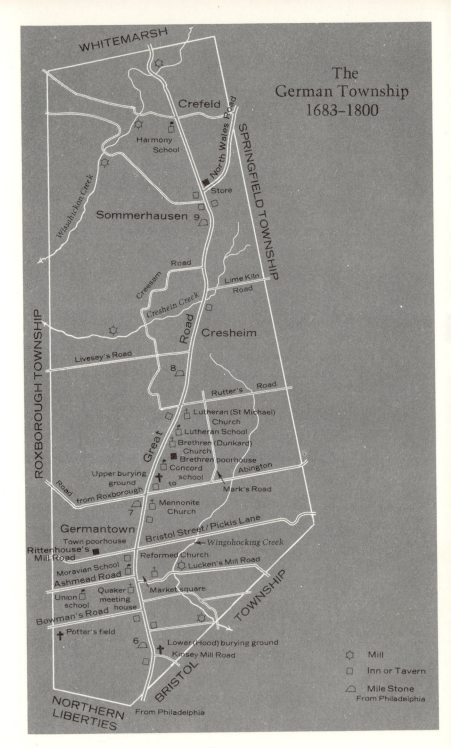

FIGURE 1

CHAPTER 1

Profile and Population of
An Urban Village

THE German Township as surveyed on December 29, 1687 and as indicated by Thomas Holme on his map of Pennsylvania, was a 5,700-acre area (8.81 square miles) lying on high, hilly ground just over 5 miles from the fast-growing city of Philadelphia.[1] It was intended to include four villages, strung along the Main Road for a distance of about 5 miles—Germantown, Cresheim, Sommerhausen, and Crefeld,[2] shown on figure 1. As time went on the whole region, and in fact many parts of the Northern Liberties and Roxborough Township lying outside the borders of the German Township, came to be known simply as "Germantown," reflecting the domination, from the very beginning, of the southernmost village in the township. In the 1790 census the word "township," a more rural term, had disappeared, and the district was called "Germantown Town."[3] Cresheim and Crefeld never really developed at all, although the former name was used occasionally to refer to more rural areas in the middle of the township. Sommerhausen, today called "Chestnut Hill," contained about 100 families

---

[1] A detail of this map, c.1687, which includes Germantown, appears as the frontispiece of John Daly and Allen Weinberg, *Genealogy of Philadelphia County Subdivisions*, 2nd ed., City of Philadelphia, Department of Records, 1966. The original is at the American Philosophical Society.

[2] See figure 1 for place references within the German Township, 1683-1800. A description of eighteenth-century roads may be found on Christian Lehmann's survey map of 1751, in Naaman Keyser, "Old Germantown," *Pa.Ger.*, XVI (1905), between pages 76 and 77. Figure 4 supplies references to other locations in Philadelphia County.

[3] *U.S. Census*, 1790, p. 196.

23

in 1790,[4] yet only 4 signers of the 308 wills recorded from the Germantown area in the eighteenth century refer to themselves as residents of Chestnut Hill. Seventy-five percent describe their residence as Germantown, although this in no way reflects the actual balance of the population.[5]

Geographically, Germantown had both advantages and disadvantages. In 1684 Pastorius described it as positively as possible to encourage settlement: "we have here wholesome pure air, charming springs, streams abounding in fish, fertile ground after it has first been manipulated by strong, assiduous arms, and all kinds of tame and wild animals."[6] It is true that the area was known throughout the eighteenth century for the purity of its air and the beauty of its scenery. During the worst of the yellow fever epidemics, which swept Philadelphia and sent city dwellers crowding into Germantown, there was almost no rise in the death rate as reflected in the burial figures of the various cemeteries. It was said that on a clear day, one could command "an extensive view of the Jerseys, and part of the City of Philadelphia"[7] from the center of Germantown.

On the other hand, the very steepness, which was so picturesque, made it difficult to cultivate the soil, and the dense thickets and heavy deciduous forests required almost superhuman effort to clear. The ground itself was unusually rocky for the area, hampering efforts at farming but providing the distinctive glimmer stone as an easily available and durable construction material. It was undoubtedly these geographical factors, as much as the original intent of the

[4] Based on figures taken from the *U.S. Census*, 1790 by Hannah Roach, "The Back Part of Germantown; A Reconstruction," *Gen. Mag.*, XX (1956), pp. 77-149.

[5] WB, Department of Wills, Philadelphia City Hall Annex, Basement. Books A through X deal with the eighteenth century. Seventeen percent of the remainder refer to themselves as being from Germantownship, and 5 percent as being from Cresheim.

[6] Sachse, *Letters*, Missive #1. Pastorius to his parents, p. 4.

[7] *Pennsylvania Evening Post*, October 29, 1776. Real estate advertisement.

founders and the natural inclination of the settlers, that led Germantown in an urban rather than a rural direction.

While there were plentiful springs to provide a good water supply for a large population and rapid streams to turn mill wheels, there was no navigable water and therefore no ready way to transport goods to market. The importance of this factor, or rather the lack of it, cannot be overestimated in relation to the failure of Germantown to develop as an independent center. Close proximity to Philadelphia and inclusion in its orbit only became important later, when Philadelphia's favored position on the water had given it the power to control the surrounding area. As Mumford put it, "the dynamic component of the city, without which it [cannot continue] to increase in size and scope and productivity . . . is the first efficient means of mass transport, the waterway."[8] Germantown had no such advantage and was forced to rely on a very poor second best in the pre-industrial age—the road.

The Germantown or Great Road was a legend in its own time, if a horror story can be called a legend.[9] There were tales of horses and wagons disappearing completely in its swampy morass during the wet weather, and of residents saddling horses merely to cross the road for a neighborly visit.[10] It required in Pastorius's day, about two hours to travel the road from Germantown to Philadelphia,[11] and by the end of the century the time had not been particularly reduced. The road was crooked, following an old Indian trail which was beaten down by the constant traffic of the early settlers. The soil was "of such a nature that in sum-

[8] Mumford, *City*, p. 71.

[9] The main road, which bisected the township, is variously known as the Germantown Road, the Great Road, the Main Road, or Main Street, the last coming more into use in the nineteenth century.

[10] See, for example, some of the stories in Townsend Ward, "The Germantown Road and its Associations," *PMHB*, 5 (1881) and *PMHB*, 6 (1882).

[11] Sachse, *Letters*, Missive #2. Pastorius to the Frankfort Company, p. 15.

mer it was ground to fine choking dust, while in winter and spring it was almost impassable for wheeled vehicles on account of the mud."[12] Still, in the most literal sense it was the main artery of life blood not only for Germantown but for the later German settlements to the north, for Reading and for Bethlehem.

Ironically, there was one way in which the poor quality of the Great Road played a positive role in the development of Germantown as an urban area, for it made the job of reaching Philadelphia from up-country so great that many rural dwellers had no urge to try. Therefore, "great stores" were opened all along the Germantownship stretch of the road, often in association with an inn, where farmers from the north and west could trade their loads of produce in return for salt, fish, seeds, and other groceries and dry goods.[13] This provided Germantown not only with a grain storage business but also with an active butcher trade for the cutting, curing, and storing of meat. In the 1780 tax returns sixteen butchers represented the largest number of taxables engaged in any trade (not counting farmers or laborers) and ranked fifth in average income on a listing of seventeen different trades.[14]

Crossroads appeared within a couple of years of the founding of the community, leading to the mills on the Wissahickon and the Wingohocking creeks. By 1751 there were fourteen roads to the north or east of Germantown Road and nine to the south or west. In the second half of the century the "inhabitants of Germantown" appeared in Quarter Sessions Court no less than twenty-eight times with

[12] Jenkins, *Guide Book*, p. 27.

[13] Although Lemon does not mention Germantown as a transport town in table 20, *Best Poor Man's Country*, pp. 120-121, his definition of this kind of development on pp. 145-146 fits this description of Germantown quite convincingly.

[14] Tax Assessor's Ledger, Germantown Township, Vol. I, 1780-83; 1785-86, Phila.Arch. (Hereafter cited as 1780 tax list.) August 22, 1780, a Tax for Redeeming Revolutionary War Bills of Credit.

petitions for the opening of new roads.[15] There are also numerous petitions from residents of outlying districts asking for roads into Germantown from Barren Hill or Roxborough or other lesser communities. By 1791 some inhabitants of Roxborough felt obliged to counter-petition the court that "so far are we from suffering any inconvenience from the want of public roads into Germantown, as good as the nature of the ground will admit of, that we every year feel that we have too many. In the space of less than four miles, there are five public roads which are supported by us at a heavy expense for the benefit of the Merchant Millers on the Wissahickon, all of them communicate to Germantown . . . with a small circuit of a quarter of a mile."[16]

Despite the large number of roads leading to and from Main Street, Germantown developed into the pattern known as a single street village, an unsophisticated layout which ran counter to rationalized growth of a markedly urban nature, since the absence of any thoroughfares running parallel to the main street prevented the formation of "blocks" on which a city is usually based. When Penn granted the land to the Frankfort Company, to the Crefelders, and to other German settlers who had joined with them in the first few years, he did not follow the pattern he himself had set for the settling of townships or villages in 1685.[17] His typical grant was to provide 500 acres per family, clustered in 10 units, with 50 acres and a house for each family placed in the center of the township to form a village and another

[15] See QS Rec. This can only be a minimum estimate as many of the records are missing, most importantly the entire decade, 1781-1789. The figure is more impressive in view of the small number of Germantown affairs in general that were brought before this county court.

[16] Ibid., December 1791.

[17] William Penn, "A Further Account of the Province of Pennsylvania and Its Improvements for the Satisfaction of Those That are Adventurous and Inclined to Be So (1685)," *PMHB*, 9 (1885), pp. 62-81.

450 acres laid out across the highways for each family, as illustrated in figure 2.

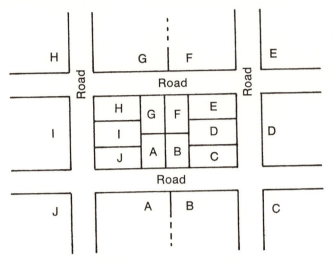

FIGURE 2. Penn's Plan for Townships, 1685.

But in Germantown, Penn granted only 2,700 acres to the 13 Crefeld families, slightly over 200 acres apiece, and an equal amount to the Frankfort Company whose numbers could not even be guessed at, since their attorney, Pastorius, was the only one who had actually immigrated. These limitations precluded any possibility that the new community would become an agricultural village of large landholders.

The nature of the terrain and conditions at the time of settlement also made Penn's plan for a square village in the center of the township impractical. There was no need to cluster together for defense; the Indians were almost gone from the area and those who remained were friendly if one remembered that "when they are drunk it is better to let them alone."[18] Wild animals were so quickly driven from

18 Julius Sachse, ed., *Falckner's Curieuse Nachricht von Pennsylvania: The Book That Stimulated the Great German Immigration to Pennsylvania in the Early Years of the Eighteenth Century*, Lan-

the area that by the 1720s it was worth a big news article when a bear was sighted in the vicinity.[19] The Germantown Road was already there and ran directly to the main settlement in Philadelphia.

Pastorius, first chief magistrate of the newly created German Township, therefore chose a different pattern in distributing the land. His plan was based on the medieval street village made up of a row of houses stretched one deep along a single highway with long, narrow gardens and fields strung out behind them.[20] The type was common enough throughout Germany and particularly in southern and western Germany where the largest proportion of Germantown settlers originated.[21]

The strung out appearance that Germantown presented was noticed by every visitor to the area over the next 110 years. In the beginning, the inhabited section was about a mile long. It appears on a map drawn about 1700[22] with houses, surrounded by little orchards, set right up to both sides of the road and behind them—nothing. The village of Cresheim appears as another little string of perhaps ten houses and a few outbuildings. There is one large house drawn at the summit of Chestnut Hill. About 50 years later, another observer described Germantown as a settlement that

caster, 1905. An interesting collection of advice, description, and attempts at scientific observation by the man who succeeded Pastorius as representative of the Frankfort Company.

[19] *American Weekly Mercury*, September 21-28, 1729.

[20] For a picture of this arrangement, see Mumford, *City*, opposite p. 318. It is called an "urban village."

[21] For a geographical and social summary of the home village of the Pennsylvania immigrant, see Thomas J. Wertenbaker, *The Founding of American Civilization: The Middle Colonies*, New York, 1938, chapter 8, "From Rhine to Susquehanna." He also describes the streets lined with peach trees, which was included in Pastorius's plan for Germantown. For the prevalence of street villages in early Pennsylvania, see Lemon, *Best Poor Man's Country*, p. 142.

[22] This map is in the Philadelphia Free Library, Logan Square, Philadelphia, but a copy is available at the PHC. It is entitled *A Map of the German Settlement including the Following Purchases.* . . .

had "only one street but is nearly two English miles long."[23] By the end of the century, in a letter listing reasons for building the Germantown turnpike, the following remark was made: "one half of the whole distance is thickly inhabited and forms almost one continued village for above five miles."[24]

There is, of course, a center to this sort of development, but it is a point on a single line rather than one formed by the intersection of two lines. This meant there was no physically anchored site around which the town could cluster, but rather a point capable of sliding with changing conditions. Pastorius did plan one cross street, forty feet wide, to be a focal point for the town and the site of the public market, cemetery, and town hall, but the population midpoint of Germantown kept shifting up the Main Road with the result that no complete community center ever emerged. It was found more convenient to establish two public cemeteries (before the churches were established with their own burial grounds), one at either end of the town. Stocks and a jail were built around 1700, but appear to have been used rarely, and were pulled down or sold to private interests in a very short time. No town hall was ever erected, the first Quaker Meetinghouse probably doubling in this capacity until the dissolution of the municipal corporation in 1708.[25] The only public building, in the sense that it belonged to the community, was the alms house, built in 1775 and housing, according to the 1790 census, ten women and two men.

[23] Adolph B. Benson, trans. and ed., *Peter Kalm's Travels in North America, The English Version of 1770*, New York, 1937, I, 49. Peter Kalm (1716-1779) was a Swedish scientist who spent over a year traveling in North America and gathering data. His eye, especially in the area of population studies, was acute, although his reasoning from the observations often displayed the limitations of his time. He was a pupil of Linne and a friend of John Bartram, therefore his access to people and places in Philadelphia was broad and varied.

[24] *Pa.Gaz.*, January 4, 1798.

[25] Marion Dexter Learned, *The Life of Francis Daniel Pastorius, the Founder of Germantown*, Philadelphia, 1908, p. 218.

In 1704 the Market Square land was purchased, but there is no record of a market building before 1741, and no indication that the market itself ever became any kind of town center. Some of the more important meeting places of the town did cluster loosely around Market Square at the place where Mill and Ashmead roads met the Great Road. The militia practiced on the green from time to time,[26] and George Whitfield preached from the balcony of a private house across from the square to a crowd said to number 5,000.[27] Some of the most prominent men of the community had their houses around the square, one of the most popular of the Germantown inns was just a few steps up the Main Road, and, after 1760, the Union School (later known as Germantown Academy) was built on Ashmead Road about 200 yards west of the market, where it filled many of the functions of a town meeting hall. The Reformed Church, second largest of Germantown's religious institutions, occupied the fourth side of the square, while the Quaker Meetinghouse was a few doors away to the south.

The rest of the public institutions and those private institutions involved in serving the public straggled all along the Great Road or, in the case of the mills, were set up at the end of more or less well-beaten trails a mile or more from the central settlement. Commercial enterprises were often marked by street signs, in urban fashion, to acquaint the large number of strangers who traveled the Germantown Road with the services available to them. The "sign of the comb" exhibited by a dealer in cures for "scald head," the "sign of the Bible and spinning wheel" hung out by a printer

[26] For example, see Christopher Saur's German newspaper, *Pennsylvanische Berichte*, November 16, 1748; *Pa.Gaz.* April 28, 1784. (Although Saur's paper changed names many times throughout the eighteenth century, it will be referred to as *Pa.Berichte.*)

[27] *American Weekly Mercury*, November 29, 1739. Anyone who has ever seen Market Square in Germantown must consider this a gross exaggeration. Standing on each other's shoulders, 5,000 people could scarcely be packed into Market Square, or even into the open area that surrounded it at the time.

and book seller, and the "three cannon" of a gunsmith, are but a few of the Germantown street advertisements mentioned in the records.[28] The inns and taverns, lining the Great Road from Bowman's Road in Lower Germantown to the North Wales Road in Sommerhausen, had their distinctive boards swinging in the breeze to beckon to the passerby, and it was in their public rooms that much of the town business was handled during the eighteenth century. Between 1778 and 1799 the Quarter Sessions Court granted an average of nine tavern licenses a year to Germantown applicants, the number rising slowly from eight to ten during the period, with uncharacteristic highs of thirteen and fourteen during the Revolutionary years.[29] Auctions, sheriffs' sales, and estate settlements, meetings for community concern, and, toward the end of the period, political gatherings all took place at the taverns. These functions of the tavern were especially important in a time when it was unthinkable that civic or organizational meetings (with the notable exception of religious gatherings) be held in the private home of any of the participants, even the chairman. Social events and community activities seem to have been far more carefully separated than they are today.

There was little in the way of public or monumental architecture to mark Germantown as an urban community. What there was contributed to the contemporary impression, noted by Peter Kalm when he traveled the area in 1748, that if Philadelphia was a city of brick, Germantown was a city of stone.[30] The earliest of the churches, the Quaker Meetinghouse, built in 1686, and the Mennonites'

[28] All of these and more are listed in the advertising columns of various Pennsylvania newspapers. The ones mentioned appeared in the *Pa.Berichte* in 1756 and 1762 and in the *Pa.Gaz.* in 1758.

[29] QS Rec. Although 1781-1789 are missing, the records before this time show approximately six per year in the fifties and seven per year in the sixties, plus a large number of indictments for running tippling houses, indicating that a good number of taverns operated without the formality of a license.

[30] *Kalm's Travels*, p. 49.

(1708), were originally log structures but were replaced by more imposing stone buildings in 1705 and 1770, respectively. The Reformed Church on the Market Square was built of the local glimmer stone in about 1733 and lent a German feeling to the area, with its steep shingled roof and its bell tower (probably added in 1762) surmounted by an iron cock, the Dutch sign of a church.[31] The stone church of the Lutherans was finished at the far end of town, complete with tower, bell, and organ, in 1752. The presence of this organ is some indication of the relative sophistication of Germantown, since at the time there were only six to be found in the entire colony.

Besides the churches, the only building to approach the status of public architecture was the Germantown Union School. There were several other schoolhouses, such as the Harmony School (1745), the Lutheran School (1745), and the Concord School (1775), but these were unimposing one-room boxes. The Union School was built in 1760 at a time when the town had just gone through a period of immensely rapid population expansion and when civic optimism was at its height. It was two stories of solid stonework, in an ambitious style of architecture. Eighty by forty feet in size with small houses on each side for the German and English masters and their students, it was probably the largest and most elaborate public building in the town. Certainly it was the most expensive. The original collection for the building totalled over £1,800, while both the Lutheran and Reformed churches had been almost completely rebuilt at around the same time for about £600 apiece.[32]

[31] Keyser, *Germantown*, p. 312.

[32] Actually, the rebuilding of the Reformed Church cost a total of £526/2/2, as itemized in the "Consistory Records of the Reformed Congregation of Germantown, 1750-1829," unpublished typescript at the Presbyterian Historical Society, Philadelphia, translated by William J. Hinke, 1937, as far as 1819. (Ref.Ch.Consis.Rec.) This information is from the accounts for 1763. St. Michael's Lutheran Church had been finished several years before, for the sum of £160; see J. W. Richards, "A Historical Sketch of the Evangelical-Lutheran

The private architecture of Germantown reflected not only changes in time, but differences in the backgrounds and conditions of the settlers. The Tinkcoms detect four decidedly different stages of development in the town: wooden huts built on Penn's plan of a three-room log building, 30′x18′, with dirt floor and ceiling, stone hearth in the gable end, wooden shutters over slit windows and clapboard roof; more permanent houses of log or stone with steep German roof or gable and a garret above the main story; the random enlargement of these houses with full stone-walled cellars, entirely underground, and extra rooms tacked on; and the traditional two-story stone house of English outline, but with pent-eaves, double Dutch door and front benches, shuttered windows, and symmetrical design.[33] The diversity of housing by the end of the period is shown in table 1.[34] The only area in which there was any uniformity was in the use of stone as a building material:

Church of St. Michael's, Germantown, Pennsylvania," 2 vols., handwritten, unpublished, 1845. Located at the Lutheran Theological Seminary. The most detailed building accounts are those of the Union School in the "Original Minute Book of the Union School of Germantown, 1757-1777," unpublished manuscript, at Germantown Academy, Fort Washington, Pa., December 24, 1761.

[33] See Tinkcom, *Historic Germantown*, pp. 27-28.

[34] United States Direct Tax of 1798, Tax Lists for the State of Pennsylvania, National Archives Microcopy #372. The section of this list that refers to Germantown has five separate parts, or schedules: A is a list of dwelling houses with information on location, dimensions, number of stories, number and dimension of windows, building materials, description of outbuildings, and names of owners and occupiers, no land over two acres was included with any dwelling; schedule B included the rest of the land within a given property and any nonresidential building, wharves, shops, etc., describing each and giving dimensions and names of owners and occupants. Both lists included the actual assessments. The other schedules—D, E, and I—were shortened versions or rough drafts of A or B. (Hereafter cited as 1798 Direct Tax.) This listing is, of course, an invaluable source of knowledge for properties in Germantown. A copy of the microfilm is on file at the Phila.Arch.

TABLE 1

GERMANTOWN HOUSING, 1798

Houses	Type of Construction			No. of Stories			Outbuildings			No. of Windows[d]				
	Stone	Frame	Other	1	2	Other	Kitchen	Other	None	0-2	3-5	6-10	11-15	Over 15
No.	403	57	24[a]	183	289	11[b]	185	64[c]	235	81	142	115	89	49
%	83.5	11.8	4.9	37.9	59.8	2.3	38.2	13.2	48.6	17.0	29.8	24.2	18.7	10.3

Floor Space
(square feet)

Houses	100-199	200-299	300-399	400-499	500-599	600-699	700-799	800-899	900-999	1,000-1,099	1,100-1,199	1,200-1,299	1,300-1,399	1,400-1,499	Over 1,500
No.	9	48	111	79	56	41	37	29	25	11	10	8	7	2	10
%	1.9	9.9	22.9	16.4	11.6	8.5	7.6	6.0	5.2	2.3	2.1	1.7	1.4	.4	2.1

SOURCE: 1798 Federal Direct Tax, Schedule A.

[a] Includes 6 brick houses; 18 log houses.
[b] Includes 6 three-story houses; 5 one-and-one-half story houses.
[c] Includes 20 washhouses; 16 stables; 22 chairhouses; 6 miscellaneous.
[d] The number of windows was not mentioned in 8 cases.

over 83 percent were built of stone, just under 12 percent were frame, between 3 and 4 percent were log (probably representing what was left of the homes of the earliest settlers), and only six houses were built of brick. Stone had begun to predominate as early as 1720, when the fronts of houses were being constructed of stone even though the kitchen or back might be of log.[35] The size, height, and number of windows per dwelling had less to do with any traditional or stylistic plan than with the owner's finances and the convenience of the builder.

Certain generalizations can be made. It was rare for a frame house to be more than one story. Typically, it would also be smaller in dimensions than one built of stone, with few windows, a smallish lot, and a lower valuation; Henry Kurtz, for example, owned a frame house of one story, 15'x20', on a lot one-eighth of an acre, containing three windows of twelve lights each, and valued at the modest sum of $200.[36] Thomas Cox's house ($1,000) embodied all the typical attributes of a Germantown house; it was a stone dwelling, two stories high, 15'x23', with four windows, eighty-eight lights, and no outbuildings.[37] Almost without exception the houses had full stone cellars. There was a fair number of very long, narrow frame buildings with very few windows, almost like converted sheds, which were classed as tenements and appear to have housed single workingmen. A typical upper-middle-class house might have been that of George Royal of Lower Germantown; valued at $1,700, it was a two-story dwelling; 30'x18' or 540 square feet in area, with twelve ten-paned windows. The most elaborate house in the neighborhood belonged to a summer resident, Benjamin Chew, and, while hardly typical, it is interesting to note its description as the upper limit on the scale of Ger-

[35] Keyser, *Germantown*, p. 118.

[36] 1798 Direct Tax, Schedule A, #40.

[37] Ibid., #82. The average house of an artisan in Philadelphia measured 17'x25' and was one-and-one-half stories high. However, unlike the Germantown craftsman, the Philadelphia craftsman's shop was usually within his house. See Warner, *Private City*, p. 17.

mantown variety: on a full two-acre lot there was a two-story stone house, 54′x44′; a two-story stone kitchen, 27′x 18′; a two-story stone washhouse, 18′x18′; a one-story stone pantry, 18′x10′. The house had thirty windows, and the assessor refused even to try to count the panes, instead giving the measurements of the windows as each 7′x3′10″. The total valuation was $7,000.[38]

The overall appearance of Germantown was for the most part more urban than that of other eighteenth-century settlements. Up-country towns, even those of considerable importance such as Lancaster, were loosely built up, the houses separated by large lots, orchards, and fields, the row houses that later came to characterize them developed after 1800.[39] The proportions of Germantown lots, as laid out by Pastorius, encouraged building right up to the front of the property line, and the narrowness of each property put the houses cheek by jowl, even when not actually sharing a party wall. While the Chew house, mentioned above, was set well back from the Great Road behind carefully planted grounds, some of the city folk who built summer homes in Germantown followed the custom of the town. In a letter describing a visit to Chief Justice William Allen's country seat, a friend complained of the dust and noise in the house because of its being set too close to the road.[40] In addition, by the end of the century, there were well over 100 separate buildings that served as business establishments for those crafts- or tradesmen who no longer worked within their homes. Most of these were small stone or frame workshops, usually one story and about 15′x16′, which crowded the edge of the road beside the owners' houses or were visible at the end of the alleys that ran behind. Some were shops, which were also tiny, although there was one great store of 540 square feet.[41]

---

[38] Ibid., #90, #266, #359, #75.
[39] Lemon, *Best Poor Man's Country*, p. 140.
[40] "Diary of Daniel Fisher," *PMHB*, 17 (1893), p. 269.
[41] See 1798 Direct Tax, Schedule B.

It is easier by far to build up a picture of the town itself than it is to acquire an understanding of the inhabitants. At the outset, one is faced with the numbers game—fascinating, but impossible to win. Germantown is as well documented as most colonial population centers, better than many, yet for most of the eighteenth century there is no way to determine beyond a question of a doubt how many people lived there at any one time. At one end is the list of the Crefeld settlers and the people who accompanied Pastorius in 1683. There were 9 in the Pastorius group beside the leader—6 men, 1 woman, and 2 children. The number of Crefelders has generally been placed at 33 individuals in 13 families, which would make the original population of Germantown 43 persons. Yet even here there is doubt. As Hocker points out in his book on Germantown, these figures are based on the ship lists of paying freights, and as children under twelve were counted as one-half fare and those under twelve months were not counted at all, it is probable that there were actually more people than traditionally thought.[42] At the other end of the scale in the census of 1790, with its explicit account of family members, whether male over or under sixteen years old, female, other free persons, or slaves. In this listing, Germantown had 556 families with a total population of 2,764.[43]

Between these two comparatively fixed points, the most complete source materials are tax lists, which give only family heads and do not enumerate other inhabitants. Therefore, it is necessary to estimate the population and determine its rate of growth through the use of average figures for family size. Pastorius recorded in 1684 that there were 42 people living in twelve houses in Germantown.[44] This would point to a household average of 3.5 members. The census figures above work out to a general average of just under 5.0 people per family in 1790, although a breakdown

[42] Hocker, *Germantown*, p. 10.
[43] *U.S. Census*, 1790, pp. 195-197.
[44] Keyser, *Germantown*, p. 110.

of the returns shows a wide variation from forty units with only 1 member, to forty-three households with 10 or more members.

One other area yields objective data that can be used to arrive at an average figure for household size in eighteenth-century Germantown. This is the compilation of material from the church registers of the period. While the problems of these sources are many—for example, only two of the five churches have usable records, and they do not deal exclusively with a Germantown congregation—they represent a large and random enough sample to be statistically valuable for a sizeable and mobile population like Germantown's.[45] When the overall baptisms for the period 1750 to 1799 that appear on these lists (minus the childhood deaths of the same period) are compared to the marriages of the years 1745 to 1794, a figure of 2.7 live children per household is obtained. Adding 2 adults per family, whether parent or some other relation, there are about 4.7 members per unit.[46] This coincides with the general pattern of Germantown population obtained from other sources.

[45] The records referred to are the church registers of births, confirmations, marriages, and burials kept by St. Michael's Evangelical Lutheran Church, Germantown (St.M.Rec.) and the German Reformed Church of Germantown (Ref.Ch.Rec.). While there are many other scattered records from the Mennonites, the Quakers, and the Dunkards, and much demographic material available from genealogies, it was felt that for general aggregate statistics it was best to use the two registers alone as a population sample of more consistency. In this way, too, the problems of incompleteness tend to smooth out. When one of the registers is deficient for a period, because of a change of ministers, for example, it is so through births, marriages, and deaths equally, and therefore does not disturb the internal relationships. It does mean, of course, that the church records are of no use in figuring actual population, but only for averages and internal population structure.

[46] The best description of using raw data to determine overall population is by D.E.C. Eversley, "Exploitation of Anglican Parish Registers by Aggregative Analysis," *EHD*, pp. 44-95. See especially pp. 76-80. Using the marriage records for the five years preceding the baptism records is fully explained there.

Do these figures make sense? Based on other estimates of household size in the colonies during the eighteenth century, they seem low indeed. It must be remembered, however, that these are gross estimates which include the single men and widows who lived in the township—7.4 percent of the total households in 1790. And the size of the Germantown family *was* small in relation to those in the rest of Philadelphia County. On the census report of 1790, only the Northern Liberties reported a smaller average (4.8), while Kingsessing was the same as Germantown at 5.0, and the rest of the townships all reported much higher averages, the largest number of members per family unit being 8.7 in Moyamensing and Passyunk. The City of Philadelphia averaged 6.6 people per household throughout its wards.[47]

One other check was made. Much of Germantown's population was composed of new arrivals from Germany, especially during the period of greatest growth around the middle of the century. With this in mind, the size of immigrating families was averaged from the ship lists wherever possible from 1727 to 1773.[48] The results are very interesting. Two general assumptions concerning the nature of German immigration have been traditionally accepted. On the one hand, it has been reported that huge families arrived to be split up pitifully and sent out as indentured servants. Others have maintained that immigration was at first largely a question of single men looking for a fresh start in life. Yet analysis of the existing records indicates that the heaviest concentration of newcomers arrived in small family groups. Only two of the ships whose lists were recorded by classification of passengers showed an average size of family under 2; once in 1738, when it averaged 1.85, and again in 1770

[47] Based on the total figures for Philadelphia County, *U.S. Census*, 1790.

[48] These estimates are made on the ships and passengers listed in Rupp, *30,000 Names*. Those used were those where the names of all males over sixteen were listed as well as the total passengers. Where sons followed fathers directly on the list, it is possible to get a corrected index for heads of household.

when the number of total passengers compared to single men fell to 1.97. There were also only two instances in which family size rose over 5; a large ship in 1733, on which 225 of the 389 passengers were children, and an even larger vessel in 1749, with a passenger list of almost 600. For all years, the average lies between 2.12 and 3.85, with the largest families coming in the late thirties, and the smallest toward the end of the period, after 1770. There are few recognizable Germantown names on the lists after 1750, so the earlier figure is probably more representative for the township. Arriving families tended to be young, judging by the small number of males over sixteen who accompanied their fathers, and by the small number of children of any age associated with married couples.

A conversion factor of 3.8 for the first half of the century and 4.5 for the second half seems sensible, not only reflecting the information given, but also taking into account the changing profile of the population. Twenty-nine new settlers and their families arrived in 1684, bringing the number of inhabitants to about 110 and more than doubling Pastorius's early-year report of 42. Nine years later, by reference to the tax list of 1693,[49] the population had almost doubled again to just under 200. Another eight years and the total was 60 families and several single people for an estimate of about 230 individuals.[50] The settlement gained slowly over the next thirty years, since the Constables' Returns of 1734 list only 89 adult males for Germantown and Cresheim together,[51] making an increase of under 50 percent for that period to about 340 people.

---

[49] William B. Rawle, ed., "The First Tax List for Philadelphia County, A.D. 1693," *PMHB*, 8 (1884). (Hereafter cited as 1693 tax list.) Pages 98-100 relate to Germantown.

[50] From Pastorius's journal, quoted in Keyser, *Germantown*, p. 110.

[51] "Landholders of Philadelphia County, Constables' Returns, 1734," *Gen.Mag.*, I (1895). (Hereafter cited as "1734 Constables' Returns.")

Tradition is the only available source of population size for over thirty years following 1734. One historian estimates the population of the town in the early 1740s as "about four hundred,"[52] while another reports that there were about 100 houses. These two estimates would appear to corroborate each other. The big leap is supposed to have come between 1745 and 1758 when, according to Margaret Tinkcom, there were 250 new houses built.[53] This would represent an enormous increase of 1,000 people or 250 percent in just over ten years. Still, it is not absolutely impossible if the general immigration figures for Pennsylvania for this period are taken into account. After this explosive period, the rate of growth stabilized again. The population rose by 52 percent in the next fifteen years to 2,128 (1767) and remained almost static at 2,164, six years later.[54] This virtual standstill actually turned into a downward trend during the Revolutionary years as the number of taxables dropped between 1773 and 1780. The change in total inhabitants was not as drastic as this might suggest, however; while the number of taxpayers fell from 481 to 423, the number of single men paying head tax in the township dropped from 89 to 32, only 1 less than the entire loss. The difference, therefore, seems to have been largely of single men rather than of families, and appears to indicate the effect of the Revolution on the bottom level of the labor

[52] S. A. Ziegenfuss, *A Brief and Succinct History of Saint Michael's Evangelical Lutheran Church of Germantown, Pennsylvania, 1730-1905*, Philadelphia, 1905. Ziegenfuss was a minister at St. Michael's and based his work on earlier figures in the materials of previous ministers. It is possible to check his work back as far as 1845, when Richards produced his book. Ziegenfuss's connection with the church, through his grandfather, went back to the eighteenth century.

[53] Tinkcom, *Historic Germantown*, p. 1.

[54] Philadelphia Tax List for 1767, University of Pennsylvania, Van Pelt Library, rare book room. (Hereafter cited as 1767 tax list.) Also, County Tax Assessment Ledger for Philadelphia County, provincial tax for 1773 (3s. in the £; 9s. per head), and 1774 (1s. 6d. in the £; 15s. per head), Phila.Arch. (Hereafter cited as 1773 tax list.)

force. The overall growth rate for the eighteen years between 1773 and the census of 1790 was 27.7 percent for the
seventeen-year period and 16.1 percent for the last ten
years of the century.[55]

The periods of population growth by average annual rate
as well as by numbers are shown in table 2. They corre-

TABLE 2

RATE OF POPULATION GROWTH, GERMANTOWN, 1683-1800

Year	Population	Mean Annual Rate of Increase[a] (%)
1683	42	
1693	200	15.60
1701	230	1.74
1734	340	1.20
1745	400	1.51
1758	1,400	9.60
1767	2,128	4.65
1773	2,164	0.16
1790	2,764	1.45
1800	3,200	1.57

[a] On the formula $A=P(e^{rt})$.

spond extremely closely to those general times of urban expansion in Pennsylvania outlined by Lemon.[56] He sees the
eras of rapid growth, both demographic and economic, as
1681 to 1700 and 1730 to 1765, with very slight development between 1701 and 1729 and a slow, somewhat erratic
pace of change from 1766 to 1800. The only way to compare Germantown with the rest of Pennsylvania and with

[55] Based on 3,220 total population for Germantown in the *1800*
U.S. Census Report, quoted by Tinkcom in "Germantown in Review,"
Germantowne Crier, 17 (September 1965), p. 76.

[56] Lemon, "Urbanization," *WMQ* (1967). In *Best Poor Man's
Country*, p. 23, he gives mean annual rates of increase for southeastern
Pennsylvania in general. His percentages differ, but the pattern of
his table is similar to that of Germantown.

the colonies at large is to even out the rate over the course of the eighteenth century. Disregarding the years of settlement, which would grossly inflate the rate of growth since most statistics begin in 1700 after initial population is determined, Germantown has an average growth rate from 1700 to 1800 of 26.6 percent per decade, which is how the figures are usually given.[57] This indicates a doubling of the population about every twenty years, a good bit faster than the Malthusian hypothesis for the colonies in general, and about the same as Benjamin Franklin's most generous estimates in *Observations Concerning The Increase of Mankind and the Peopling of Countries*.[58] By comparison, the colonies taken together averaged almost exactly the Malthus estimate of 34.5 percent per decade, and Pennsylvania stood well above average with a decennial increase of 43 percent.[59] During the period between 1720 and 1775, the city of Philadelphia increased from 10,000 to 24,000 inhabitants, for a mean growth rate per decade of 16 percent, while Germantown, during the same time, was experiencing a kind of population explosion of 32 percent per decade.[60]

[57] See J. Potter, "The Growth of Population in America, 1700-1860," in *Population in History: Essays in Historical Demography*, eds. D. V. Glass and D.E.C. Eversley, London, 1965, pp. 631-688, for a summary of American population statistics of the eighteenth century, their validity, sources, and method of utilization.

[58] Ibid., p. 632, text and footnote.

[59] Ibid., p. 639, Table I (d).

[60] The rate for Philadelphia is based on figures provided in Warner's *Private City*, p. 12. They are much lower than the traditional population figure of 40,000 used by Carl Bridenbaugh in *Rebels and Gentlemen: Philadelphia in the Age of Franklin*, 1942, rpt. New York, 1962, p. 3. A check of the 1773 tax list shows taxables of 3,703 in the City proper, 615 in Southwark, and 1,033 in the Liberties. Using the conversion factor of 4.5, this means a population of about 23,000. On the other hand, correcting the tax figures by rates obtained from Bridenbaugh's numbers, one would still only have a figure of about 27,000 in 1776. This independent use of the 1773 tax list would seem to corroborate Warner's smaller figure. Another view disputing Warner's figures and arguing for a conversion factor of 6.27, which

Throughout the entire colonial period, the sex and age mix of Germantown's population was remarkably even, never reflecting the extreme frontier conditions of Pittsburgh, for example, where, in 1761 the population consisted of 278 men to only 69 women and 35 children.[61] The number of women in Germantown was always close to the number of men, and there were almost as many children as there were adults. By 1790 females outnumbered males 1,394 to 1,343, and the estimated number of female adults was 775 as compared to 746 adult males.[62] This is interesting in view of the fact that in all of the vital statistics available for Germantown throughout the period, entries for males outnumber those for females by a small margin.[63] Among the total 5,041 births recorded, of those whose sexes were known 2,603 were boys, and 2,367 were girls. In childhood deaths boys outnumbered girls 352 to 293, and adult males whose burials are registered are listed at 643 compared to 541 females. The slight surplus of females over males in the census,

---

yields a population of 33,482 for the urban area in 1774, is presented by John K. Alexander, "The Philadelphia Numbers Game: An Analysis of Philadelphia's Eighteenth-Century Population," *PMHB*, 98 (1974), pp. 314-324.

[61] "Pittsburgh in 1761. A Return of the Numbers of Houses, of the Names of the Owners, and Number of Men, Women and Children in Each House at Fort Pitt, April 14, 1761," *PMHB*, 6 (1882), pp. 344-347.

[62] These estimates are arrived at by assuming the same ratio of adult to juvenile females as persists among males. The statistical justification for this is found in T. H. Hollingsworth, *Historical Demography*, The Sources of History: Studies in the Uses of Historical Evidence, Ithaca, N.Y., 1969, p. 49 and passim.

[63] The following statistics are gathered from St.M.Rec., Ref.Ch. Rec., Hood Cemetery Records, AbMM Rec. (on microfilm at Swarthmore College Library, except for the burials which are in the Collections of the Genealogical Society, HSP), and the "Records of the Upper Burying Ground," Peter Keyser, ed., *PMHB*, 8 (1884) and 9 (1885). Records of the other churches have no information on these points since these churches practiced adult baptism and opened no graveyards until very near the end of the eighteenth century.

however, ties in with hypotheses made by sociologists in relation to this proportion as an index of urbanization.[64]

There are no sources comparable to the tax lists, census reports, or even the ship registers for quantified study of the variety of life-styles, simple or elegant, followed by the burgeoning population of Germantown throughout the eighteenth century. A small number of estate inventories (forty-five) are available for 15 percent of the wills probated in Philadelphia by Germantowners between 1708 and 1799.[65] There are certain drawbacks, of course, to the use of such limited documentation for a general study. For one thing, it is difficult to determine the range of life-styles from the inventories, since the poorest elements with no property to leave are not represented at all. The size of the problem is illustrated by the fact that items such as silver plate and servants' time occur more than twice as frequently in the inventories as they do on the most complete of the tax lists.[66] It is also impossible to be sure that the inventories were honest and complete—that many items were not removed before they were enumerated or that the evaluators did not routinely fail to include certain categories of goods. There is no compelling reason to believe that this was the case, however. Inventories were not used for tax purposes,

[64] See, for example, Duncan, "Community Size," *Cities and Society*, p. 41.

[65] That only 310 wills from Germantown are recorded at City Hall for the eighteenth century, shows that there was a severe problem of failure to legalize property ownership by Germantowners in general. There are no copies of the inventories to match the Will Books for the eighteenth century. Those still in existence are filed in the Registry of Wills, Philadelphia City Hall Annex. They are indexed by the name of the legator, the year, and a number. The number matches that of the will as copied in the Will Book. Occasionally, the original copy of the will is also in the folder with the inventory, and once in a while there is also a final accounting of the actual value and distribution of the estate by the executors. References to Inventories or Accounts that follow will be to the originals and will cite them by name, year, and file number.

[66] 1780 tax list.

and common household properties may be missing from a single inventory, yet appear regularly on others, supporting the idea that when they were not reported, it is because they were not part of the estate. The inventories were regularly made by prominent citizens in a semiofficial capacity, rather than by members of the family or by close friends who might have had some personal motivation. Finally, they were made very quickly, usually before the funeral, which took place within two days after death, so there was little opportunity for removal of items. Thus, while bearing in mind the shortcomings of the inventories and their potential for inaccuracy, there is still much valuable information to be gained from their study, particularly in helping to build a picture of certain models or types of life-styles across the time spectrum of the period.

Understanding of the setup of Germantown homes is helped by knowledge of the method in which inventories were taken. For the most part, the appraisers began in the bedchamber of the deceased, probably with the very bed on which he was laid out, and proceeded from there around the second floor or through the other bedrooms, then through the downstairs living quarters, the storeroom, and finally, to the outbuildings, sheds, barns, etc., and the fields in which any standing crops required enumeration. It is possible, as in the case of the inventory of George Riter, to determine that a servant slept behind the kitchen and that he (or she) had "an old couch, a chest, four wood bottom chairs and a bed pan" but no stove or fire.[67]

The inventories make very clear the way in which the life-style of people in Germantown became more sophisticated in relation to household comfort and decor throughout the eighteenth century. Pastorius, for example, was a cultured and comfortably secure gentleman. Yet the contents of his house betray the frontier conditions that still existed in Germantown when he died in 1720. His furniture

---

[67] George Riter, Inventory, 1794, #103.

consisted entirely of two bedsteads, a chest, a trunk, a desk, one table, three chairs, a kneading trough, and a stove. One lantern and one candlestick provided the household with light and one chamber pot with the necessities. In addition, there was the usual complement of iron and brass kitchenware and some pewter. No china or earthenware crockery is listed. Each of the beds had a bolster, pillow, blanket, and a pair of sheets, and there were four extra pairs in a chest. There were five towels, eight tablecloths, and four napkins. That exhausted the luxury. The library is worth recording in full as it was considered extremely large and much admired. Many of the books were texts, in quantity, used by Pastorius's pupils during the time he kept the Court School, and the "six quire of paper" must also date from his schoolmaster days.

An English Bible in quarto and an other in octavo
french books (sic)
English books
a Greek Testament
Latin books
14 Dictionarys
high Dutch Books
Low Dutch books
100 primmers[68]

The simple inventory of the effects of Lenert Streepers, one of the original Crefelder settlers, serves as a model for the rural establishment of the time, bearing in mind that Pastorius was living what was considered a town life. In the one bedchamber was a bedstead with its clothes and a chest with a few pieces of "linin woolin" in it, a few tablecloths, and napkins. No other sleeping accommodations were listed even though Streepers had four sons not yet old enough to be put out to trades who presumably lived with him and

[68] Francis Daniel Pastorius's inventory, dated January 25, 1719/20, is available in Learned, *Pastorius*.

his wife.[69] In a storeroom next to the bedroom were found ten bushels of rye and six bushels of wheat, thirty-six pounds of wool, and three deer skins. The only other room in the house contained a chest of drawers, a cupboard, table, trunk, a moulding trough and chairs, various kitchenware, including a churn, some pewter, and some earthenware. A gun, plow, harrow, wagon and gears, a grindstone, scythes and sickles, a strawbench and knife were in one part of the barn, while the rest housed cows and young cattle, hogs, sheep, horses, mares, and colts. Standing in the field waiting for harvest were wheat, rye, and oats. The plantation itself contained 184 acres.

From 1750 on there was a marked increase in the number of luxury items mentioned in the inventories. This applies particularly to household goods, such as walnut or mahogany furniture, rugs, curtains, pictures, desks, looking glasses, and clocks, but there is also a larger proportion of people who own table silver, tea services, watches, and jewelry of silver or gold. The only extra possessions of value that were as common in the early part of the century as later appear to have been technical instruments such as compasses and telescopes, and these are found among the effects of the original settlers who came far better equipped than the immigrants who immediately followed them. By the end of the century, the standard of living as measured by these criteria had risen considerably, although careful study of the inventories shows that certain kinds of luxuries were more typically owned by the urban Germantowner than they were by his rural counterpart. In 1794, for example, George Riter, a farmer, left an estate valued 50 percent higher than that of the tradesman, Jacob Frailey, who died in the same year. Yet beyond a comfortable excess of the necessities, Riter's home boasted only a looking glass, a 34-hour clock, a desk, a walnut table, six china cups and saucers, and four silver spoons. Frailey, on the other hand,

[69] Lenert Streepers, WB E, p. 56, #58. Inventory, 1727, #58.

possessed a silver watch, in addition to the clock, the looking glass, two walnut tables—dinner and breakfast—, a walnut desk, bookcase, and corner cupboard, a mahogany table and stand, eight windsor chairs, and five silver teaspoons. Finally, about 1 percent of the value of Frailey's estate was made up of books, an item completely lacking in the rural listing.[70]

The possession of books is another interesting factor in the Germantown life-style of the eighteenth century, which can be illuminated somewhat by the inventories. Books represent the only item consistently owned by more than half the sample throughout the whole period, and, like the compass and the telescope, seem to have been part of the regular gear brought over by the earliest settlers. One of the very poorest men, who had no real property at all and a very small personal estate, left twenty books which comprised 5 percent of his total worth,[71] and J. F. Ax, who could not even write (he signed his will with his mark), had a small shelf of them in his kitchen.[72] As the century progressed, the value and importance of books to Germantowners, both financially and as status symbols, seem to have declined, and prosperous tradesmen commonly averaged less than 0.5 percent of their appraised value in books, and if they had any at all, they were frequently stacked away out in the shed, according to the evidence of the inventories.[73] Only the very richest, most acculturated of the permanent residents ever boasted anything like a gentleman's library. Charles Bensell included "between six and seven hundred volumes of books, in folio, quarto, octavo and duodecimo, being a collection of physical and historical authors &c" in an inventory of goods taken from his house during the

[70] George Riter, Inventory, 1794, #103; Jacob Frailey, Inventory, 1794, #30.

[71] Daniel Geissler, Inventory, 1745, #11.

[72] John Frederick Ax, WB O, p. 206, #155. Inventory, 1768, #155.

[73] See, for example, Derick Keyser's will and inventory, copies of which are on file at the PHC.

British occupation of Germantown.[74] Many of these were undoubtedly professional, as Bensell was a doctor.

The real difference in private life-styles, and, in fact, in the profile of the town as a whole was made by the advent of the summer visitor. Jones has pointed out that as the economy of a country becomes more complex and diversified, many of its functions split up, creating cities "with specialist activities like education or trade or even government."[75] It was the increasing complexity and urbanization of nearby Philadelphia that superimposed upon the development of Germantown a specialized function as a vacation resort; it was found to be ideal for the establishment of country seats, particularly for men of affairs who needed to be within a day's journey of the city. The Shippens had discovered the town as early as 1714,[76] and James Logan began work on Stenton in 1728. By mid-century the area was dotted with the vacation homes of prominent Philadelphians, and more and more were added in the second half of the century. Those who didn't buy, rented, and local families did a thriving business by renting out spare rooms and apartments.

The steady stream of Philadelphia visitors and Philadelphia influence became a flood with the yellow fever epidemics of the 1790s. The first epidemic in 1793 did not create much permanent change. While both the federal and state governments were temporarily located in Germantown and rooms were almost impossible to obtain, a crisis was avoided since Congress was not in session. By the time the cool weather set in, Germantown had returned to normal. By 1797 when the next big epidemic struck the city, Germantown had a reputation as the place to go, and busi-

---

[74] Inventory of items left in the house of Charles Bensell when he left Germantown at the approach of the British, September 24, 1777. Printed in the *Pa.Gaz.*, March 10, 1779.

[75] Jones, *Towns*, p. 84.

[76] "1714 List of Property holders" in Keyser, *Germantown*, p. 44.

nesses as well as families and individuals moved out at once. The township began to look more like the suburbs and less like a small city. During the next two summers, which also saw increased health hazards in Philadelphia, the changes in Germantown became better established and, in many cases, permanent. Only five announcements in the newspapers related to the location of Philadelphia enterprises, including the tax office, in Germantown for the "sickly season" in 1797. There were over thirty such ads in the summer months of both 1798 and 1799.[77] The businesses included insurance companies, banking offices, and merchants' headquarters, as well as smaller establishments—perfume shops, shoe stores, dry goods shops, and the like. Some of the businessmen who ran these shops settled permanently with their families and contributed to changing the character of the local population in the nineteenth century.

There is no doubt that there was a large gulf that separated the summer people from the local residents at every level and particularly at the top, where the Philadelphians were not merely wealthy city folk but, like the Allens and the Shippens, among the richest people anywhere in the province. On the Scull and Heap map of 1750, there was only one local Germantown businessman—Theobald Ent—who had a home worth classifying as an estate, and at the end of the century the elegant homes of the Johnsons and the Bensells were tax rated at less than half of that of one of the richest of the summer residents.[78]

The actual financial gap is perhaps best seen through an examination of the subscription list for charitable donations to relieve the Philadelphia poor during the epidemic of 1797.[79] The idea of such a collection had been suggested

[77] This information has been compiled from Jenkins, "News," GHS.

[78] 1798 Direct Tax, Schedule A. Benjamin Chew's house is valued at $7,000, while those of the Johnsons and the Bensells are each rated at $3,300.

[79] *Pa.Gaz.*, October 9, 1797; *U.S. Gazette*, October 14, 1797. The list of names and amounts was given in the *Pa.Gaz.*, November 1, 1797.

at a meeting of Philadelphia citizens living in Germantown held at the Union Schoolhouse in October of that year. Twelve hundred dollars was subscribed immediately, and a committee was appointed to canvass the town. This committee was made up of 11 men, 6 of whom were regular vacationers in Germantown and 5 of whom were newcomers living in the township purely because of the unhealthy conditions in Philadelphia. The final list of contributors included about 225 names; the contributions totaled $4,421.70. This included 4 business firms and 14 anonymous donors. Of those individuals whose names were given, 95 were not familiar to the Germantown area; they were mostly English or Irish; they gave an average of $29 apiece, including one gift of $200, with most donations in the $20-$50 range. Twenty-seven regular summer people gave an average of almost $39 apiece, for a total of over $1,000, with 4 gifts of $100 or more. By contrast, there were only 85 local Germantowners on the list, and the comparison of their donations with those of the Philadelphians is well worth making. First, and possibly most interesting of all, over half of them (53) gave in shillings and pence instead of American currency. None of the summer people and only a few of the unfamiliar donors were using this kind of money as late as 1797. Second, there was a large difference between the size of their gifts and those of their more affluent visitors. The average donation in dollars and cents was only $9.27, with 1 person giving $50 and 5 offering less than one dollar. The average of those who used the old-fashioned currency was 9s. 6d.

The difference in generosity toward the suffering poor between the local Germantowner and the Philadelphia refugee was at least as much psychological as it was financial, and hints of underlying resentment between "townies" and summer people appear in many sources. Certainly the lines between very rich, English, and Philadelphian were fairly well established in Germantown as early as 1755, when Christopher Saur complained that "Poor people are not able to let their children be boarded, nor can they clothe them properly to go to school with those of high rank, *so that this privilege belongs only to the rich and to the English.*"[80] Near the end of the century, a local voter saw unfair political influence being wielded in the township by its nonresidents: "In Germantown, when by the casualty of the yellow fever, that town felt the weight of influence of the fugitive gentry from the city, 184 votes were given for Morgan, and but 44 for Israel. At the late election, when the freemen of the district had the opportunity of exercising their opinions uninfluenced, Israel had 265 votes and Morgan 283. So that in the former instance Morgan had a majority of 140 votes out of 228, and in the latter a majority of 18 out of 548."[81]

For their part the summer people were apt to condescend to the townsfolk, to find them quaint or amusing, and largely to ignore them, except when there was a difference of interest. When a jury of local residents laid out a new course for Wissahickon Avenue in 1763, the result displeased James Logan and Rebecca Venables, two of the most important sometime residents, who immediately appealed to the Quarter Sessions Court and arranged for the appointment of a new set of road viewers—all English and all Quaker.[82] Those who had come to Germantown to enjoy gentry life as described by Jane Austen at the end of the eighteenth century had no interest in the urban future of Germantown; their interest was rather in keeping it as quiet and rural as possible. The bill in the State Assembly that authorized the turnpike and made it easy to bypass the town was almost wholly their work. Such opposition to the new road as occurred was engineered by ambitious local

---

[80] From an *Open Letter* by Christopher Saur, September 16, 1755, quoted in Samuel Edwin Weber, *The Charity School Movement in Colonial Pennsylvania, 1754-1763: A History of the Educational Struggle Between the Colonial Authorities and the German Inhabitants of Pennsylvania*, Philadelphia, 1905, p. 58. Emphasis supplied.

[81] *Aurora*, February 28, 1798. Letter to the editor.

[82] QS Rec., December 1763.

tradesmen, who lost out two ways, for not only did the road cut into the potential of their businesses, but when the subscription book for buying shares in the turnpike was opened, over their objections, it was city gentry like the Chews, the Haineses, and the Logans who profited.[83]

In the long run the summer people had their way. The intangible excitement of the street scene that goes to make up a city atmosphere seems to have flourished briefly in Germantown and then petered out. To Peter Kalm in the 1740s, "the inhabitants were so numerous that the street was always full,"[84] yet by 1811 a guidebook described Germantown as "a summer retreat for a number of citizens, and excepting its airy and elevated situation . . . it has little to interest or detain strangers."[85] There was no regular market, and the semiannual fairs that were held around mid-century were dull and uninspired. There were no public executions or floggings; a sermon by Whitfield was a high point of the century. True, there were militia reviews on the green from time to time, but this was no urban phenomenon; Jane and Eliza Bennett would have felt right at home among the spectators. Theater, which gave Philadelphia such a cosmopolitan appeal, never came to Germantown, and the only show in town was a miniature architectural model "done by an illiterate shoemaker, intended when put together as a representation of Jerusalem."[86]

Social life was basically a private affair. The very wealthy provided their own amusements within their homes and grounds with house parties and visiting patterns similar to

[83] See, for example, the *Daily Advertiser*, June 1793; *National Gazette*, June 15, 1792; *Federal Gazette*, March 13, 1795; *Pa.Gaz.*, April 18, 1798.

[84] *Kalm's Travels*, p. 49.

[85] James Mease, *The Picture of Philadelphia, Giving an Account of Its Origin, Increase and Improvements In Arts, Sciences, Manufactures, Commerce and Revenue*, Philadelphia, 1811, p. 351. This rare book may be found in the Phila.Arch.

[86] "Extracts from the Diary of Hannah Callendar," *PMHB*, 12 (1888), p. 454. See also Anthony Sultser, Inventory, 1761, #101.

those of the English gentry of the time. Weddings, baptisms, and funerals provided family entertainment for middle- and lower-class Germantowners. Important expenses in the final accounts of various estates almost always include beef, cheese, and beer for the funeral. It was not uncommon for the entertainment expenses of a funeral to come to 10 percent of the total value of the estate![87] The number of inns in Germantown has already been mentioned, and these were the center for community social life. In addition there were a number of illegal "tippling houses," which operated throughout the period, and evidence of at least two whore houses.[88]

Yet in many ways the warm, close, almost claustrophobic life of a traditional village seems to have been missing. Main Street was constantly filled with strangers—passing drovers, guests of summer visitors, refugees from the yellow fever, itinerant tradesmen on their way to or from Philadelphia. People in the churches didn't always know each other. One man on the Great Road could lose three cows and another a few doors away find them, and the fact would never be known until both advertised in the newspaper.[89] An article in Christopher Saur's newspaper illustrates "modern urban" indifference instead of the supposed neighborliness of frontier villages: in 1747 there was a fire at the home of a prominent Germantown citizen. While spectators stood around and refused to help, the entire building burned to the ground, and after the family had left the scene for the night, the household items, which had been saved and were standing about on the ground near the ruin, were stolen by the loiterers.[90]

[87] See, for example, Catherine Seaman, Accounts, 1744, #96, or Peter Rittenhouse, Accounts, 1782, #100.

[88] QS Rec., passim.

[89] See the *Pa.Gaz.*, April 15, 1762. It is probable that in a true village society word of lost and found cows would have gotten around without recourse to newspaper columns.

[90] *Pa.Berichte*, February 16, 1747.

In sum, however, there is very little in the life-style of Germantown to show why the community should not be left far down at the village end of the urban-rural continuum. It is necessary to turn to the tangibles—the use of land, the mobility of the population, the industrial occupations of the breadwinners—to see the ways in which village life was really just a facade behind whose placid surface changes in community development were constantly taking place.

CHAPTER 2

To The Highest Bidder:
The Economic and Social Value of
Land in a Mobile Society

"A town's economic activity is its mainspring,"[1] and, by definition, in an urban community this activity is nonagricultural in orientation. Yet the land itself is far from irrelevant. It is of vital importance both economically and socially, although attitudes toward owning and holding land have very different sociological implications in an urban context than they have in a peasant society. The conditions and status of a large landless portion of the population and the patterns of distribution of wealth in such a situation affect the whole social structure. Moreover, the land itself has great economic worth both in the colonial setting where it is the first commodity for trade and at a later time when its limited availability continually increases its value. This economic value, however, lies not in its potential for feeding a family or even in the long run for producing a salable surplus. Rather, its usefulness lies in its location in relation to the growth of the population—in its potential as a site for houses and shops and markets.

In colonial America, towns were created instantly rather than through slow organic development over a period of decades and centuries. The tendency to utilize the land in a specific way, whether urban or rural, was therefore heavily influenced by the first leaders in a community. New England settlements whose founders came from parts of England where open-field systems and agricultural villages were the custom, usually reproduced a similar pattern, even

[1] Jones, *Towns*, p. 91.

58

where the majority of the newcomers were craftsmen or servants and had not been trained as farmers at all.[2] The fact that the inhabitants resided "side by side along the streets of the villages rather than dwelling on separate and distant farms outside the village center"[3] did not turn rural communities into cities or even urban towns. Instead, as long as the land continued to feed the people, these communities remained agricultural population clusters. The trend in Andover, for example, was for families to move within a generation from the town to their farms outside the village.[4] Those who came to Pennsylvania with the express purpose of farming "organized the space into dispersed farms and open country neighborhoods rather than agricultural villages."[5]

The founder of Germantown, Francis Daniel Pastorius, was from an urban background. His father had been a citizen and burgher of a populous German town; Pastorius himself attended four universities and practiced law in Frankfurt am Main before coming to America.[6] He was quite well acquainted with William Penn, whose attitude toward the colonies as mercantile and productive was pronounced,[7] and his objectives for his "Germanopolis" closely paralleled those of the proprietor for Philadelphia. In preparation for life in the New World, Pastorius had his own sons learn, not farming, but weaving and shoemaking.

[2] Greven, *Four Generations*, p. 44.

[3] Ibid., p. 43.

[4] See Greven, "Family Structure," *WMQ* (1966).

[5] Lemon, *Best Poor Man's Country*, p. xiii.

[6] Learned, *Pastorius*. Although old fashioned, this biography of Pastorius is complete and includes excellent selections of appropriate German records and Pastorius's own writings in German. Most of the background information on Pastorius comes from this source. While Pastorius's papers are available at the Library Company of Philadelphia, for most purposes this secondary book is eminently satisfactory.

[7] Mary Maples Dunn, *William Penn: Politics and Conscience*, Princeton, 1967. See, for example, pp. 64-65: p. 178, passim.

As legal representative of the Frankfort Land Company in the colonies and as chosen leader of the Crefeld immigrants, Pastorius was responsible for the first division of lands in the German Township. The manner in which he handled this chore indicated not only a knowledge of classical ideas on the city[8] but an interest in the urban definition of the economic value of land. In the original plan, Germantown was to be broken into forty-four grants of approximately 50 acres each, Cresheim into eight lots averaging 110 acres apiece, and Sommerhausen into eight lots ranging from 75 acres to 200 acres; Crefeld was not divided at that time.[9] (See the map of the German Township, figure 1.) Germantown properties were each laid out in two separate parcels. "On account . . . of the favorable location of some parts and the unfavorable location of others, *thus causing great difference in worth*, each was allowed only part of his land in the middle of the town, taking the remainder from the so-called side-lots."[10] The advantage of location to which Pastorius refers is that of centrality rather than soil conditions; like William Penn, he laid out his lots on a grid plan, with little accommodation to geographical factors.

Twenty-one town lots were thus laid out on the west side of the Great Road from a point opposite the road above Kinsey's Mill to the "Road from Roxbury to Abington," and twenty-three town lots were laid out on the east side of the Great Road, for the same approximate distance. Side lots were numbered to correspond to the town properties and marked off to the north and south of the main area, nearer the township lines and frequently off the Great Road alto-

[8] For example, Plato's emphasis in the *Laws* that each citizen should have two lots—one within the city, one outside. Mumford, *City*, p. 179.

[9] The original lot plan is in the Grund und Lager Buch, Germantown General Court, HSP. This was the plan of the first division as made and drawn by Pastorius. A copy of the lot plan is in Keyser, *Germantown*, between pp. 42 and 43.

[10] Pastorius, quoted by Keyser, ibid., p. 37. Emphasis supplied.

gether. For the most part the country lots were on the same side of the road as their "downtown" counterparts, but to make the grant sizes more even the side lots toward Roxborough above the Abington Road stretched across Germantown Road to Mark's Road.

If Pastorius really intended to divide Germantown land equally, he failed to achieve his goal. While the median holding per person of town lot and side land considered together was 49 acres, the properties were not actually equal

TABLE 3

ORIGINAL LAND DISTRIBUTION, GERMANTOWN, 1689

	West of the Great Road					East of the Great Road			
Lot No.	Town Lot (acres)	Main Rd. (linear perches)	Side Lot (acres)	Total Acres	Lot No.	Town Lot (acres)	Main Rd. (linear perches)	Side Lot (acres)	Total Acres
1	23	14.4	27	50	1	15	14.4	35	50
2	22	14.4	27	49	2	16	14.4	33	49
3	44	28.8	55	99	3	18	14.4	31	49
4	22	14.4	12	34	4	20	14.4	29	49
5	21	14.4	25	46	5	22	14.4	15	37
6	21	14.4	28	49	6	23	14.4	26	49
7	42	28.8	57	109	7	24	14.4	25	49
8	20	14.4	29	49	8	62	42.1	62	124
9	40	28.4	59	99	9	30	14.4	20	50
10	20	14.4	30	50	10	66	28.8	33	99
11	19	14.4	30	49	11	35	14.5	14	49
12	19	14.4	30	49	12	76	27.0	23	99
13	19	14.4	50	69	13	145	50.0	29	176
14	49	36.0	76	125	14	40	14.4	9	49
15	49	36.0	75	124	15	20	7.6	5	25
16	19	14.4	30	49	16	39	14.5	10	49
17	20	14.4	30	50	17	19	7.6	5	24
18	10	7.2	15	25	18	39	14.8	11	50
19	20	14.4	24	44	19	38	14.8	11	49
20	50	36.0	70	120	20	19	7.4	6	25
21	10	7.6	14	24	21	19	7.4	6	25
SOURCE: Grund und Lager Buch, lot plan.					22	37	14.8	12	49
					23	37	14.8	12	49

in size: the mean acreage per grant was a much higher 61 and the standard deviation from the mean an incredible 33.18. The same wide variation existed among the town lots considered separately. In this case, the median lot was 22 acres, the average acreage was 29, and the standard deviation was 15.06.[11] The importance of street frontage to an urban land holder was also recognized. Although one cross street was planned, Main Street was the only thoroughfare of any significance for commercial activity. Each town lot, therefore, was provided with a minimum of 125 feet on Germantown Road and stretched all the way back to the township lines at Roxborough, Bristol, or Springfield. There was more equality in terms of frontage than there was in total acreage; the median lot was slightly over 14 perches on Germantown Road, the average slightly over 18, with a standard deviation of 6.4.[12]

The intention of the settlers to create a town as opposed to an agricultural village was clearly established in the "Laws, Ordinances and Statutes of the Community At Germantown, Made and Ratified From Time to Time in the General Court at that Place."[13] The fundamental articles "for the greater and more rapid growth of this place" included provisions for dividing the town lots still further, with the true town property being those two- to four-acre plots that lay directly along the road: "That since Germantown is laid out like a town and every whole property contains four acres, every half property two acres, no inhabitant here shall be entitled to build his dwelling except upon the aforesaid four or two acres respectively, without ob-

[11] This data is collected from table 3. Lot #13 on the east is not included in the calculations as it represented unsold lands of the Frankfort Company rather than a regular lot. When it was sold in 1689, it was divided into three parts.

[12] A perch, which is the measurement used most consistently for Germantown land in the eighteenth century, is the same as a rod: 16½ linear feet, 272¼ square feet.

[13] Pennypacker, *Pa.Ger.*, IX, pp. 319-339. These laws were passed August 28, 1691.

taining first the consent of the community and then that of the General Court."[14] They further stipulated that the owner of side lands must not build on them until after he had established his own family in Germantown. The fine for violating this restriction was an enormous £25![15]

The community grew slowly at first. To make sure that the whole township was settled before undue density built up in any one location, an addition was made to the above ordinance, 12ᵐᵒ26ᵈ1701/2: "anyone who already has his dwelling upon said four or two acres may not himself or have anyone else build a dwelling or stable upon land lying back of it."[16] The result of this attitude was that although many of the lots changed hands between the original grant in 1689 and a survey taken in 1714, none was broken up, and in only one case was a town lot sold away from side lands remaining in the hands of an original owner.[17] There was even a slight degree of consolidation. There were only thirty-seven separate owners listed in 1714, two of them owning three separate properties each and three of them owning two apiece.

By 1734 the situation had begun to change. In the Constables' Returns of that year[18] there were eighty-nine property holders in Germantown proper and in Cresheim. The size of an average lot in Cresheim had dropped from 110 acres to 73, and the average in Germantown was under 29 acres per owner. This made Germantown the place with the smallest average landholdings in the county outside of Philadelphia city; Lower Dublin was next with holdings over twice as large, at 61 acres per landowner.[19]

---

[14] Ibid., p. 322.

[15] Hocker, *Germantown*, p. 37.

[16] Pennypacker, *Pa.Ger.*, IX, p. 338.

[17] Keyser, "Lists of Property Holders, 1689, 1714," *Germantown*, pp. 37-41.

[18] "1734 Constables' Returns."

[19] These figures omit the Northern Liberties for which land returns were only fragmentary. However, among the figures that are available, there were four, out of a total of sixty-three inhabitants,

The next complete figures on landholding in Germantown are not available until 1767, and by then a quantum leap had been taken in the direction of urbanization: the mean property size in Cresheim was now down to 26.36 acres, while that of the Germantown part of the township averaged 10.92. Even more significantly perhaps the medians were 11 and 5 acres respectively.[20] Of course, this in no way measures up to a true metropolis. The original Philadelphia city block was set up to be only an acre, with the stipulation that four houses be built on it as quickly as possible.[21] The plan for density in Germantown was from the beginning two to four times as generous. By 1774 Warner finds the average house lot in the city to be just over 800 square feet,[22] while twenty-five years later, Germantown could still boast a much larger average of over one third of an acre.[23]

Some of the steps along the road to this change to a small city can be perceived through the real estate advertisements relating to Germantown that appeared in the Pennsylvania papers during this period. From 1729 through 1799, 308 offerings of Germantown property were made to the public for sale. The first great leap in Germantown real estate came not too long after those 1734 Constables' Returns. While there were only 7 ads for the township in the 1730s, the number in the 1740s jumped to 47 and remained around this number until the 1790s, at which time it jumped again, this time to 70. Of these, 42 percent involved the sale of cleared

---

who had over 100 acres, while three of Germantown's freeholders had a top of 100 acres. This compares even more dramatically with Lemon's averages for size of holdings in Chester and Lancaster counties throughout the century. *Best Poor Man's Country*, pp. 89-90.

[20] 1767 tax list. The total properties were 74 for Cresheim, 122 for Germantown.

[21] Sachse, *Letters*, Missive #2, pp. 19ff.

[22] Warner, *Private City*, p. 17.

[23] 1798 Direct Tax, Schedule A. The exact average is 15,697.93 square feet.

land for building purposes and another 13 percent empha-
sized the land value of the property rather than the house
that stood on it. Over one-quarter involved schemes to break
larger holdings into smaller ones, increasing the density of
the township. In the earlier decades, these properties usually included rural features—woodlots, orchards, barns,
stables, and the like. However, they also invariably stressed
the advantage of frontage on the Great Road.[24] In the forties
at least two schemes were abroad to sell land for speculative
development. Joseph Shippen planned a "German Square"
to be 300 feet on a side, divided by a center road. The lots
were to range from 40 to 100 feet in frontage. Paul Kripner
divided his land on Market Square and the cross street into
21 small lots, some on the main road, some on the lane. The
time, however, was not yet ripe, and neither of these plans
was successful. The properties were bought instead in sev-
eral-lot chunks by prospering Philadelphia gentlemen to be
used as country seats.[25]

By the end of the century land pressure had become too
great for any but the wealthiest to continue to maintain
large plantations. In 1791 there were seven properties listed
that were over 100 acres, and by 1798 this number had
dropped to three.[26] The pattern that was often followed
may be seen in the distribution of the Neuss (Nice) plantation. On the 1714 survey Cornelius Nice owned 75 acres
in Cresheim. During the course of the next twenty years he
disposed of 25 acres, and in the Constables' Returns of 1734
he was charged with only 50. In 1759 his heirs broke the
plantation into seven lots, added eight others which Cornelius had acquired in upper Germantown, and arranged the
whole into a development for the highest bidder. The "plan

[24] For example, see the *American Weekly Mercury*, March 1-8,
1736/7; April 14-21, 1737.

[25] For the details of these plans see Margaret Tinkcom, "Germantown in Review," *Germantowne Crier* (17 September 1965).

[26] State Tax Assessor's Ledger, Germantownship, 1791. Manuscript located in Phila.Arch. (Hereafter cited as 1791 tax list.) 1798
Direct Tax.

of the Whole could be seen at Christian Lehmann's" who was the surveyor and mapmaker of the area.[27] The rising value of land near the center of Germantown frequently made it far more profitable for an owner to break up his holdings and sell them bit by bit. Land pressure due to immigration was beginning to be felt as far out as Sommerhausen by the 1740s, and part of this area began to be subdivided in a nonrural manner. Single-acre lots were being purchased by craftsmen in relatively remote areas as early as 1743, and land speculation in the "suburbs" included the conveyance of small lots on ground rent on the condition that at least one good, livable house was to be built on each property within a specified period of time.[28]

Although specific information on land holdings in Germantown becomes available in 1767, the material cannot be easily compared with later lists since there is no assignment of land to renters, leaving the actual size of properties controlled by an individual uncertain. The separation of owned and rented land into usage parcels occurs for the first time on the tax list of 1780, which may then be compared with the one for 1791 and the exhaustively complete 1798 Federal Direct Tax, completing the picture of an urbanizing settlement of less than metropolitan size in the eighteenth century. Looking at figure 3, it can be seen that by 1780 no part of the Germantownship could function as a farming community; the median size of a land holding (including those in the more remote parts of Cresheim and Crefeld) was only six to ten acres, with only 14 percent of the individual properties over thirty acres, the amount of land that Greven feels could support an eighteenth-century family.[29] If Lockridge's figures are used, the lack of agricultural independence in Germantown becomes more obvious, since he suggests

[27] *Pa.Gaz.*, July 5, 1759.

[28] Roach, "Chestnut Hill," *Gen.Mag.* (1956), p. 88. The complicated nature of land transfers and breakups in Chestnut Hill is clearly shown throughout this basically genealogical article.

[29] Greven, *Four Generations*, p. 224.

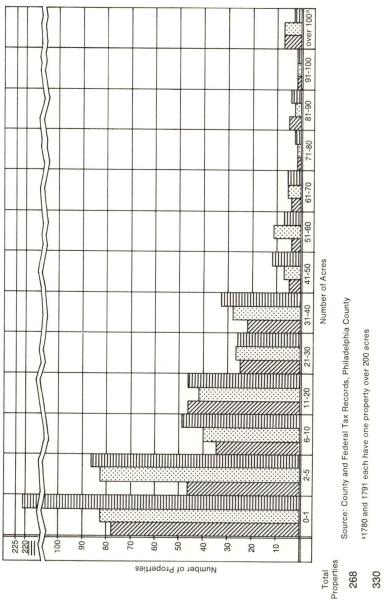

FIGURE 3. Germantown Properties Compared by Size: 1780—1791—1798.

Source: County and Federal Tax Records, Philadelphia County

[a]1780 and 1791 each have one property over 200 acres

Number of Acres

Number of Properties

KEY   Total
       Properties

1780   268

1791   330

1798   488

that in New England it required sixty to ninety acres to sustain a family of six with a small surplus.[30] In the imme- diate Philadelphia area, even taking into account the greater fertility of the soil on the Lancaster Plain, and perhaps a longer growing season, Lemon found that as much as sixty to seventy-five acres fell short of needed acreage for family support.[31]

Nor did the inhabitants of Germantown think of them- selves as rural folk. From 1773 (when the first complete figures were available) through the rest of the century, the number of taxpayers who listed themselves as farmers or who could be determined to be employed on farms never rose higher than 15 percent.[32] To compare this with the rest of Philadelphia county: in 1773 there were no farmers listed within the city wards, with the exception of one in Dock Ward, although there were several graziers; only those di- visions outside the city proper that were larger in popula- tion than Germantown reported fewer people engaged in agriculture, with 5 percent for Southwark and 8 percent for the eastern part of the Northern Liberties. On the other hand, in the underpopulated western section of the North- ern Liberties only 14 of the 466 ratables (3 percent) reported an occupation other than farming. In the surrounding town- ships, a tanner in the Manor of Moreland and two millers and a carter in Lower Merion were the only taxpayers re- porting an occupation, the inference being that the others were in some way or another deriving their incomes from the land.[33] Of course, it would be ridiculous to assume that

[30] Lockridge, *A New England Town*, p. 149.

[31] Lemon, *Best Poor Man's Country*, p. 91.

[32] This is based on analysis of the 1773 tax list, the 1780 tax list, the 1791 tax list, and A list of the Taxable inhabitants residing within the County of Philadelphia, taken agreeable to an Act of Assembly en- titled an "Act to provide for the Enumeration of the Taxable in- habitants of this Commonwealth" passed the 10th day of April, 1793, Phila.Arch. (Hereafter cited as 1793 Septennial Census.) All of these lists give occupations.

[33] It is impossible to judge whether a man was really involved in

all the people in the townships were exclusively farmers, only that they basically thought of themselves as such and that they saw agriculture as their chief means of support. If they were also smiths or innkeepers or the like, this was evidently considered secondary, a kind of service to their communities rather than a primary source of income.

The striking change that came about over the last twenty years of the century was the enormous growth in the number of holdings of less than two acres and the considerable growth in the two- to five-acre category. The number of individual properties increased 23 percent between 1780 and 1791, and jumped another 48 percent between 1791 and 1798. While the number of larger holdings did not appreciably diminish, they came to constitute a smaller percentage of the total. This leads to the conclusion that the trend was to chop just a few perches off the front of one's property and sell that portion as a house lot rather than to divide holdings into smaller even shares among one's children, for example. The amazing leap from 83 lots under two acres in size (25 percent of the total) in 1791 to 221 lots (representing 45 percent of the total properties) in the same category in 1798, should be especially noted.

One other factor should be considered in relation to the density of settlement—the number of houses built on each property. Multiple houses on a single property were not necessarily rental units but may have been used for the families of workmen on the place, for married sons, or for aged parents. Table 4 also indicates the number of properties on which no dwelling is listed at all, thus giving an index to the amount of unsettled land still within the township. The 1798 federal tax is not suitable for this kind of comparison, since it set an arbitrary limit of two acres on each domestic property in Schedule A and did not distinguish vacant land

---

farming, since the 1773 tax list does not list size of holdings, only a general valuation and final rating for each taxable citizen.

TABLE 4

HOUSES PER SINGLE PROPERTY, 1780, 1791

Houses per Property	1780				1791			
	Size of Property (acres)				Size of Property (acres)			
	0-5	6-20	Over 20	Total	0-5	6-20	Over 20	Total
0	18	6	7	31	6	9	3	18
1	136	74	52	262	148	60	57	265
2	1	5	5	11	12	10	13	35
Over 2	—	2	5	7	1	2	9	12
Total	155	87	69	311	167	81	82	330

SOURCE: Philadelphia County tax lists, 1780, 1791.

from cultivated back fields in Schedule B. It may be observed, however, that on a total of 488 properties of less than two acres apiece, there were 543 houses, meaning that roughly 10 percent of the lots had more than 1 dwelling. As an indication of a trend, the percentage of holdings of all sizes with more than 1 house had doubled from 7 to 14 between 1780 and 1791.

The difference between the traditional peasant village and its more rapidly changing counterpart involves more than the patterns of land holdings and the use of property. The attitude of people toward the land on which they live and the value they place upon it, whether intangible or speculative, tell a great deal about the community as a whole, about where it stands on the urban-rural continuum. For both Lockridge and Greven, the basic fact about land in the New England village was the family attachment to it.[34] Williams also noted, in relation to the modern English village of Ashworthy, that the "traditional values of all

[34] Kenneth A. Lockridge, "The Population of Dedham, Massachusetts, 1636-1736," *EHR*, 19 (1966), pp. 322-323; Greven, *Four Generations*. See also Edward S. Penzel, "Landholding in Ipswich," *Essex Institute Historical Collection*, 104 (1968), pp. 303-328.

peasant societies is in their passionate attachment to the land."[35] The attitudes of a vanished and largely inarticulate population are hard to discover, of course, except by indirection, but the extent to which there was any intention to hold on to the homeplace can be determined for at least part of the Germantown population by reference to the wills and deeds of the period.

Wills were almost as frequently arranged to dispose of family land holdings as they were to perpetuate them. Although it is obvious that real estate is included in the general effects of most of the 308 Germantown legators recorded during the period, it is directly mentioned in only 177 of the wills. Of these, there are 25 cases in which no children are involved, leaving 152 times in which parents (almost exclusively fathers) had an opportunity to leave their homeplace to the family. Almost half (46 percent) did not choose to do so, but rather directed that the estate be sold, frequently at public auction, and the cash proceeds be divided up; immediately, if the children were of age, or after maintaining the family as a whole, if they were still minors. Provisions for the widow were also made out of the cash return. In only 4 cases was it stipulated that the oldest son should have the first opportunity to purchase before the property was advertised for general sale. The decision to leave the children with cash, rather than land, was not based primarily on the sex of the children, since in only 11 percent of the cases where fathers left the home to be sold were there no sons alive to inherit, and in one-third of the cases where it was left to a single child it was given to a daughter and away from sons. Forty-four percent (33) of those who left their family home to the children as a land holding left it to be equally divided among sons and daughters, usually after the death or remarriage of the widow. Since the property was rarely large enough for actual division, this meant practically that the father was taking no real interest in who inherited the family home, but was

---

[35] Williams, *Ashworthy*, p. 56.

leaving it to his heirs to make their own decision.[36] The deeds of those properties that can be traced over a useful period of time (thirty years or longer) throughout the century indicate that, in these cases, the children themselves sold the whole and divided the money about as often as they released their shares to one of their own number.[37] This attitude toward the land as a speculative rather than a traditional thing of value changed very little during the century. Only a slightly higher proportion of the properties left to be sold, as compared to those left directly to children (93 percent to 87 percent), appeared in wills dated after 1740,[38] and there was no particular change in the rate of turnover among the deeded properties, which averaged about 1.16 times per decade, with 62.2 percent of the new owners being unrelated to previous holders.

The effect of the treatment of land as a commodity was to promote a high degree of mobility among Germantown residents, since it left them free to decide rationally rather than emotionally the question of whether to move or stay. Each course could be considered on the basis of whether it "would improve their material position or at least prevent a decline in status."[39] Although recent research has indi-

[36] For other aspects of inheritance in relation to family structure, see chapter 8.

[37] Deeds in Brief and Commission Reports for Properties along Germantown Avenue, PHC. (Hereafter cited as Deeds in Brief.) Much of the material in these deeds is by recital, since property so frequently went unrecorded throughout the period, and there are only 25 that provide a really continuous record of the ownership of specific pieces of property. Still, they are valuable as they indicate long-term patterns of transfer for the area, which are not available in coherent form from any other documents, and over half of them cover at least 100 years.

[38] The size of the percentages in both instances reflects, of course, the fact that only 16 of the total 152 wills were for the period prior to 1740.

[39] Lemon, *Best Poor Man's Country*, p. 71. All of chapter 3, "Movements of Pennsylvanians," pp. 71-97, is valuable as a comparison to the following pages on Germantown mobility.

cated that seemingly immobile peasant or rural persons move more than has previously been thought,[40] the amount of mobility and population turnover in eighteenth-century Germantown is closely related to the general development of the township as a village of urban character. While one must acknowledge all the difficulties, set forth by Lemon, of studying the factor of mobility in relation to Pennsylvania colonists in particular, the effort is still necessary to a complete study of this nature, even if the results can be only tentative.[41]

Mobility was not a new way of life for many of the immigrants to Germantown. There is much evidence, especially among the earliest arrivals whose paths are most easily traced, that they had already moved several times in Europe before coming to the colonies. In 1665 an ancestor of one of the first Germantowners wrote a poem in which he described the flight of his family and much of his congregation (he was a Mennonite preacher) from the countryside into Worms and later to Kriegsheim, where the group settled until many of them removed to Pennsylvania in 1684.[42] After being settled for perhaps only a generation or

[40] See, for example, Williams, *Ashworthy,* for the importance of short distance migration among rural folk, and D.E.C. Eversley, "Population, Economy and Society," *Population in History,* p. 40, on physical mobility in England by the seventeenth century. Peter Laslett, "The Study of Social Structure from Listings of Inhabitants," *EHD,* pp. 165-166, mentions a turnover in persons of 61 percent between 1676 and 1688 in Clayworth, England, much larger than would be supposed. While Greven found colonial Andover extremely stable (*Four Generations,* p. 268), Lemon mentions a rate of 30 percent for Chester and Lancaster counties in Pennsylvania in the latter part of the eighteenth century; *Best Poor Man's Country,* p. 73.

[41] Lemon lists, among other factors, the unimportance of township government, filing of records by county, the variety of churches in any one community, and the general inadequacy of Pennsylvania record keeping; *Best Poor Man's Country,* pp. 72-73. All of these difficulties affected the Germantown material.

[42] Pennypacker, *Pa.Ger.,* IX, pp. 172-174. A poem by Ylles Kassel, ancestor of Johannes Kassel of Germantown, who came with the Kriegsheim group.

so after the Thirty Years' War, many were displaced again by the French invasion of the Palatinate (1688-1689), moving into the Netherlands and then on across the seas.

Although conditions in the Palatinate improved during the next fifty years, the fact that the electors John William (1690-1716) and Charles Philip (1716-1742) were Roman Catholic placed the Reformed and Lutheran people of the territory under the financial and religious strains of petty persecution. Largely for these reasons emigration, even during peaceful times, continued heavy until it was halted by the French and English wars. Swiss immigrants, moved by similar impulses, migrated first to the Palatinate, then to America.[43] The first Germans to come to America were often quite well to do; most had enough, not only to pay for their passage but also to buy land on arrival.[44]

Contemporary reports would seem to indicate that by the middle of the century, the main drawing card was the amazing ability of Pennsylvania to produce abundant food supplies. It is perhaps worth quoting two examples of the kind of literature that reached Germany in this period and that must have appealed to the already dissatisfied peasant there. Peter Kalm discussed the bountiful supply of food in a scientific way, attempting to find the natural causes for the phenomenon: "The annual harvest . . . always affords plenty of bread for the inhabitants, though one year may be better than the rest. . . . It is likewise to be observed that the people eat their bread or corn, rye or wheat quite pure and free from chaff and other impurities . . . the inhabitants

[43] Wertenbaker, *Middle Colonies*, chapter 8, gives the most concise account of these waves of immigration, which are largely ignored as a social phenomenon by historians. For general conditions, social and economic, in Germany and the surrounding areas at the time, see M. S. Anderson, *Europe in the Eighteenth Century, 1713-1783*, New York, 1961.

[44] Frank R. Diffenderffer, "German Immigration into Pennsylvania Through the Port of Philadelphia, 1700-1775: Part II, The Redemptioners," *Narrative and Critical History*, Part VII, Pa.Ger., X (1899), p. 142. (Hereafter cited as "Redemptioners.")

could not remember any crop so bad as to make the people suffer in the least, much less that anybody had starved to death, while they were in America. Sometimes the price of grain rose higher in one year, on account of a great drought or bad weather, but still there was always sufficient for the consumption of the inhabitants."[45] Gottlieb Mittelberger, who wrote of the horrors of the system of "redemption" as applied to the German immigrant and who in general attempted to discourage German settlement in America, also saw food as an important factor: "Provisions are cheap in Pennsylvania. The people live well, especially on all sorts of grain, which thrives very well, because the soil is wild and fat. They have good cattle, fast horses and many bees. The sheep which are larger than the German ones, have generally two lambs a year. . . . Even in the humblest and poorest houses in this country there is no meal without meat, and no one eats the bread without the butter or cheese, although the bread is as good as with us."[46]

A very large number of those who eventually settled in Germantown first lived in some other part of Pennsylvania or in one of the other colonies. Those who had fled the famine of 1709 went first to England and then to New York, and when conditions there failed to offer them adequate support, a few proceeded to Germantown. Many of the best-known families in Germantown in the later part of the century—the Dewees, the Ashmeads, the Bringhursts, the Rittenhouses, and the Bensells, to name just a few—had started out elsewhere in the colonies. This was often necessary since the cost of land in the township was high, and as time went on it was harder for the newly arrived immigrant

[45] *Kalm's Travels*, pp. 285-286.

[46] *Gottlieb Mittelberger's Journey to Pennsylvania in the Year 1750 and Return to Germany in the Year 1754, containing not only a Description of the Country According to its Present Condition But also a Detailed Account of the Sad and Unfortunate Circumstances of Most of the Germans That Have Emigrated or Are Emigrating to That Country*, trans. Carl T. Eben, Philadelphia, 1898, pp. 64-65.

to afford the settled areas. A clear indication of this pattern is found in the fact that after the resumption of immigration in 1761, recognizable Germantown names appearing on the passenger lists almost vanish,[47] although the number of new surnames on the Germantownship tax lists continued to grow.

The settlers of Germantown were, therefore, people whose attachment to the land had already been severely weakened by years or even decades of mobility. How much of that pattern of impermanence remained after settlement in Germantown may be quickly summarized by a survey of the demographic events recorded in the town during the eighteenth century.[48] Thirteen percent of all the individual listings for births, marriages, and deaths involve surnames that appear only once in the records: that is, over 1,000 of the 8,000 entries investigated had no relationship at all to any other item in any church or cemetery record. The large number of marriages involving transients is understandable since Germantown was a resort area and therefore popular as a place to get married. Yet it is truly astonishing in its implications that one out of ten persons buried, and one out of twelve babies baptized were, in some sense, strangers to the community.

It is also possible to make a somewhat more complete investigation of mobility through a study of surnames within the township from 1689 to 1798. Actually, the family unit is a more useful subject for analysis in this regard, since disappearance of an individual is so often due to death or poor record keeping, especially when the facts cover a very long period. The length of time over which family names appear on the various tax or census lists is a basic indication of the permanence of the residence of the family unit within a community, independent of the reasons that cause the

[47] Rupp, *30,000 Names*, p. 351.
[48] These statistics are gathered from St.M.Rec., Ref.Ch.Rec., Hood Cemetery Records, AbMMRec., and the "Records of the Upper Burying Ground," *PMHB*, 8 and 9.

Table 5

Population Mobility in Germantown, 1689-1790
Based on a Study of Surnames

List on which Name First Appears	(a) No. of Persons This List	(b) No. of Surnames This List	(c) New Surnames This List		(d) Single Appearance This List			(e) Names from (c) Remaining 20 Years Later		(f) Names from (b) Remaining 20 Years Later	
			No.	% of (b)	No.	% of (b)	% of (c)	No.	% of (c)	No.	% of (b)
1689	48	40	—	—	12	30.0	—	—	—	18	37.5
1693	52	42	16	38.0	13	31.0	81.0	3	19.0	14	33.3
1714	43	39	20	51.2	6	15.5	30.0	9	45.0	14	35.9
1734	89	70	51	72.8	19	27.1	37.2	26	51.0	35	50.0
1767[a]	473	328	282	85.8	101	30.8	35.8	120	42.6	156	47.6
1773	481	356	181	50.8	106	29.8	58.5	62	34.3	125	35.1
1780	423	253	67	26.6	43	17.0	64.2	18	27.0	73	28.9
1790	556	324	125	38.5	82	25.3	65.6	—	—	—	—

SOURCE: Philadelphia County tax lists, 1693, 1767, 1773, 1780; Federal Direct Tax, 1798; *U.S. Census Report*, 1790; List of Property Holders, 1689, 1714; 1734 Constables' Returns.

[a] The large jump in this year represents a change in tax keeping records from listing owners only to listing renters as well.

disappearance of any particular individual. Those families that seem to vanish but are actually still present in the female line are balanced by those surnames that recur decade after decade and would seem to point to a high degree of stability while, in fact, there are two, or even more, completely unrelated groups of the same name. Actually, the number of either of these cases is quite small in eighteenth-century Germantown, although there are a few examples. The name "Klostermann" appears on the list of property owners in 1689 and is never seen again, leading one to believe, perhaps, that the family moved on; yet the name was that of a single woman who married Pastorius himself, bore him two sons, and remained one of the very few people to have descendants present in Germantown throughout the entire period. As a practical matter, the loss of the name has little effect on a study of stability, since the patriarchal principle was so strongly evolved in the community that a continuation through the female line was not considered particularly meaningful.

On the other hand, a common name like "Keyser" or "Miller" was held by more than one family from the very beginning, and the records are often too incomplete to be sure which individuals belong to which group and whether or not family stability is really indicated by the evidence. For the purposes of this study the problem was solved by giving each surname the value of one, rather than trying to report on each household within a given group.[49] The name "Miller" appears on every list considered and is counted as if the same family is continuous throughout the century. Because of the large number of individuals with this name, it is likely that some do belong to a common line and that one unit at least is properly considered among the stable families of the township.

---

[49] The size of families in relation to the number of units of kinship groups living within the community is, of course, extremely important in considering the sociological structure of the family, as well as that of the community. See chapter 8.

Nine different lists of property owners and taxpayers were used to arrive at the breakdown of information on Germantown mobility that appears in table 5. While they cover the period from 1689 to 1798, the last, of course, could not be used to indicate ongoing mobility, although it was employed as an end check for the rest of the century. Actually mobility is somewhat understated in this study, since the first, third, and fourth include only property owners, while single men who owned no land and worked for an employer were among the most unstable elements of the population. To equalize this, persons who were present on those lists that included renters and head taxers but were missing on adjacent ownership lists were considered to be in continual residence unless there was outside information to the contrary. In all other cases, discontinuous surnames were classed as different families, again unless there was independent information concerning their relationship.

In all, there are 2,165 entries on the nine lists that cover the period of this study. Of these 1,472 could be established as separate individuals, the rest being duplicate listings of those who survived from one list to another. It is in itself somewhat astonishing that, in a group of tax lists between which the interval is over twenty years only once and is frequently under ten, less than one-third of the entries were repeats. The 1,472 persons represented 782 different surnames, as nearly as can be determined.[50] Forty-eight and

---

[50] A major problem in Germantown history is to decipher the spelling of names in order to sort them into family groups. It is not only a question of eighteenth-century spelling, which is free in any case, but of German pronunciation in the ears of English bureaucrats. It is often possible to relate one name to another by pronouncing it out loud quickly in German and considering the phonetic transcription of the actual sound—for example, it is not too difficult to determine that "Pencil" is "Bensell" when one takes into account frequent German reversal of "b" and "p." "Veafer" for "Weaver" and even "Tidwiler" for "Ditweiler" are also readily decipherable. It requires more imagination to spot the eight different spellings of "Toulesan" from its original to "Dulesang," and it is only luck that Simon

eight-tenths percent of the family names only appeared once, while there were only 3 surnames present on all nine lists. Thirty percent of the family names were represented by at least one member for twenty years or more, leaving another 22 percent who were not transient, but who remained for less than a generation. This contrasts most sharply with findings on New England villages where Lockridge, for example, listed 63 family names in 1648 in Dedham, and forty years later, found only 57, with an increasing majority who belonged to one of the 30 clans present before 1648. In addition, any given year turned up less than 1 percent immigration or emigration by adult males.[51] It is smaller, however, than Lemon's findings of over 5 percent removals of individuals per year in Chester and Lancaster counties.[52]

While attachment to the land was not necessarily deeply felt by those who owned property, or who were married, the most mobile sector of the Germantown population appears to have been that which was least encumbered. The lists in which the greatest permanence of residence can be observed are those that contain no renters and very few single men. Of those who owned their homes in 1780, almost 60 percent were still present in 1798, while only 27 percent of the rental families remained. While the proportions of single men and married men who appeared only

---

Vogelgesang was recognized as the same person as "Kazongen, Simon Foulk," whose will was probated by an English clerk (WB W, p. 138, #73). It must also be remembered that names were frequently translated, especially around mid-century; for example, "Koenig" became "King." Finally, in the first part of the eighteenth century, it was not unknown to follow the Dutch custom of dropping the last name entirely and using the father's given name (with an "s" appended) as a surname. Thus, the son of Adam Hogermoed became Matthias Adam Hogermoed, and, eventually, merely Mathew Adams. For these reasons, as well as for the basic ones of underregistration and misplaced taxpayers, any numbering of inhabitants or sorting of families must be recognized as having a fairly high likelihood of error.

[51] Lockridge, *A New England Town*, pp. 63-64.
[52] Lemon, *Best Poor Man's Country*, figures 22 and 23, pp. 74-75.

once tended to be about the same over the space of a generation, 73 percent of the bachelors disappeared, as compared to only 58 percent of their married counterparts. Renters and single men who stayed in the township had usually changed their status by the time of the next record; 70 percent of the 1780 renters who were still listed in 1798 had become owners. There are also many examples, although there is no way to quantify them, of single men who married into the established families and became owners as well as householders through their new relationships to resident Germantown families.

It was significant for the stability of the community as a whole, however, that many of the most important families in the town at various periods of its history failed to establish a tradition of permanence. For this, Germantown's original land distribution and its specific geographic situation are largely responsible, together with the larger historical trend toward mobility. Those whose real interest was in becoming squires of landed estates never had any way of accumulating enough property in the Germantownship. Even the first settlers had been encouraged to move on by the very nature of their land grants. Only a small percentage of the German purchase was in Germantown itself, the rest having been laid out in the rich, western part of what is now Montgomery County (see figure 4). A tract of over 22,000 acres was surveyed by Penn and titled to Daniel Falckner and Johannes Jawert as representatives of the Frankfort Company in 1701; this area was known as Falckner's Schwamp, and huge chunks of it were acquired by Germantown families who either moved out themselves or deeded the property to the next generation. Jan Lucken, for example, a weaver who arrived in America in 1683, owned one of the original 50-acre sections in Germantown.[53] By 1697 he had sold this land, although he kept his house and the small lot on which it stood until he died there in 1744. He had also received 500 acres in Towamensing

[53] Lot #6, east side; table 3.

81

and another 500 near present-day Doylestown. None of his eleven children inherited his Germantown property although a few of them lived just over the line in Bristol Township. Most of his heirs were provided for out of those extensive properties in the further reaches of the county.[54]

A year after Penn had granted the rest of the Frankfort Company land to Falckner and Jawert, the Crefelders in Germantown received an extra 6,000 acres in settlement of their claims against the proprietary. These were bought up by Matthias van Bebber who added 915 acres of his own and received a patent on the whole tract in Skippack township (often called Bebber's township) on February 22, 1702. This area was largely colonized by Mennonites both from Germany and from Germantown, the latter frequently being men who had been Quakers until the Keithian controversy.[55] By 1745 most of the influential Mennonites seem to have moved to Skippack, as judged by the names on a letter to the Dutch Mennonites sent from America in that year.[56]

The relatively high value of the Germantown land meant that those who had property both there and up-county and desired to farm could use the sale price of the more expensive land as capital with which to set up a really well-stocked establishment. This also encouraged the early settlers to move away from the township. Thus, Abraham OpdenGraff, who by rights of survivorship came into over 2,000 acres of Pennsylvania land that had belonged to his brothers as well as to himself, sold the 828 acres that had been laid out in Germantown as early as 1704 and moved to Perkiomen in the so-called Dutch township. His move was probably also prompted by the fact that he had been heavily involved in the Keithian troubles, and was frequently called before the court as a result of his naturally quick temper.[57]

[54] From an unpublished genealogy of the Lucken family, GHS.

[55] Pennypacker, *Pa.Ger.*, IX, p. 193.

[56] J. G. de Hoop Scheffer, "Mennonite Emigration to Pennsylvania," Samuel Pennypacker, trans., *PMHB*, 2 (1878), pp. 134-135.

[57] Pennypacker, *Pa.Ger.*, IX, p. 200. Also see "The Records of the Courts of Record held in the Corporation of Germantown from the

Those who followed the early settlers adhered to much the same pattern, and as might be supposed in a community where the population moved so frequently, the rental of property became more important than would be the case in an average colonial rural settlement. Lemon places the percentage of tenants in Chester and Lancaster counties at 27 and 36 respectively in the 1750s, and 27 and 32 in the 1780s; the borough of Lancaster had 41 percent rented property in 1758, with no later information given.[58] In Germantown, on the other hand, from 1767 on (the first time that such statistics become available), less than half of the adult taxables (43 percent) were land owners.[59] Of the remaining 56 percent (269 individuals), 26 percent rented their own establishments and 30 percent appear to have been landless. It is interesting to note that although single men accounted for only 15.6 percent of the ratables on this list, they make up 42 percent of the totally landless, indicating a combination of hired labor and single sons of age still living at home. While the figures do not compare to Philadelphia, where, by 1774, according to Warner, only 19 percent of the families owned their homes, they are impressive enough. The breakdown on the 1780 tax list for Germantown is even more complete in showing the kind of property held by the inhabitants. At that time, 181 residents owned their homes, 65 rented landed properties on which they paid the taxes, 85 rented tenements involving

---

first day of the eighth month, Anno 1691 and thenceforward from time to time. Thus transcribed by ordre [*sic*] of a General Court held at the said Germantown the twenty-sixth day of the tenth month in the year 1690," manuscript, HSP. (Hereafter cited as Records of the Court of Record.) This is a nineteenth-century English transcript of an earlier German court record which seems to have disappeared. Part of it is reprinted in *Collections of the Historical Society of Pennsylvania*, I, pp. 243-258. The references here are to 21^{d}1mo 1703/4 and passim.

[58] Lemon, *Best Poor Man's Country*, p. 94.

[59] Unless otherwise noted, the information in the following section is taken from the tax lists of 1767, 1780, 1791 and the 1798 Direct Tax.

no land at a fixed yearly rate, 10 were sharecroppers work-ing the property "to the halves," and 69 were totally land-less, being housed by their employers or parents either within the main house or in an outbuilding on the property. Of this last number, 41 were married men, presumably with families, and 28 were single.

The percentage of resident owners stood at 40 in 1791. The tax list for this year did not separate the renters of tenements from the completely landless, but, as a group, the two categories accounted for 229 of the total 499 taxpayers. Sixty-nine households were established in rented properties, and 201 homes were owner occupied. Of these last, 24 were still paying ground rent or other "perpetual" obligations. It is impossible to measure 1798 in the same terms because, due to the intent of the tax, landless taxables were not men-tioned at all. However, there is no reason to believe that the pattern in this category varied from that established in the areas of ownership and rental. By that year 262 householders owned their property, and 222 were renting. The ratio of owned to rented properties was about eight to seven, much the same as it had been in 1780.

Rented properties on which the residents paid the taxes in 1780 differed only slightly from the owner-occupied properties of the same period in size and value. The dif-ference may be seen in table 6. There was a slight tendency for rented lands to be smaller, and the average value of all rentals was somewhat smaller, except in the categories of six- to twenty-acre estates, and twenty-one- to fifty-acre plantations, where the value of rented land was greater than that of owner-occupied. Two factors operated to unbalance the statistics in these size ranges. In the first place, there were a large number of elaborate "gentlemen's seats," which were rented rather than owned, thus inflating values of large rental properties. In addition, a group of local farmers were working their own estates of approximately the same acreage, which deflated the value of owned land, since

TABLE 6

OWNER- AND RENTER-OCCUPIED PROPERTIES
COMPARED BY SIZE AND VALUE, 1780

Size (acres)	Owner Occupied		Renter Occupied	
	%	Av. Value (£)	%	Av. Value (£)
0-1	28.2	5,100	36.9	3,750
2-5	18.5	6,413	18.6	6,666
6-20	29.6	9,324	27.7	11,666
21-50	17.6	13,523	7.7	14,500
Over 50	6.1	19,500	3.1	15,000
Not given	—	—	6.0	4,166
Total	100.0	10,722	100.0	9,291

SOURCE: 1780 tax list.

NOTE: The average property values are based on the midpoints of
data grouped in £5,000 intervals. The high cash valuations reflect
the inflation of the war years, but the relative values are equivalent
to those of noninflation years.

farming was never a terribly profitable part of Germantown's economy.

The real and growing difference between the landholder
and the renter can be seen in the 1798 Direct Tax list, which
describes tenement and fixed-rate rentals as well as landed
ones. While only three owner-occupied properties were
rated below $300.00, there seems to have been a kind of
standard tenement rated far below this, usually occupied
by workmen in the owner's business, associated with the
better owner properties. This small dwelling, usually valued
uniformly at $200.00, was a one-story frame building, 16'x
18', on a forty-perch lot (somewhat less than one-quarter
of an acre), and having two twelve-over-twelve windows.
Overall, the gap can be seen in the assessment of 65.8 percent of the rented properties at under $1,000, while 73.6
percent of owner-occupied lands were valued at over
$1,000. As in the earlier period, the more expensive rental

85

TABLE 7

OWNER- AND RENTER-OCCUPIED PROPERTIES
COMPARED BY VALUE, 1798

Assessed Value of Property ($)	No. of Owners	No. of Renters
Under 299	3	47
300-599	31	54
600-999	35	45
1,000-1,999	72	44
2,000-4,999	101	31
5,000-9,999	17	—
10,000 and up	3	1
Total	262	222

SOURCE: Federal Direct Tax, 1798, Schedules A and B.

properties were most often gentlemen's estates rather than rented farms or businesses.

Those aspects of the quality of housing that accounted for the disparity in value of owner and rental properties are clearly shown by separating the two in relation to building characteristics. In every respect, those people who rented their homes had less substantial, less comfortable accommodations than those who owned their own places. This was true even when such rented houses as country seats and large family places, still owned by widowed mothers but carried by the son or eventual heir, are figured into the

TABLE 8

OWNER- AND RENTER-OCCUPIED PROPERTIES COMPARED BY QUALITY, 1798[a]

	Building Material (%)			No. of Stories (%)			Outbuildings (%)			Windows per House[b] (%)				
	Stone	Frame	Other	1	2	Other	Kitchen	Other	None	0-2	3-5	6-10	11-15	Over 15
Owners (N-262)	89.3	8.3	2.3	26.4	69.8	2.9	49.6	15.6	34.8	10.2	24.3	27.5	21.6	16.5
Renters (N-222)	76.1	15.8	8.1	50.7	47.6	1.7	24.8	10.4	64.8	24.9	36.2	20.4	15.4	3.2

[a] Based on the 484 properties analyzed in table 1.
[b] Only 476 of the properties listed windows.

averages along with more modest freeholdings and tenements.

The corollary of renter is landlord. In Germantown the majority of those who rented out property let only one place, often directly behind their own houses. Therefore, nothing that could be called a landlord class ever developed on any large scale. Out of sixty-four people who rented property in 1779,[60] forty-five leased only one property, ten had two properties from which they derived income, three had three tenants, two had four, and one each had five, six, or seven. Only one man could truly be called a landlord in the sense that the major part of his income was derived from rentals. This was John Johnson, a direct descendant of two of the original settlers, who leased out sixteen properties for term, and collected ground rent from twenty-two others. After he died, his family split up the property so that, by 1798, the largest landlord in Germantown was still a Johnson, but he held only six places, while another son had three, and the estate of a third rented out one tenement. Widows, however, found the rental of property a useful way to make money, and while in 1779 there were only five who rented out property, by 1798 eighteen widows were receiving income on a total of twenty properties.

The use of rental properties was not merely residential, but commercial as well. Lots were rented out for their income, and country seats were frequently rented after the English custom, especially as Germantown became more and more popular as a summer resort: "For rent to a gentleman's family for the summer season. A Large, two-story

[60] State Tax Assessment Ledger, Philadelphia County, 1776-1779, Phila.Arch. (Hereafter cited as 1779 tax list.) The tax lists for these dates present a problem as they were made during and after the confusion of British occupation and the aftermath of the Battle of Germantown. Despite their somewhat uncertain character, they are useful for sorting specific elements, such as rental properties, head tax, and the like which the appraiser tended to separate.

stone house with four rooms on each floor, a large entry, a piazza and a kitchen. In a pleasant situation near middle Germantown with a garden, orchard and stable if wanted."[61] The summer visitor became as time went by an extremely important factor in the economic life of the community, and the tourist industry had great impact on many areas of business life besides land value.

Business properties as well as houses were frequently rented rather than sold. As early as 1735, a brick kiln with a supply of dug clay was offered for rent in Cresheim.[62] The taverns in the area were continually changing managers, although retaining the same owners. When William Hoffman died in 1758, his widow advertised his smith shop for rent rather than for sale,[63] and the Shoemaker family, although moving to Philadelphia, remained absentee landlords in Germantown throughout the century, not only renting out their family dwelling in the town, but also a tanyard on their property, to a succession of tenants.[64]

One other factor should be mentioned before leaving the topic of rental. There was a definite trend, as congestion increased toward the end of the century, to rent out part of a house or a few rooms. The first recorded instance of this development was in 1752 in an advertisement for Stephen Benezet's house in Germantown as suitable for one or two families.[65] By the nineties, especially during the periods of the yellow fever epidemics in Philadelphia, it became common practice to offer a few rooms with the "use of the kitchen and cellar" for rent for the season.

It is almost impossible to figure actual land values for

[61] See, for example, *Pa.Gaz.*, July 2, 1747; January 10, 1781; May 23, 1765.

[62] *American Weekly Mercury*, April 17-24, 1735.

[63] *Pa.Berichte*, August 19, 1758.

[64] 1780 tax list, 1791 tax list, 1798 Direct Tax. Also see *Dunlap's Advertiser*, January 21, 1791.

[65] *Pa.Gaz.*, May 21, 1753.

eighteenth-century Germantown.[66] Buildings were rated together with the land; even in the Direct Tax of 1798 where houses were assessed separately, improvements, such as stables and barns, were not. It is frequently impossible to tell whether a given piece of land had been improved, whether it was pasture, orchard, or field. Certainly no complete statistical analysis can be made under these circumstances. Still, some suggestive examples can be cited, not only from the tax lists, but from inventories, deeds, and sheriffs' deeds registered in Common Pleas Court records.[67]

Pastorius is reported to have bought land for the Frankfort Company at a rate of less than one shilling per acre at the time of settlement in 1683. Penn himself pegged the price at £20 for 500 acres or something under two shillings per acre. In 1720 John Wister bought 500 acres in mid-Germantown at the rate of two shillings per acre.[68] This would all appear to apply to uncleared land. In the 1720s, the standard 50-acre property with house and some improvements was inventoried at £80.[69] Ten years later, Henrich Stalfelt's 14½-acre "plantation" was considered to be worth £30.[70] The boom in Germantown land value had begun in earnest by 1735, when 152 acres were valued at £300.[71] Unfortunately, beyond this point, the amount of

[66] This is generally true throughout the colonies. See, for example, Greven, *Four Generations*, pp. 128-129. Lemon attempts some sketchy evaluations based on deeds (*Best Poor Man's Country*, table 13, p. 69), but as the price in one period alone is indefinite from 4 shillings to £30, the results are not terribly useful.

[67] Sheriffs' Deeds, Court of Common Pleas Records, 1736-1800, 4 vols., Phila.Arch. Of a total of 2,122 recorded sales of property in Philadelphia County made by the sheriff between 1736 and 1800, only 99 relate to Germantown.

[68] Keyser, *Germantown*, p. 28.

[69] Samuel Pastorius, Inventory, 1722, #246; Georg Adam Hogermoed, Inventory, 1723, #293.

[70] Henry Stalfelt, Inventory, 1732, #264. While this shows something of a rise over the ten-year period, speculation in Germantown land had obviously not yet begun.

[71] Henry Holesapple, Inventory, 1735, #426.

land was not specified in the inventories, so the material cannot be used for comparison.[72]

Location and use of the land came, of course, to play a large part in its commodity value. While early development of the township suggested an undifferentiated pattern of land use, which is common to the preindustrial form of the city,[73] concentration of business slowly built up in the lower part of Germantown during the course of the century. In the 1740s, properties were frequently advertised as being suitable for either the country home of a gentleman or business use, such as the house and lot on Main Street which were "fit for a gentleman or tradesman" or the house and garden offered for rent as "best situated for business or pleasure." By the 1750s and later, however, land in that part of town was more apt to be listed as "convenient for tanner, tavern or shopkeeper, being in a part of the Town where all the Trade centers," or simply "fit for smith or other tradesman."[74]

While all types of properties continued to be scattered throughout the township—the largest store was at the far end of Sommerhausen, the most spacious of wealthy estates near the Market Square—the price of comparable properties was much determined by their availability to central Germantown. In 1753, for example, unimproved land sold for £17/6 per acre in mid-Germantown, for £7 per acre on the Wissahickon Creek, and for £4/6 in Sommerhausen where development was just beginning.[75] Assessments on the

[72] Even the 1767 tax list is useless for these purposes, since valuations are figured on the ratable's total estate, including cows, horses, servants, etc. There is no separate assessment of his land.

[73] See, for example, Jones, *Towns*, p. 40 and passim.

[74] Any newspaper ads from Jenkins, "News," make the point. See, for example, *Pa.Gaz.*, August 21, 1746; April 21, 1748; August 29, 1751; May 10, 1753; August 13, 1761; *Pennsylvania Journal*, June 8, 1779.

[75] Sheriffs' Deeds, Volume A, June 6, 1753: lender, Benjamin Shoemaker; debtor, Immanuel Kolgesser; buyer, George Smith. June 26, 1753: lender, David van Horne; debtor, Peter Rock, dec'd; buyer,

1780 tax list generally showed that an acre in the village of Chestnut Hill was worth 50 percent more than an acre of mill land by the Wissahickon, and a quarter-acre-lot on the Market Square was twice as valuable as a whole acre in Chestnut Hill, or eight times as much per acre.[76] In 1787, at Sheriff's sale, two empty lots near the center of town, totaling 150 square perches (a shade over an acre) were sold to pay the debts of Abraham Jones for £270 (about £260 per acre), while the creditors of Matthias Gensel could only collect £450, or about £12/18 per acre, on his 34¼ acres of unimproved land "near Cresheim."[77] The difference was somewhat less noticeable when a building was involved. The 1798 Federal Direct Tax rated standard tenements on the back lands of Cresheim at $110 and exactly similar models just off the Great Road in central Germantown at $200.

This urbanization of the land, and its importance for building and commerce, meant that its value was less and less determined by its suitability for farming. After 1780 farm lands consistently rated lower than those owned by craftsmen, and, as a rule, the larger the property, the less its valuation by the acre. In the inflated currency of 1780, properties of over fifteen acres were generally rated below £1,000 per acre, while those of less than five acres were usually over £2,000 per acre. The same overall profile held true in 1791, although a more careful rating of the value of the houses themselves led to greater variations within the categories. Schedule B of the Federal Direct Tax rated non-residential properties in 1798 and shows that the same pat-

---

John Johnson. June 6, 1753: lender and debtor, same as above; buyer, John Gardner.

[76] 1780 tax list. For example, Henry Cress, a hatter, with one acre in Chestnut Hill was assessed at £3,000; Charles Hay, a miller, with five acres, at £10,000; and Widow Delaplaine with one-quarter acre was valued at £6,000. Each of these properties had one house. These assessments, of course, are in the inflated money of the war period, but their relative values are comparable.

[77] Sheriffs' Deeds, Volume C, January 29, 1787 and May 29, 1787.

TABLE 9

AVERAGE PRICE PER ACRE,
NONRESIDENTIAL PROPERTY, 1798

Acres	Improved Land ($)	Unimproved Land ($)
0-.9	622	319
1-5.9	165	71
6-10.9	100	50
11-20.9	73	45
21-39.9	67	35
40 and over	49	—

SOURCE: Federal Direct Tax, 1798, Schedule
B.

tern was even more apparent at the end of the century. As is to be expected, the smaller the overall property, the greater the value of improved over unimproved acreage.

There are other indicators, small but salient, that point to the decreasing availability of Germantown land for rural purposes by the end of the eighteenth century. The lumber business, which was thriving enough in the township in 1759 for its citizens to petition the Quarter Sessions court for a new ferry and road across the Schuylkill to a saw mill in Merion,[78] had dwindled by the eighties to the point that the "Tanners of Germantown" regularly advertised for lumber and bark.[79] By 1780, only 59 percent of the tax-payers were assessed for cows. While this sounds like a large number, it is necessary to remember that the keeping of a cow for the family milk supply was not uncommon even in the urban atmosphere of Philadelphia.[80] Of the 251 ratables

[78] QS Rec., December 1759.
[79] See, for example, *Pa.Gaz.*, April 19, 1786; April 18, 1787.
[80] Warner, *Private City*, p. 17.

93

who did own cows in Germantown, only 28 percent had more than one, with only 3 people reporting as many as five. The 1798 Direct Tax records only 40 percent of the properties with any sort of barn and 23 percent with stabling facilities.

It is easy to attribute much of the urban pattern that developed in eighteenth-century Germantown to rising land values, which made the agricultural use of lands with high speculative potential financially unattractive. While this is undoubtedly a factor, it should be clear by now that it was far from being the basic cause. In New England villages, where traditional communities became established, the scarcity and rising price of land contributed to the mobility of younger sons in later generations but did not prevent at least one branch of the family from keeping enough land to continue farming and living within the old structure.[81] Those who had settled in Germantown were different from the very beginning; they lacked the psychological drive of a peasant society to make their homeplace or community a symbol of family strength and continuity. The founders had intended to create a town and had laid out lots that never could have supported an agricultural economy, according greater importance to frontage on Main Street than to conveniently arranged fields, and regarding the location of a lot as more vital than the quality of its topsoil. Later arrivals were quick to build, subdivide, and sell. Those fathers who felt they had established a homestead were often overruled posthumously by children who wasted no time in selling out to the highest bidder and moving on. Seventy percent of Germantown's families remained for less than a generation, and community structure in terms of acquiring a traditional leadership suffered thereby. Even the most influential families often pulled up roots that had scarcely had time to take hold, and the large number of renters left little permanent record beyond an entry on the tax list and a

[81] Greven, *Four Generations*, p. 156; p. 224.

marker in the burying ground. Those who did remain broke
their holdings into smaller pieces to accommodate an ever
greater number of these semitransients, increasing the density of the town and widening the gap between those who
stayed and those who passed through. An interesting picture of small city development emerges, lacking the explosive qualities of metropolitan growth, but with a tempo and
pace of change that may prove to have been typical of
countless American urban villages.

CHAPTER 3

The Urban Village as an Industrial Center

CONTRARY to the title of Carl Bridenbaugh's well-known book, there is no such thing as a "city in the wilderness." Even the smallest crossroads hamlet must draw customers and goods from a surrounding, more rural population. According to classic theory, the preindustrial market town relies on an area that can be circumscribed by a circle with a four- to five-mile radius. This embraces the distance one can manage to walk in something over an hour, thus making a round trip, with business conducted in between, feasible in a single day. The larger and more complex a town or city becomes, the more complicated its dealings in relation to the surrounding region and the larger the area it must service. The primary service area of Philadelphia came to be a circle with a thirty-mile radius, the distance traveled one way by a loaded cart over the roads of the period.[1]

From the time of Penn's first decisions regarding his new

---

[1] A good, though rather old, brief summary of the relationship of the city and the region, including discussion of Christaller's basic theory of the central place of the city, can be found in Edward Ullman, "A Theory of Location for Cities," *The American Journal of Sociology*, 46 (May 1941), pp. 853-864. A more recent, though basically similar account appears in Jones, *Towns*, pp. 85-89; pp. 93-103. Lemon, in *Best Poor Man's Country*, chapter 5, "Territorial Organization of Towns, Counties, and the Region," deals with this question exhaustively in relation to colonial Pennsylvania but ignores Germantown almost completely, no doubt because he concentrates on the backcountry and because the information for Germantown was not readily available. Much of what follows in this section is an attempt to integrate the developments in Germantown with his schema.

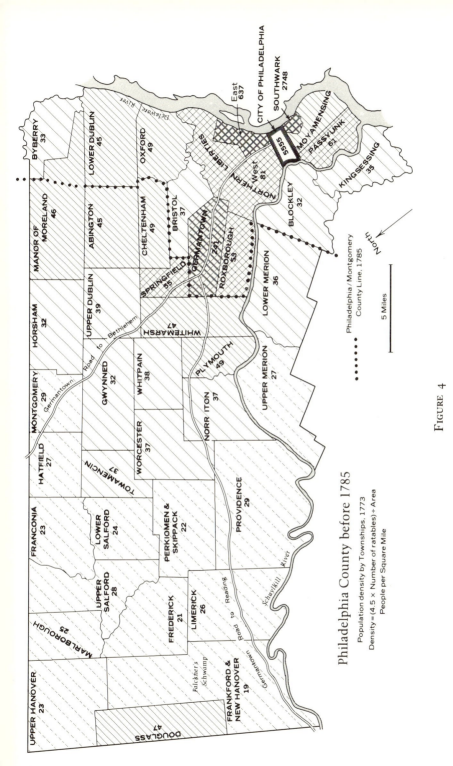

Philadelphia County before 1785

Population density by Townships, 1773

Density = (4.5 × Number of ratables) ÷ Area
People per Square Mile

FIGURE 4

Source: Daly and Weinberg, *Philadelphia County Political Subdivisions*; L. E. Wilt, *Map of Montgomery County* (Harrisburg, Pa., 1946); *Philadelphia County Tax List, 1773*.

colony, there was no doubt that Philadelphia was to be the central place within Pennsylvania, and for the colonial period, at least, it dominated not only the entire settled part of this colony, but a good portion of the Jerseys as well.[2] As late as 1800, the city of Philadelphia still contained 20 percent of the total population of southeastern Pennsylvania.[3] People tended to spread out from the center in a fairly regular pattern, and almost all urbanization within thirty miles of the center was inhibited by the overwhelming importance of the metropolis. Even county seats, if they fell within the circle of Philadelphia's sphere, failed to develop independently, despite the attraction of their administrative functions, which helped more distant local centers to prosper. The town of Bristol, for example, miles away up the Delaware River beyond the rural outskirts of Byberry township, grew very little after 1720 and never succeeded either as an independent population center or as an economic unit.[4] In nonurbanizing areas, such as the townships of Kingsessing, Blockley, and Lower Merion, population growth was hindered rather than helped by geographical barriers to the city.

Having stifled the development of other significant population centers in the area, Philadelphia assumed most of the functions required of urban concentrations. Lemon lists these as public administration, commerce, transport, and processing. He also ranks successful central places in higher or lower order, depending on the number and complexity of their participation in these fields: high-order towns would not only provide the basic services of the shopkeepers and blacksmiths of the small town, but would also in-

[2] For the best discussion of Penn's planning and location of Philadelphia, see Hannah Benner Roach, "The Planting of Philadelphia, A Seventeenth Century Real Estate Development," *PMHB*, 92 (1968), pp. 3-47; pp. 143-194.

[3] Lemon, *Best Poor Man's Country*, p. 123. For density throughout the area and period also see ibid., figures 7-10, pp. 44-47.

[4] Terry McNealy, "Bristol: The Origins of a Pennsylvania Market Town," *PMHB*, 95 (1971), p. 510.

clude more specialized activities such as clockmaking or wholesale dealing.[5] Philadelphia stood alone as a fifth-order town, and only a few distant places, such as Lancaster, reached fourth-order status before the end of the century. Fourth-order towns usually performed the governmental functions of local county seats, for "although commerce was the compelling interest of many persons, concentration resulted primarily from the location of courthouses."[6] There were almost no processing or industrial centers, since this kind of work in a prefactory society traditionally took place in the open countryside or as cottage industry.[7]

Germantown was an exception to almost all the foregoing general rules. To be sure, in the final analysis it failed to achieve total independence as a mature city, primarily because it lacked an administrative function around which it might have organized the surrounding territory. Even its own people were forced to look toward the metropolis for the legal necessities of business and personal life. Proof of this may be found in the fact that at no time throughout the eighteenth century did any permanent resident of Germantown list his occupation as a lawyer; not on wills, not on tax lists, not in township documents of any kind. There were any number of summer people who followed the profession—the Chews and William Allen being perhaps the most successful and prominent examples. Early in the century Pastorius earned his living as a conveyancer and notary, writing leases, mortgages, deeds, articles of agreement, wills, marriage certificates, and transacting other legal business. Christian Lehmann performed these functions for his neighbors later in the period. But the former regarded himself primarily as a teacher, the latter as a mapmaker and nursery owner. Most Germantown legal business was, perforce,

[5] Lemon, *Best Poor Man's Country*, pp. 118-121.

[6] Ibid., pp. 140-142. For a most interesting discussion of the founding and growth of Lancaster, see Jerome H. Wood, Jr., "The Town Proprietors of Lancaster, 1730-1790," *PMHB*, 96 (1972), pp. 346-368.

[7] Lemon, *Best Poor Man's Country*, p. 122.

taken to Philadelphia, where the courts were located. If, when Montgomery County was formed out of Philadelphia County in 1785, Germantown had been included and made its seat, Germantown might have become a more completely autonomous regional headquarters, but it lay much too far from the geographical center of the new division to make this possible, and it remained a suburb of Philadelphia in the legal sense.

On the other hand, while Germantown lay only about five miles from the center of Philadelphia, its population grew steadily if not spectacularly, and it acquired its own little complex of satellite townships, interrupting and complementing the smooth flow of population outward from the metropolis. One reason for this was the existence of the relatively underpopulated and rural district known as the "Northern Liberties west," which separated the growing town from the exploding city, contrary to the general principle that land will fill up in concentric rings around a central population point. This not only provided a kind of buffer zone but, with a density of only 81 people per square mile compared to 241 for Germantown by 1773, it offered an opportunity for the acquisition of cheaper land to second- and third-generation Germantowners who could not afford the skyrocketing real estate prices of their hometown. Many who chose to move into the Liberties were the sons of those who had not been among the original settlers, and for whom the early grants in the outlying districts were therefore not available. They were often small craftsmen and tradesmen, rather than farmers, and were not all sorry to move their businesses a little closer to the main market in Philadelphia. An examination of the Sheriffs' deeds of partition in the Court of Common Pleas during the period turns up dozens of cases indicating that, whenever possible, Germantowners were buying up Liberty lands at sale prices. Baltes Reser, a tanner, was typical, having acquired twenty acres in the western Liberties in 1754 for £388, far less than an equivalent piece of land would have cost in the lower end of the Germantownship.[8] The popularity of the Liberty land was also enhanced by the Germantown Road, which bisected it, providing easy access both to the markets of the city and the family, church, and social life of the old hometown. By 1773 a rather special relationship had built up between the Northern Liberties and Germantown, with over forty families of Germantown connection clustered just along the Main Road in the western Liberties and twenty-five more in the eastern Liberties.[9] This is in contrast to a relatively small number of families who appear to have moved into the other surrounding townships— Springfield, Roxborough, or Bristol—supporting Lemon's thesis that, although short-term migration was frequent in seventeenth-century England, it was not usual among eighteenth-century Pennsylvanians.[10]

As the economic center of its own region, Germantown was less a typical market town and more a place of permanent shops and wholesalers ready to deal in raw materials. Although a market house existed as early as 1741, it seems to have been used but little: "Newspaper advertisements mention it as a point of reference when a house or other piece of property in the area was offered for sale. . . . Of the market *per se*, little was said. Travelers who commented favorably on the Philadelphia markets are silent on the subject of Germantown's. . . . Elizabeth Drinker spent weeks in the summer of 1793 . . . across the Germantown Road from the market house but never mentions it."[11] Yet private enterprise with the more rural folk from surrounding townships and from far upcountry as well was a noticeable part of the relationship of the town to the countryside. By 1798 there were twelve permanent stores, stone or frame structures, standing independently from the home of the

[8] Sheriffs' Deeds, Volume A, p. 137.

[9] 1773 tax list.

[10] Lemon, *Best Poor Man's Country*, p. 72.

[11] Margaret Tinkcom, "Market Square," *Germantowne Crier*, 19 (September 1967), p. 71.

owner or manager, to cater to wholesale or retail trade. While most were small (only about 15 feet square) there was one great store of 540 square feet at the junction of the two branches of the Main Road in the upper part of the township.[12] In addition, of course, there were dozens of entrepreneurs who ran small businesses out of their homes. Between 1731 and 1800, well over 100 advertisements for Germantown businessmen appeared in area newspapers. In addition to sales of both manufactured items such as saddles, gloves, or guns, and basic items such as seed, they offered to buy raw farm goods, such as hog skins or wheat.[13] One rather prosperous wholesale merchant, for example, sold "all kinds of goods for country people: will take farm products in trade."[14] The attempt to service the large number of Pennsylvania German farmers who were located inland rather than on waterways where transportation would have been easier, led to an important cart- and carriage-making industry in Germantown and the subsequent development of the so-called Germantown wagon.

It was craft and processing, raised to a surprisingly complex and sophisticated level, rather than commerce and trade, that formed the backbone of the economic system in Germantown and made it unique among Pennsylvania towns.[15] The economic pull of Philadelphia was far too strong for Germantown manufacturers to resist when it came to selling their own merchandise, but this very closeness to the metropolis made the town an attractive place for industrial production, particularly of those items that required a certain amount of space for their manufacture. The degree to which Germantown business and industry had progressed beyond the cottage stage by the end of the

12 Joint property of John and Enoch Rex, 1798 Direct Tax, Schedule B.

13 See Jenkins, "News," passim.

14 *Pa.Berichte*, August 17, 1759.

15 See Lemon, *Best Poor Man's Country*, table 20, pp. 120-121; p. 147.

century is marked by the large number of men whose work was no longer done at home. There were, of course, the usual separate working establishments to be found in most towns, not necessarily industrial in nature, although the number in relation to the population was quite impressive. There were twelve mills within the township borders along the Wissahickon and Wingohocking creeks—eight grist mills, a saw mill, a corn mill, an oil mill, and a chocolate mill —and just over the line on the Roxborough side of the Paper Run was the famous Rittenhouse paper mill. There were slaughter houses, bark houses, malt and brew houses, and bake houses, fifty-one in all. But beyond this, there were eighty-five craftsmen of the type usually associated with home industry who had set up shops in separate buildings unconnected to their homes, frequently in a completely different section of town.[16]

The ratio of workshops to stores in 1798 stood at 7:1, evidence that the most highly organized enterprises in Germantown were preponderantly craft, as opposed to trade, operations. The bias in this direction is even more marked if one considers the occupations of individuals employed, rather than merely the number of separate shops in which they worked. Before the Revolution, there were eleven craftsmen paying taxes in the township for every shopkeeper, merchant, innkeeper, or other trades- or serviceman.[17] By comparison, in the city wards of Philadelphia the overall ratio was 3:1 in favor of the crafts, and in the outlying districts of the eastern Northern Liberties and Southwark, it rose to 6:1 and 7:1 respectively. During the same period Lancaster and Reading both showed a ratio of around 3:1, similar to that of central Philadelphia, al-

[16] This information is all gathered from an analysis of Schedule B, 1798 Direct Tax.

[17] This is based on an occupational analysis of the 1773 tax list for the entire county of Philadelphia. Craftsmen included all those who listed themselves under a specific occupation, even if it was not a manufacturing skill. Tradesmen included all those engaged primarily in commerce from huxters and innkeepers to brokers and merchants.

though their suburbs were rural rather than industrial; a few years later (1783), York, Pennsylvania had about 3½ craftsmen for every taxpayer involved in trade.[18] In Lemon's system of town classification, Germantown, therefore, is clearly a processing town and is not a mere transport point, although the designation involves far more than the simple transformation of raw agricultural goods as he implies.[19]

The large number of craftsmen in Germantown, which had a high proportion of German settlers, is not too surprising, since there is a good bit of evidence that the immigrants who arrived from Germany had long been craft-oriented people. Wertenbaker sees this as largely due to conditions in Germany during the seventeenth and eighteenth centuries where, because of the many trade restrictions along the Rhine, there were more local industries than in places where the movement of goods was easier.[20] Many of those who became farmers in the New World may have done so because "there was not much of a demand for bakers, glass blowers, millers, engravers and some other classes of handicraftsmen."[21] One of the poorest of the waves of immigration, the Palatines who left Germany in the "starving time" of 1709, was considered by contemporary opinion to be made up of uneducated farmers, although 34 percent of its members were actually skilled craftsmen.[22]

The settlers of the German Township wasted no time. In 1685 a Philadelphia merchant, Robert Turner, wrote to William Penn: "The manufacture of Linnen by the Germans goes on finely, and they make fine Linnen: Samuel

[18] Lemon, *Best Poor Man's Country*, table 23, p. 128, gives the percentages from which these ratios may be figured.

[19] Lemon, "Urbanization," *WMQ* (1967), p. 505.

[20] Wertenbaker, *Middle Colonies*, p. 262.

[21] Diffenderffer, "Redemptioners," *Pa.Ger.*, X, p. 120.

[22] Frank R. Diffenderffer, "The German Exodus to England in 1709," *Narrative and Critical History*, Part I, *Pa.Ger.*, VII (1896), p. 307, presents an occupational breakdown of the 1709 immigrants. While most of this group went to New York, they are quite typical of the early German settlers.

Carpenter having been laterly there declares they had gathered one Crop of Flax and had sowed for the Second and saw it come up well."[23] At the same time one of the original Crefelders was writing to his father in Germany: "We already begin to spin flax. If any reputable spinsters who like to work desire to come here, we should receive them all."[24] By 1698 Pastorius wrote home that "the inhabitants of this city [Germantown] are for the most part tradespeople, such as cloth, fustian, and linen weavers, tailors, shoemakers, locksmiths, carpenters."[25]

While spinning and weaving may have been thought of as the principal industries of Germantown, many other crafts, trades, and services sprang up quickly. Of the 220 men who listed their occupations in their wills prior to 1773, 26 different categories were mentioned besides farmer or weaver. These included other fabric handlers such as tailors and dyers; metal workers like blacksmiths, locksmiths, and brass founders; leather crafters like tanners, cordwainers, and saddlers; millers and papermakers; carpenters and masons; ministers and doctors; and several other specialty occupations. By 1773 there were 46 definite occupational categories reported and by the Septennial Census of 1793, there were 60.[26] Table 10 provides a comparison of those two years in regard to jobs and numbers involved.

Problems that arise in discussing the two lists together include the large number of men who do not list any occupation at all in 1773 and the fact that single men in that year were listed merely as "head tax" rather than by job description. Internal and structural analysis of the list, together with comparison to other sources, makes educated,

[23] Hocker, *Germantown*, p. 23.

[24] Sachse, *Letters*, Missive #7, Herman OpdenGraff to relatives at home, February 12, 1684, p. 33.

[25] *Germantowne Crier*, 8 (September 1956), p. 23. Letter from Francis Daniel Pastorius to his father, May 30, 1698.

[26] 1793 Septennial Census.

TABLE 10

OCCUPATIONS LISTED BY GERMANTOWN TAXPAYERS, 1773 AND 1793

Category	No. Workers 1773	1793	Category	No. Workers 1773	1793
I *Fabric Crafts*			IV *General Crafts and Industries*		
Stocking weaver	20	19			
Weaver	11	22	Clockmaker	5	6
Tailor	12	20	Printer	2	10
Hatter	6	13	Bookbinder	3	3
Dyer	4	3	Typemaker	–	1
Fuller	1	1	Painter	3	3
Breeches maker	1	2	Limner	–	1
Glover	–	1	Basketmaker	–	1
Collarmaker	–	1	Rope maker	1	–
			Starchmaker	1	1
Total	57	82	Powdermaker	1	1
II *Leather Crafts*			Total	16	27
Skinner	7	8			
Cordwainer	17	22	V *Metal Crafts*		
Saddlemaker	8	4	Blacksmith	11	26
Saddletree maker	1	9	Coppersmith	–	1
Harness maker	2	4	Miner	1	–
Tanner	10	18	Tinman	–	1
Total	45	65	Total	12	28
III *Woodworking and Building Crafts*			VI *Food Production*		
			Miller	6	14
Turner	2	5	Millwright	–	2
Cooper	26	43	Millstone cutter	–	3
Cedar cooper	–	13	Baker	4	2
Carpenter	9	30	Butcher	10	21
Mason	10	11	Total	20	42
Joiner	8	–			
Nailer	–	1			
Windsor-chair- maker	–	1			
Total	55	104			

TABLE 10 *Continued*

OCCUPATIONS LISTED BY GERMANTOWN TAXPAYERS, 1773 AND 1793

Category	No. Workers 1773	1793	Category	No. Workers 1773	1793
VII *Transportation Crafts and Services*			IX *Professionals*		
Coachmaker	8	1	Doctor	3	7
Chairmaker	1	23	Pastor	1	2
Chair trimmer	–	2	Schoolmaster	4	4
Wheelwright	6	9	Barber	–	1
Currier	1	2	Total	8	14
Carter	8	17	X *Other*		
Drover	–	3	Farmer	28	68
Coachman	–	1	Gardener	1	1
Total	24	58	Laborer	52	78
VIII *Tradesmen*			Head tax (no occ. given)	83	–
Innkeeper	4	8	Occ. not given	42	11
Shopkeeper	8	9	Total	206	158
Tobacconist	1	1			
Merchant	1	–	Total all occupations	457	597
Lumber dealer	–	1			
Total	14	19			

SOURCE: County tax, 1773; Septennial Census, Philadelphia County, 1793.

though tentative guesses possible.[27] Of those who listed no occupation, it would seem that twenty were probably general laborers, ten were farmers, eight would probably have been considered gentlemen, and four were some sort of skilled craftsmen. The single men on the list divided up as follows: category I, three; category II, twelve; category III, four; category IV, five; category V, one; category VI,

[27] This was done by combining information from other sources—wills, census reports, deeds, etc.—concerning the occupations and families of specific individuals and the factor of their placement on the tax list. Because of the methods of the assessors, workers for a larger craftsman usually follow, or occasionally precede, him on the list.

three; and category VII, nine. Two of those paying head tax were general laborers, and five were undoubtedly farmers as were most of the twenty-one other "head taxers" of whom it is impossible to be certain. The other twenty-five single men of age in the township were living at home with their fathers or widowed mothers and helping out in the family business or on the farm.

Distributing the 1773 information according to the above assumptions, there are interesting conclusions to be drawn concerning the changing economic patterns of Germantown. In the twenty-year span represented by the two lists, there was a 30.6 percent increase in the number of ratable, employed men. The greatest percentage increases—73, 115, 83, and 76 respectively—took place in the specific craft areas represented by categories III, V, VI, and VII, all areas affected particularly by an increase of local population and a need for housing and servicing the rapidly proliferating summer trade. This is even true of the transportation crafts; the influx of city people brought many customers to the carriage shops of John Bringhurst and Noah Townshend, the former having achieved lasting local reputation for the receipt of an order for a "chariot" worth £210 in gold from George Washington.[28] On the other hand, the smallest percentage increase occurred in the oldest, best established craft areas, in fabric work and leather crafts. There was also no significant increase in the number of totally new specialized fields such as clockmaking. The tremendous growth of farmers was apparent rather than real, since many of the same men had been designated "not given" in 1773.

The increases in the number of men involved in some of the more specialized crafts between 1773 and 1793 indicate, to a great extent, the enlargement of existing businesses; craftsmen with 2 names following them in the earlier list often had 4 or 5 by the later enumeration. One reflection

---

[28] Jenkins, *Guide Book*, p. 43.

of this was the jump in the number of general laborers, a condition consistent with growing urbanization.[29] An examination of the relative wealth of men engaged in different occupations in 1780 makes the point even more clearly.[30] In many of the occupations, a wide variation between the average and the median value of an occupation, as well as placement on the tax list, points to large shops with wealthy entrepreneurs and a considerable contract labor force working under them. For example, a total of 15 chairmakers reported a net value that ranged from £40,060 in the case of John Bringhurst, to £1,860 for Thomas Waterman who worked for him. Despite an occupational average of almost £7,000, only 4, in fact, were worth over £6,000. The median for these craftsmen was a much lower, and more informative, £3,540. The other areas where a variation between mean and median of over £1,000 indicates the existence of wide-spread employer-employee relationships were among the skinners or skindressers, carpenters, and farmers. While the wealthiest of the 53 farmers reporting was rated at £10,060 for his occupation, the median of the group was at £2,080, £1,400 below the average. This would seem to support Warner's statement that farms were more apt to have large work gangs than were businesses.[31] With the rapid breakup of farms during the 1780s, this situation changed quickly. By 1791 an analysis of 36 land-holding farmers indicates that 61 percent of them had no male employees at all, not even grown sons; 16 percent reported 1 full-time worker, 22 percent reported 2, and none supported more than that. The trend among the crafts, on the other hand, was to larger shops. Of 162 land-holding craftsmen,

---

[29] Lemon, *Best Poor Man's Country*, p. 8, discusses the increase of unskilled labor in urban situations.

[30] This list is the most suitable for use in this way, since it is the only one to rate occupations separately from property. The actual pound value is tremendously inflated because of the Revolution.

[31] See Warner, *Private City*, p. 6.

56 percent had no workers, 31 percent reported 1 employee, 7 percent reported 2, while 6 percent had 3 or more workers (the largest number was 5).

Seventeen new occupations were listed in 1793 that had not appeared in 1773. For the most part, these represented some improved specialization of skill, another indication that Germantown craftsmen were moving in the direction of an urban, industrial, rationalized economy. In addition to general clothing makers, by 1793 there were a glovemaker and a collarmaker; there were cedar coopers as well as coopers and a windsor-chairmaker rather than the simpler joiner. There were two men who did nothing but trim "chairs," as the small riding conveyances of the time were called. There were smiths who dealt only in copper and tin and three drovers who specialized in transporting cattle to the greatly increased butcher trade in the town. The millstone cutters had separated themselves from the masons, and those who made only "chairs" no longer placed themselves in the more general category of coachmakers.

There was, of course, no reason why a worker could not change his job or learn a new trade, if he was dissatisfied or saw a way to better his material situation. Lack of guild restrictions was a noteworthy feature of colonial life in general. In 1754 Gottlieb Mittelberger had written: "No trade or profession in Pennsylvania is bound by guilds . . . if any could or would carry on ten trades, no-one would have a right to prevent him."[32] The earliest settlers were frequently forced by conditions to change their jobs almost as often as they changed their addresses. Reynier Jansen, for example, arrived in Germantown from Holland and was made a citizen of the town in 1699, designated as a "lacemaker." By December of the same year, he was known in Philadelphia as a merchant, and just two years later, when he was recorded as dealing in Germantown land, he referred to himself as a printer.[33] Throughout the century there was

[32] *Mittelberger's Journey*, p. 56.
[33] "Laws, Ordinances and Statutes of the Community at Germantown, Made and Ratified From Time to Time in the General Court

always a certain amount of anticipation of the "jack-of-all-trades" approach to earning a living which became so typical of nineteenth-century America. Christopher Saur was not only a printer and publisher, he was also called at different times "a clockmaker" and "maker of mathematical instruments."[34] The number of men who possessed such widely varied skills was, however, extremely limited.

It is possible to trace the careers of 194 men who listed their occupations more than once during the years between 1767 and 1790.[35] Two-thirds of these were listed as following the same trade for the entire period during which they could be followed, while for the other one-third there is a discrepancy in the listing of some kind or another. Obvious changes in vocabulary account for some of these, such as the 3 men who were initially known as stocking weavers, and later came to call themselves "hosiers." The change from joiner to carpenter or the reverse may represent the same situation, although since it happens in both directions and since there is a subtle difference in the work, it is possible that each man was considering the type of job on which he was engaged at the time the listing was made. Disregarding these cases, about 20 percent of those who changed occupations did so within a very narrow range, moving from one craft to another that involved working with the same materials or utilizing the same markets. Those who moved from cordwainers to tanners, or from saddlemakers to harness makers, or even from printer to typemaker, could be placed in this category. Another 20 percent made a much more radical shift, moving completely from one area of

at that Place," Samuel Pennypacker, ed. and trans., *Pa.Ger.*, IX (1898), p. 190.

[34] Keyser, *Germantown*, p. 249.

[35] This includes material from the tax lists of 1767, 1773, 1774, and 1780, as well as wills and deeds recorded during the period. Extending in time any further made it difficult to be sure whether one was dealing with the same person, or a father and son or other person of the same name, and would have increased the probability of error more than it would have added hard information.

expertise to another: that these were individual preferences appears from the fact that no two sets were identical, the examples ranging from bookbinder into linen weaver, cooper into typemaker, joiner into a cordwainer, stocking weaver into preacher, and doctor into farrier, to name a few. A smaller number, about 17 percent, indicated a failure to succeed in their chosen craft, slipping from a definite designation to the lower classification of "laborer," while only 8 percent who were initially listed as "laborers" appear later as possessing some specific occupation, all of a lesser order of skill, such as farmer or spinner. This last statistic is probably misleading, however, since much of the general labor was done by single men, who were recorded only as "head tax" or by a large number of individuals who first appear without any classification at all, and are only listed once by occupation, so that they were not taken into account in this analysis. Seventeen percent of those who changed jobs were farmers who sold off most of their land and either descended to the class of laborer or entered one of the lower-order crafts. Finally, it is interesting to note that there was a large group (18 percent) who were first recorded as craftsmen, but on the tax list of 1780 appear as "farmers." This would seem to be a situation in which the affairs of the community were being affected by the Revolution, since all but a few in this group were either Quakers or Tories who were paying double for refusal to take the oath of allegiance. Why this should have been so is unclear; perhaps there was some kind of a boycott against them because of their political attitudes, and they could not gain employment in their chosen trades, perhaps they felt it was more discreet to lie low. In any case, 3 of these men, for whom later wills could be found, had, after the Revolution, left farming and were once more practicing their earlier trades.

While there were no guilds as such in Germantown, there was from time to time a certain amount of corporate or group action on the part of the community at large or of certain trades in particular. An attempt to define a corporate business aspect for the town was written into the laws passed by the General Court on December 18, 1696: "In order that the benefit of our best and most complete brand of the clover leaf registered in Philadelphia, may be preserved strictly for the community, all inhabitants of Germantown who sell their own horses, marked with said clover leaf, or exchange them or otherwise part with them to any one who does not belong to our Corporation, shall before parting with the horse, burn upon him addition to such clover leaf, with the stamp prepared for the purpose, the letter 'G', under penalty of ten shillings fine."[36]

The fabric makers of Germantown cooperated early with each other, and an Englishman describing conditions in Pennsylvania in 1690 wrote home to his friends that "five miles off is a town of Dutch and German people that have set up the linnen manufactory which weave and make many thousand yards of pure fine linnen cloth in a year."[37] As late as 1759, the Reverend Mr. Burnaby reported that the Germantown linen and stocking makers still stood as a group with their goods for sale on the edge of the road on the north side of Market Street near Second in Philadelphia.[38] In 1795 the constitution of the "Germantown Society for Promoting Domestic Manufactures" was issued. It sought to promote the materials turned out by mills in the lower end of the town. Every member, from the president George Logan on down, was expected to "be clothed in the manufactures of his country, if not inconvenient to himself," and the Society undertook to "engage a storekeeper to receive and sell on a low commission, any thread, woolen, linen, or any other domestic manufacture brought to him."[39]

There were a few other examples of group cooperation in business in eighteenth-century Germantown. As men-

[36] "Laws," *Pa.Ger.*, IX, p. 333, #47.
[37] "Some Letters . . . From Pennsylvania, London, 1691," Samuel Pennypacker, ed. and trans., *Pa.Ger.*, IX (1898), p. 185.
[38] Ward, "The Germantown Road," *PMHB*, 5, p. 386.
[39] Ibid., p. 367.

tioned earlier, the tanners of the community banded together to advertise in the *Pennsylvania Gazette* for lumber.
In 1786 those engaged in the various aspects of coachmak-
ing, which had become big business in the vicinity, presented a petition to the State Assembly stating "that the act
for laying a tax upon pleasurable carriages has greatly dis-
tressed them in the carrying on the aforesaid business, and
praying the said tax, or a part thereof, may be discontin-
ued."[40] But beyond these instances, the business life of the
community was a relatively individualistic one—the first
element of what Warner calls the privatism of economic
life which has an individualized structure of work.[41] If there
were six hatters in Germantown in 1773, they were completely free to cut each others' prices and steal each others'
workmen. The latter was frequently done as can be seen by
noting the large number of workmen who change employers between the 1773 and 1774 county tax lists.

Business life, however, had its interdependent side as well.
It can be no coincidence that butchers were among the most
successful businessmen in the township, considering the
number of leather crafts that were being followed. The
Rittenhouse and Dewees paper mills used the linen waste
that was left from the production of the weavers. The
establishment of Saur's printing press led to "the most extensive book manufactory in the British American colonies."
At the height of his success, Christopher Saur's business also
generated enough work for the creation of several binderies,
a paper mill, an ink manufactory, and a foundry for German
and English type, in addition to the printing company itself.[42] An interesting example of a group of interconnected
businesses is that set up by John Bringhurst, a successful

[40] *Pennsylvania Evening Herald*, November 15, 1786, from Minutes
of the Pennsylvania Assembly, November 9, 1786.

[41] Warner, *Private City*, p. 5.

[42] Keyser, *Germantown*, p. 63 cites this as coming from Bishop,
History of American Manufactures, Vol. I, p. 182, with no other
bibliographical information.

coachmaker and one of the wealthiest men in town. For years two of his sons were listed as working for him, but they emerge on the 1780 list with trades of their own, one as a "chairtrimmer," the other a "saddle-tree" maker. Even a third son who appears to be an independent blacksmith is mentioned in the tax list of 1809 as a "manufacturer of iron work for carriages."[43]

The estate accounts tell many stories of intricate networks of debts built up among the various businessmen of the township. Johannes Gress, for example, died in 1752, leaving an estate valued at £298/5/1 and twenty-six business debts of £25 or less, which totaled £151/7/1. Over half of these were in the community itself and the others were in the surrounding area of Springfield township, which is not surprising, since he lived and worked in Sommerhausen, close to the township line.[44] Derick Keyser, a wealthy tanner, died four years later, leaving an estate of £2,564/17/0½. After funeral expenses, there were eighty debts large and small to be discharged. Twenty-nine of these were bonds and interest owed to other craftsmen in the town. From two neighbors evidently lending money jointly, there were six separate loans ranging in amount from £9 to £16. His largest debt was a set of twelve bonds to another local businessman, worth over £106. It would seem that money lending was a sideline for many Germantown entrepreneurs. Then there were smaller sums owed the blacksmith, the miller, and the local shopkeeper. Together with £72 of bad debts, this amounted to over £800 of outstanding financial business on the part of one successful tanner.[45]

If the extent of the business done by Derick Keyser was unusual, the pattern was fairly common, perhaps because

---

[43] 1780 tax list, passim; for the tax list of 1809, see "A List of the Inhabitants of Germantown and Chestnut Hill in 1809," Thomas H. Shoemaker, ed., *PMHB*, 15 (1891) and 16 (1892).

[44] Johannes Gress, Accounts, 1752, #12; final accounting, February 15, 1764.

[45] Derick Keyser, will and inventory on file at PHC.

Germantown suffered periodic cash shortages, as did much of colonial America. Georg Keamer, a hatter who died in 1771, had 42 small local debts to be discharged, none of them over £10. He also owed on a bond and interest £27/2 —all this on an estate worth only £264/17/5½. William Streeper, a local farmer, had somewhat wider connections. In addition to the local debts he was responsible to six outside lenders, one of whom had advanced him £130. His debts actually totalled over half of his estate.[46] How easy it was to go deeply into debt in a semi-informal setup such as this is shown in the estate of Jacob Frailey who died in 1794, leaving over £1,000. By the time his local debts, amounting to 106 separate items, most of them business related, were discharged, there remained only £313/13/7 to divide among the heirs.[47]

In a fairly sophisticated money economy such as Germantown's, payment in labor or in kind was relatively rare. If such informal, personal exchanges took place, there is no record of them, and the large number of money debts between individuals would seem to indicate that this was the more usual way of doing business. Even the widow's share of an estate was much more commonly in the form of rents or profits on the property than it was in goods or services to be provided by the other heirs. Only in the field of community projects did one see occasional contributions of time or goods where the donor was unable to pay cash but wished to be included. Among the charter members of the Lower Burying Ground in 1738 were several men who gave bushels of lime, a product much in demand for cemeteries. Still, they represented only a few percentage points of the total membership list.[48] When St. Michael's Lutheran Church was

[46] William Streeper, Accounts, 1773, #348; final accounting, October 22, 1783.

[47] Jacob Frailey, Accounts, 1794, #30; final accounting, March 21, 1796.

[48] Minute Book and Record Book of Burials, Hood Cemetery, Germantown, photostat, HSP. (Also known as the Lower Burying Ground.)

formed and took up its first building subscription, there were a small number of people contributing nails, shingles, and lime, while one man contributed three days' use of his team.[49] As the century wore on, there were fewer and fewer of these sorts of donations, and after 1760 there appear to be none at all. Contributions to the fire companies, the Reformed Church, and the Concord School were all strictly cash.

The growing urban quality of Germantown business is indicated, as Margaret Tinkcom points out, by the way in which the occupational list of 1793 refers to those who make shoes as "cordwainers" or shoemakers while the list of 1809 calls them "shoe manufacturers."[50] This is not, however, a sudden change which took place like magic at the beginning of the industrial nineteenth century. Although the majority of businesses were one-man affairs throughout the eighteenth century, they were neither simple cottage industries nor even solely the kind of entrepreneurial affairs that Warner describes as run to fill the specific orders of specific customers.[51]

Spinning had passed slowly from its place as the staple occupation in the township during the course of the first hundred years. In the earliest of the estate inventories, the spinning wheel was almost always mentioned. There was often more than one, and they were usually in the main room of the house. By 1725, in the inventory of Maria Margaretta Zimmerman, the spinning wheel was still found in the kitchen although among a collection of goods that must have been stacked in a corner; it was referred to as "an old spin wheel." Twenty years later it was most frequently found in a small bedroom behind the kitchen, probably belonging to an indentured servant, and by 1768 it was to be

[49] Little Book I, St. Michael's Archives, St. Michael's Church, Germantown. 1739 List of Building Contributors.

[50] Tinkcom, "Germantown in Review," *Germantowne Crier*, 17 (September 1965), p. 75.

[51] Warner, *Private City*, p. 6.

found on John Frederick Ax's estate out in the shed with "three new bridles, an old gun and an anvil, rasp, etc." Thrifty as they were, the Germantowners rarely threw anything out, and as late as 1794, the estate of Jacob Frailey, which included such finery as walnut and mahogany furniture, five silver teaspoons, and a silver watch, still boasted the old family spinning wheels sitting out in the barn with the "grind stones" and a "quantity of hay."[52]

The inventories also testify that in many instances industry was far more complex than is usually supposed for the so-called preindustrial period. While it is conceivable that Derick Keyser, the tanner, was working to order and had 370 hides, tanned and untanned, 17½-dozen calf skins and 19½-dozen sheepskins in his tannery, only to fill customers' requests,[53] the goods on hand itemized in the inventory of Johannes Gress can only reflect a business that was conducted on the principles, if not with the techniques, of mass production. As Gress was not a particularly wealthy or powerful man in the community but was rather of the middling sort, the contents of his workshop may be considered something of a model for a fairly successful Germantown business. This quantity of goods on hand, as well as the large amount of raw material and number of tools, represents a considerable investment on the part of the craftsman and would scarcely be undertaken in a small village without the expectation that the goods would find a commercial market. The number of tools points to a three-man shop which is born out by reference to the servants' time. A check of his will shows that Gress had two small daughters and no sons so that this was the likely extent of his labor force.[54]

---

[52] This progression is quite common, but see, for example; Maria Margaretta Zimmerman, Inventory, 1725, #345; Wagner, Inventory, 1744, #112; John Frederick Ax, Inventory, 1766, #155; Jacob Frailey, Inventory, 1794, #30.

[53] Derick Keyser, Inventory, February 25, 1756, PHC.

[54] Johannes Gress, WB K, p. 19, 1752, #12.

FROM THE WORKSHOP OF JOHANNES GRESS: INVENTORY, NOVEMBER 19, 1752

STOCK IN HAND:

3 dozen hats @ 12 sh.
5 beaver hats @ 30 sh.
4 hats @ 11 sh.
2½ dozen boys' felt hats
   @ 3 sh.

1¾ dozen hats @ 15 sh.
3 dozen felt hats @ 3 sh. 4d.
2 dozen felt hats @ 4 sh.
36 half-made felt hats

MATERIALS ON HAND:

12 gross coarse hat cord
   @ 1sh. 6d.
1 lb. thread
12 lb. wool @ 10d. per lb.
6 oz. beaver hair
11 muskrat skins
57 raccoon skins @ 1sh. 6d.
2 reams and 13 quires brown
   paper (for wrapping)
34 pieces of cord to tie up
   hats

2 gross hat buttons
163 lb. wool @ 10d. per lb.
12 lb. wool @ 6d.
5 lb. racoon hair
20 beaver skins and 38 lb. hair
   @ 6sh. per lb.
29 fox skins @ 1sh. 6d.

WORKSHOP TOOLS:

14 hatter's bows and strings
2 hat benches
copper dyeing kettle
old copper pot
6 hat brushes
fulling board and kettle
hand saw

2 wool card benches with
   cards
2 iron plates
iron pot
3 iron rollers, 2 stampers,
   2 flat irons
3 dozen hat molds
81 lb. brazil wood
slate and inkhorn

The remaining time of two servant men; one, 8 months, the other 10 months. . . .

A public auction in 1795 of the remaining stock of John Bringhurst, coachmaker, also shows the extent to which Germantown craftsmen were willing to tie up capital in advance of sales. Considering that the material and labor that went into each completed product was, of necessity, large in the coach-manufacturing business, the number of ready-made vehicles is remarkable. They included a second-hand chariot, a riding chair, a coachee, a chariot, a phaeton, a sociable, and an unspecified number of chair and sulky bodies, coachees, and other carriages. Leftover materials also indicate parts made up in advance—steel springs, hubs, spokes and felloes, and axle trees.[55]

The view of Germantown as an increasingly urban community is further supported by a growing unevenness in the distribution of wealth. The first division of land by Pastorius and the differing economic conditions of the earliest Germantown settlers insured that the community would never be economically homogeneous. Here is another marked difference from the essentially agricultural villages of New England which, in their earliest generations at least, did maintain a kind of economic balance.[56] The earliest tabulations for the rural sections of Philadelphia County also show a relatively even distribution of property between rich and poor, or, more accurately, between more or less comfortable. In 1693 virtually all of the outlying districts reported a normal curve of tax valuation. That is, by dividing the pounds of assessed value into even groups and using the section into which the greatest number of people fall as a center, there are approximately the same percentage of ratables above and below this plurality grouping. In the city of

[55] *Pa.Gaz.*, April 16, 1795; an advertisement for an auction to be held on April 23, 1795, at 9:00.

[56] See, for example, Powell, *Puritan Village*, pp. 107ff., and Greven, *Four Generations*, pp. 45ff. The last noted that while the intent was to create a hierarchy of rank and wealth, the bounds were actually quite narrow. Demos, *Little Commonwealth*, notes the widening gap between rich and poor, p. 37.

Philadelphia, however, the curve was positively skewed, with a far greater percentage of taxpayers being assessed below the central grouping than above it. The trend in Germantown was similar to that of the city, although not as extreme; there, the central category was an assessed valuation of £ 50-99, held by 57 percent of the ratables, while 33 percent reported less than this and only 10 percent reported more.[57]

By 1773 the community was becoming far more sharply stratified in respect to wealth. In general, craftsmen and farmers varied in wealth to about the same degree; 8 percent of each could be found among the richest people in the community, 40 percent of each among the poorest of the taxpayers.[58] Only three men were assessed at over £ 100. Two of these were millers, John Gorgas and John Paul, and one was the landlord, John Johnson. The first and last of these listed no occupation at all, although it is probable in any other community that they would have been classed as miller and gentleman, respectively. Those who called themselves "gentlemen" rated well above the average, as did shopkeepers, while schoolmasters rated generally low, due to the fact that they were usually itinerant and owned no land. The laborers, as might be expected, ranked the lowest in the community with none in the richest category and 94 percent in the poorest.

Among the various crafts, a hierarchy of wealth was also slowly emerging. By 1780 the distinctions between one line of work and another were as marked as those between

---

[57] 1693 tax list. The other exception to the general finding was the Welsh tract, but this was because it was not yet broken up into townships. Lemon cites a relatively even distribution of wealth in 1693 in Chester County, with the top 40 percent of the ratables paying 60 percent of the taxes, while the bottom 60 percent paid 40 percent, but comparisons are difficult since he uses taxes paid rather than estate valuation. *Best Poor Man's Country*, table 1, p. 11.

[58] Actually, what follows gives a slightly rosy picture of the economic structure of Germantown. The sixty-three head taxers, who were generally among the poorer members of the community, are not included since they paid a flat rate and were not assessed.

TABLE 11

DISTRIBUTION OF WEALTH, GERMANTOWN, 1773

	Rated Value (£)														Total Ratables by Occupation
	6	8	10	12	14	16	18	20	22	24	26	28	30	Over 30	
No. of craftsmen	91	33	33	24	4	8	6	1	3	2	2	2	6	9	225
No. of farmers	15	3	2	5	–	–	2	1	1	1	–	–	–	3	33
No. of laborers	48	1	1	1	–	–	–	–	–	–	–	–	–	–	51
No. with no occupation listed	20	5	7	7	–	2	–	1	1	–	1	2	–	9	55
No. of others[a]	6	4	4	4	2	4	–	1	1	–	1	1	1	6	35
Total ratables each valuation	180	46	47	41	6	14	8	4	6	3	4	5	7	28	399
Cumulative % of ratables	45.0	56.7	68.4	78.7	80.2	83.7	85.7	86.7	88.2	89.0	90.0	91.2	93.0	100.0	

SOURCE: County tax, 1773.

a Includes doctors, widows, shopkeepers, schoolmasters, innkeepers, and gentlemen.

craftsmen and common laborers, and in some cases more so. In the grossly inflated money of the Revolutionary years, the tanners were found to be the wealthiest, with an average vocational worth on the county tax list of £7,337. The chair- and coachmakers followed at £6,917, with millers next at £5,780. Hatters and skinners were also rated above £5,000. Butchers fell into the £4,000-5,000 range, and blacksmiths, innkeepers, farmers, and skindressers were over £3,000. The rest of the leather crafts, along with most of the building and woodworking trades (coopers only excepted), tailors, and wheelwrights, ran businesses worth between £2,000 and £3,000. Of all the categories with enough representation to make averaging a useful device, only those in the fabric crafts and general laborers were valued at less than £2,000. Poorest of all were the linen weavers, which may help to explain why, as a designation, they had disappeared by 1793.

When it came to percentages at the top and bottom of the scale, Germantown reflected a trend that was generally becoming clear throughout the colonies. Even in rural areas stratification was noticeable by the third quarter of the century.[59] In the cities a proletariat had actually begun to develop by the time of the Revolution. As early as the seventeenth century in Boston, the 5 percent at the top controlled 25 percent of the wealth while the 20 percent at the bottom had only 3 percent. By 1771 the situation was even more unbalanced; while the lowest 20 percent of the population still controlled about 3 percent of the assessed taxable wealth, the top 5 percent had increased its share to something over 44 percent of the total.[60] In Philadelphia, by 1774, 89 percent of the taxable property was held by 10

[59] Lemon, *Best Poor Man's Country*, pp. 10-12.
[60] For an interesting comparison of seventeenth- and eighteenth-century wealth in Boston and the development of a proletariat, see James A. Henretta, "Economic Development and Social Structure in Colonial Boston," *WMQ*, 22 (1965), pp. 75-92.

percent of the taxpayers.[61] The trend in the rural areas was never as sharp, although the plight of the poorest group was even worse in Chester County by 1800 than it was in the city, with the lowest 30 percent of the inhabitants paying only about 4 percent of the taxes. The middling sort fared better, however, since the upper 40 percent altogether was only rated for about 80 percent of the wealth.[62] Germantown, as an urban village, fell somewhere between the steep changes of the cities and the gentler curve of the countryside. In 1773 the 10 percent at the bottom had 4.5 percent, and the top 10 percent controlled 36.5 percent of the wealth. Less than twenty years later the direction in which Germantown was moving had become obvious; the bottom 10 percent now accounted for less than 1 percent of the property, the top 10 percent for over 40 percent.[63]

Evidence of increasingly unequal division of the economic pie is not the same thing as evidence of the existence of more people who were actually classified "poor." This designation was very specifically applied to people whose means of support were such that they, or their families, were in actual danger of being unable to survive, not merely to those who might happen to find themselves on the bottom of the economic ladder but whose chances of rising were tolerable, or who were, at least, in no imminent danger. There were, of course, always some people in the German-township who were regarded as poor. Among the earliest actions taken by the Court of Record was the waiving of the six-shilling fee for becoming a citizen for two worthy but indigent elderly, residents.[64] Although a public poor-

---

[61] Warner, *Private City*, p. 9.

[62] Lemon, *Best Poor Man's Country*, p. 11; p. 84.

[63] Based on analysis of 1791 tax list. By comparison, in the United States today the top 20 percent of the population receives 45 percent of the total income, the bottom 20 percent receives 4 percent: Herbert J. Gans, "The New Egalitarianism," *Saturday Review*, May 6, 1972.

[64] Records of the Court of Record, admission of Maria Margaretta Zimmerman, widow, 25^d 11mo 1694, and "the blind man, Cornelius Plockoy," 25^d 11mo 1694/5.

house was not built until 1775, both the Brethren and the Mennonites ran special establishments long before this time, and donations to the poor were frequent in the wills of the period. But by 1790, there were only twelve people—ten women and two men—who lived in the poorhouse, and as late as 1798, only eight men whose taxes were abated by reason of their being "poor."[65] Except for the abatement list for the 1786 funding tax, which was heavy in single men who wandered into the township following the Revolution, and on which the number of poor rose to thirty-three, there was no other time during the whole of the recorded period, from 1767 on, when there were more than sixteen so listed, and in most years the number was a single digit.

Having one's taxes abated was not necessarily a sign of poverty. It more generally indicated a temporary embarrassment, as the two lists of 1779 and 1780, taken during the Revolution, show clearly. Twenty of the twenty-nine who received abatement on the former list were comfortable property owners and tradesmen who were regarded as having "suffered much by the enemy." In 1780 thirty-nine fell into this category, although in this year the assessor failed to assign any reason for his generosity. Even when a man was listed as being "encumbered," it did not mean that the wolf was at the door; such a designation was given to a vacation resident and one of the richest men in the entire province, Joseph Shippen, in 1767. Widows' taxes were more or less regularly abated, even when they were in the upper economic brackets of the town, as were those of people who could be classed as "aged" or "sickly." Other conditions that appeared to soften the tax collector's heart

[65] This information and that which follows comes from the Allowance and Abatement Ledger, Philadelphia County: for the Funding Tax, 1785; the County Tax, 1792-95; and County and Hearth Taxes, 1796, Phila.Arch. Allowances made for Germantown for the 1786 Funding Tax on April 15, 1791. The 1779 tax list presents a problem, as internal evidence indicates the date may be wrong, but it is definitely a Revolutionary list and may be used with caution. See also 1780 tax list.

included "having many children" (usually six to ten), having a "sickly wife," or taking care of one's "old mother."

Nor does poverty seem to have been a permanent condition, for throughout the last thirty years of the century, at least, the tax lists indicate no build up of a hard-core, persistent group of poor families or individuals. One reason for this was the mobile nature of eighteenth-century Pennsylvania society in general. In Germantown, as in Chester County, very few of those classed as poor appeared on the list more than once; by the time of the next tax they had either died or left the area, perhaps moving elsewhere to seek a better situation.[66] The special quality of the economic situation in Germantown enabled its inhabitants to provide for themselves and their families, since an industrial community with good access to markets and a generally short labor supply means opportunity, if not plenty, for those who can work. Its location within the radius of Philadelphia's primary circle of influence kept Germantown from developing as a fully articulated urban society of even fourth-order importance, but it provided a continual stream of customers for both mass and specialty goods. There were three basic markets for the businessmen of the township to serve—the city itself, the rural people of both the surrounding townships and the areas along the roads to Bethlehem and Reading, and the summer people. Each of these separate markets brought ready cash into the local economy, and because of their widely differing consumer needs provided the prerequisites for the growth of a widely varied and flourishing industrial center, within the limits of eighteenth-century colonial technology.

[66] Lemon, *Best Poor Man's Country*, pp. 84-85.

CHAPTER 4

With a German Accent: Patterns of Acculturation in an Eighteenth-Century Urban Village

THE URBAN cast of colonial Germantown, as indicated in its patterns of land distribution, its economic system, and the mobility of its population, was matched by its equally urban heterogeneity. Since the traditional society of a village requires a common background of breeding and custom, there is hardly any community in the American colonial experience that can really be considered homogeneous in the sense of Old World cultures. Even the seventeenth-century New England village of Sudbury, which appears remarkably uniform in its makeup from a vantage point distant in time, was replete with differences that required formal rules and impersonal decisions to insure a smoothly functioning community.[1] This was an almost accidental nonconformity, however, compared to the deliberate wooing of various ethnic and religious settlers that led to the peopling of Pennsylvania. The proprietor, probably of mixed background himself (his mother is thought to have been Dutch), encouraged such immigration both as a practical and a moral matter. And there was never any real intention to set things up so that there would be separate German or Dutch or English areas.[2] Land was not refused to homogeneous groups who desired to settle, of course, and the method by which the Amish successfully retained their old ways right into the twentieth century shows how effectively social patterns might be maintained in an isolated situation. But Penn did

[1] Powell, *Puritan Village*, especially pp. 185-186.
[2] For a discussion of mixed patterns of settlement, see Lemon, *Best Poor Man's Country*, pp. 46-49.

not regard a desire to perpetuate cultural identity of prime importance when contrasted with more pressing economic considerations. Pastorius found this out almost immediately: "Concerning the 15,000 acres, two great difficulties presented themselves, namely: W. Penn does not want to give them all in one parcel, so that so great a tract should not remain desolate and unoccupied, nor on the Delaware River, where everything is already taken up by others. However, after I had many times by word of mouth, as well as by writing, represented that it would be very prejudicial for us and our German successors to be even located among the English, . . . he at last granted me a warrant to have our land all together, provided we would, within a year's time, place thirty families upon the 15,000 acres . . . but in case there are not thirty families, he will not promise to give land all in one tract."[3]

It is somewhat ironic that, with Pastorius's express intention of "receiving a separate little province, so that we could the more provide ourselves against all oppression,"[4] the community he founded was perhaps the most mixed society for its size on the entire continent. Even the eight men who accompanied him included one Swiss and one Englishman. In addition, he was linked from the very beginning with the Crefeld immigrants, whose national backgrounds were largely Dutch. The 1689 list of land owners added a French Huguenot to the mix, and a few years later the Swedes were also represented. The owners of the central ground around the Market Square in 1730, who were the most influential and important citizens in the township, included not a German name among them: Hans Bensell, a Swede; James Delaplaine, a Huguenot; and John Ashmead and George Bringhurst, of English descent.[5] The Germantown heterogeneity runs true to form, however, and the last named is found, on close examination, to have had a German mother

[3] Sachse, *Letters*, pp. 22-23.
[4] Ibid.
[5] Tinkcom, *Historic Germantown*, p. 7.

who had emigrated to England as a young woman, married an English husband, and then moved on to America with her four children when she was left a widow.[6] Nor is there any proof of homogeneity among those of unquestioned German roots, for they came as individuals from almost every German state, with little in common besides their language, and differences of dialect often nullified even this similarity. The original settlers must have been difficult for any of the others to understand, since they are thought to have spoken "Crefeld-Hollandish," a *lingua franca* derived from a Lower Rhenish dialect.[7]

The variety of ethnic backgrounds in Germantown was surpassed, almost at once, by the diversity of religious belief and practice. After all, religious offshoots flourished in general in the seventeenth and eighteenth centuries, and even among those of a single nationality there were a number of possible church affiliations. Pastorius's domestic staff included a Roman Catholic, a Lutheran, a Calvinist, an Anabaptist, a member of the Church of England, and a Quaker.[8] In 1690 a minister of the Dutch Reformed church visited Germantown and reported to the Classis of Amsterdam: "This village consists of forty-four families, twenty-eight of whom are Quakers, the other sixteen of the Reformed Church [among whom are] the Lutherans, the Mennists [*sic*] and the Papists, who are very much opposed to Quakerism and therefore lovingly meet every Sunday."[9]

An awareness of heterogeneity as a special condition of New World life appeared as early as 1702, in *Falckner's Curieuse Nachricht von Pennsylvania*, in which the author

[6] See Josiah Granville Leach, *History of the Bringhurst Family With Notes on the Clarkson, De Peyster and Boude Families*, Philadelphia, 1901. Privately printed, this book also includes useful portraits of early members of the Germantown branch of the family. Located at GHS.

[7] Joseph Henry Dubbs, "The Reformed Church in Pennsylvania," *Narrative and Critical History*, Part IX, *Pa.Ger.*, XI (1900), p. 67.

[8] Sachse, *Letters*, p. 10.

[9] The Reverend Rudolphus Varick of Long Island, quoted in Hocker, *Germantown*, p. 27.

included a section on "How to conduct oneself [in Pennsylvania] circumspectly and inoffensively toward the divers sects." He reflected that "this is a difficult question, and one almost impossible to answer, and still harder to observe." He had no ready-made solution to the problem, however, and merely suggested adherence to one's own piety, and acceptance of the fact that many different groups were going to have to live together.[10]

The basic effects of forming a new society out of such individualistic roots have been pointed out by Oscar Handlin, in discussing the immigrants of the nineteenth century. "Strangers in the immediate world about them, the immigrants often recognized, in dismay, the loneliness of their condition. Their hesitant steps groped around the uncertain hazards of new places and exposed them ever to perilous risks. No one could enjoy the satisfaction of confidence in his own unaided powers . . . the social patterns of the Old World . . . could not be imposed on the activities of the New. . . . What forms ultimately developed among immigrants were the products of American conditions."[11] These generalizations are no less true of the seventeenth- and eighteenth-century settlers and seem particularly applicable to the non-English newcomers to Pennsylvania. Again and again, Falckner returned to the theme of loneliness and the necessity for acculturation. On the one hand, he saw the freedom of being unattached as a great advantage, largely because it allowed one to follow the new ways without restriction: "This is to be remarked, that those who come into this country are at liberty, if they so desire, even if they have no friends. No one questions them, and no suspicion or rumor arises upon their account. They are entirely at liberty to do the same as they see other inhabitants do."[12] His advice therefore, was to learn to acculturate: "Seek to make

---

[10] *Falckner's Curieuse Nachricht*, p. 97.
[11] Oscar Handlin, *The Uprooted: The Epic Story of the Great Migrations that Made the American People*, Boston, 1952, pp. 170-171.
[12] *Falckner's Curieuse Nachricht*, p. 211.

one or more good friends, to whom you can disclose your intentions, projects and manner of living. Do not stand upon your own head, but take advice from the experience of others. In the mean time one need not act hastily, but await with patience the Divine dispensation, until one learns fully how to establish oneself according to the custom of the country."[13]

It is difficult to find any shortcut to describing the way in which acculturation proceeded in Germantown, now that "melting pot" is a dirty word. Even before the environment of the colonial experience had worked on the settlers of Pennsylvania, they had tended to have much in common, regardless of national background, by virtue of their relatively similar social and economic roots in western Europe. Lemon, for example, finds very little difference between the cultural patterns of one group and another when it comes to the occupation, organization, and use of the land.[14] He recognizes in rural areas, a continuance of a certain amount of nationalistic feeling, language, kinship, and denominational adherence, because the immigrants arrived in large groups and settled in segregated areas.[15] In the undifferentiated neighborhood patterns of Germantown, however, such separation was never a factor, and by the end of the colonial period the real cultural gap came between rich and poor; more specifically, between the homes and lifestyles of the wealthy summer people, whether their names were William Allen or Caspar Wistar, and the tenement living of the poor or landless, which were the same for Thomas Duke or Baltes Isenminger.

Marriages were responsible for a great deal of actual intermixture. Neighbors of similar economic and social standing were apt to marry even if their ethnic (or religious) backgrounds varied. Members of a church took wives from among the congregation despite differences in nationality.

[13] Ibid., p. 95.
[14] Lemon, *Best Poor Man's Country*, p. 18.
[15] Ibid., p. 43.

Of the marriages recorded in the Lutheran and Reformed churches of Germantown during the eighteenth century, 18 percent took place between an English and a non-English partner. Of these, about half involved an English man with a German or Swiss female, and about half worked the other way.[16] Early examples of acculturation by marriage are numerous. James Delaplaine, a Huguenot, who arrived in Germantown in 1692, married an English Quaker, while one of his sisters married a German Lutheran and the other a Dutch Quaker.[17] Ashmeads and Bringhursts, neighboring upper-class families on Market Square, continually intermarried throughout the eighteenth century despite religious differences, and at least one, John Ashmead, was married in the Reformed Church to a German girl, in a German service, as late as 1791.[18] Even where both partners to a marriage were of German descent, they were frequently from parts of Germany that had little in the way of common culture, so that the resulting new family had to form new patterns of its own, apt to be more like those of its neighbors in the New World, than in line with any long established traditions of the Old.

As a practical matter, the German settlers quickly recognized the importance of becoming naturalized. A petition for such a purpose was presented to the Governor's Council, 15^d 3mo 1706, by Johannes Koster and "one hundred and fifty high and low Germans."[19] This petition was more than a simple request for confirmation of property rights, however. It requested English citizenship not only for the "security of property and the ability to sell, trade and inherit the same," but also for the purpose of becoming participants in the colonial political process, "that they may be capable of Electing and being elected, to serve in Assembly

[16] Compiled from the marriage registers, St.M.Rec. and Ref.Ch.Rec.
[17] Pennypacker, *Pa.Ger.*, IX, pp. 186-187.
[18] John Ashmead married Hany [*sic*] Reiter, Ref.Ch.Rec., Marriage: April 17, 1791.
[19] *Pennsylvania Archives*, Colonial Records, II, 241-242.

and other Offices." Furthermore, they asked for the right of Mennonites to affirm rather than swear, as the law specifically allowed Quakers to do. The bill was passed by the Assembly and signed by the Governor in 1709, although the provision regarding oath taking by groups other than Quakers was not accepted until 1743.[20] Over thirty German-towners, both German and Dutch, were included in this first naturalization.

As the century wore on, naturalization became more a form and less a sign of acculturation; the first petition cited twenty-two years of loyalty to England as a reason for citizenship,[21] but by mid-century new arrivals were being taken directly from the ship to the mayor's office to sign their naturalization papers. The necessity for following this step remained valid as shown by the fact that, as late as 1760, the Privy Council Committee for Plantations recommended against a bill that would have allowed the heirs of unnaturalized persons to inherit without having to satisfy the escheat of proprietary rights.[22] The first action in the new land, therefore, in addition to having practical significance, provided the immigrant with symbolic expression of his new status as the citizen of a new country and of his break with the traditions of the past.

Another step in the acculturation of the Germantown immigrant was the gradual weakening of his ties with the Old World. One of the most revealing places to check for this is among the wills of non-English settlers who died in

[20] Ibid., IV, 638. February 3, 1742/3, "A Bill for naturalizing foreign Protestants as are settled, or shall settle in this Province . . . who . . . do conscientiously refuse the taking of any Oath."

[21] Ibid., II, 493. September 29, 1709.

[22] Ibid., VIII, 545. June 1760. Practically speaking, escheat was not much of a problem and seems to have been solved most of the time by fairly easy compromise. Lemon does mention one instance of a Schwenkfelder who had trouble with an old grant of Frankfort Company land in Philadelphia County: *Best Poor Man's Country*, pp. 86-87.

Germantown.[23] The conclusion reached from studying this evidence is that most men had put the personal relationships of youth behind them when they embarked for America. Only 7 percent of the Germantown wills mentioned people in the old country at all. Of these, almost half left gifts to brothers and sisters, nephews and nieces, and cousins, in that order. Two left sums to unspecified relatives in Switzerland or Holland. Around the middle of the century, there was evidently a form will, which directed that any relatives in Germany or America who made claims on an estate should be paid off with a shilling, and a few of the Germantowners used this form. In addition, there were two cases where the legacy was specifically denied to potential heirs abroad—a sister and brother, who had received the testator's share of the old country patrimony, and a wife who had refused to emigrate. Sentimental attachment appeared present in only three cases: one in which money raised on a small lot owned by the deceased in Germantown should be paid to the Meeting of his little hometown in Germany, and two in which the names of the German relatives were not known, but the successful American wished to leave a "remembrance." Mention of German bequests grew less and less frequent as time passed, and most of those who left money abroad had neither children nor other relatives in this country. Only once, during the whole century, did a legacy lead to any kind of recorded dispute between heirs in Germany and those who lived in Germantown. While a paid advertisement appeared in the newspapers setting forth the position of the foreign claimants, the matter was dropped without being settled, in or out of court.[24]

[23] While this material was culled from all available eighteenth-century Germantown wills, the following are examples of some of the types: Paul Wolf, January 6, 1708/9, WB C, p. 149, #115; Adam Snyder, November 2, 1736, WB F, p. 16, #14; John Adam Gruber, May 20, 1763, WB M, p. 528, #298; George Heebner, November 30, 1773, WB P, p. 487, #344.

[24] See *Pa.Gaz.*, June 20, 1765. The problem involved one of the original Crefeld families where both brothers had originally intend-

It is impossible, of course, to know the extent of personal communications between the stay-at-homes and the immigrants, and there is only a small amount of evidence indicating the maintenance of formal contact between the Old World and the New. General information concerning Pennsylvania was disseminated in pamphlets by Penn, Falckner, and Mittelberger. Letters home were occasionally printed and circulated in the old country; in the seventeenth century there were those from Pastorius and the OpdenGraffs relating directly to Germantown, while an eighteenth-century letter from Caspar Wister told of conditions throughout the colony.[25] Many of the visible ties to the Old World that remained were those of religious organizations. Although official communication between North American and Dutch Mennonites ceased by 1758,[26] the Lutheran church in Germantown still used ministers sent out as missionaries from Halle as late as 1789. When the church was built and a parsonage added in 1752, money was raised not only from local sources, but with considerable assistance from Germany. There were 300 florins from the ecclesiastical authorities of the Duchy of Würtemburg and over 50 pounds from Hesse-Darmstadt.[27] While the Reformed Church was never as well

---

ed to migrate, but only one actually arrived in America. This first generation had settled the problem by having all the family property in Holland go to the brother who stayed and all land granted in Pennsylvania settled on the brother who went. It was only a few generations later that the European connection objected, the land values in Germantown having grown far faster than those in Holland. Actually, the Germantown branch of this family (Streepers) was one of the very few stable units that remained on its land throughout the entire period of this study. (There is still a Streeper listed in the Philadelphia telephone book, living on what was once part of this property.)

[25] These works include Penn's "Further Account," *PMHB*, 9; *Falckner's Curieuse Nachricht*; and *Mittelberger's Journey*; as well as Sachse, *Letters*, and a "Letter From Caspar Wister, 1733," *Pa.Ger.*, VIII (1897), pp. 142-144.

[26] Scheffer, "Mennonite Emigration," *PMHB*, 2, pp. 134-135.

[27] Ziegenfuss, *St. Michael's*, p. 17 for information on funds for the church. Also contains a complete listing of the pastors.

organized as the Lutheran and its ministers were frequently
unordained, they are known to have come directly from
Germany at least until 1779.[28] The Schwenkfelders, too, are
known to have kept in touch. In 1767 Melchior Schultz, an
American member of the original group of immigrants,
wrote home, not only describing the agricultural and political setup in Pennsylvania and comparing it to Germany,
but including a map with the homesteads of all Schwenkfelder families indicated and a key to distances around
Pennsylvania.[29]

The role of Germantown as a center of German affairs,
both concrete and cultural, has been much exaggerated. It
has been traditionally accepted, for example, that most
Germans came first to their "own township," rented and
worked for a while, and then moved on, but even at the
very beginning of the eighteenth century there were many
more German immigrants than ever saw Germantown. In
fact, most of those who arrived during the initial period of
immigration from 1700 to 1705 did not funnel through
Germantown at all, but went directly to other settlements
like Oley and Amity in the western townships.[30] Those who
remained in Germany, however, did tend to fix on the township as the place where the American dream was being
realized, as the "el dorado" of the New World. "Many
Newlanders boast that they are rich merchants in Pennsylvania, that they sail in their own ships, and own houses in
Germantown," warned Christopher Saur, trying to expose

[28] See the list of pastors in Ref.Ch.Consis.Rec.

[29] *The Genealogical Record of the Schwenkfelder Families: Seek-
ers of Religious Liberty Who Fled From Silesia to Saxony and
Thence to Pennsylvania in the Years 1731 to 1737*, Samuel K. Brecht,
ed., New York, 1923, p. 84.

[30] Theodore E. Schmauk, *The Lutheran Church in Pennsylvania,
1683-1800*, vol. I, "The Church Prior to the Arrival of William Penn
in the Seventeenth Century and Prior to the Arrival of Henry Melchior Mühlenburg in the Eighteenth Century," *Narrative and Critical
History*, Part IX, *Pa.Ger.*, XI (1900), pp. 212ff.

the redemptioner trade in mid-century.[31] Saur, himself a Germantowner, probably had much to do with this attitude, since his German paper was certainly the most influential of its kind in the colonies and was widely circulated in both Germany and Pennsylvania. His press became a clearing house, not only for general information on problems of immigration and living conditions, but also for individual communications needs. He regularly reported the movements of German businessmen to and from the city, and from one part of the county to another. During the period of enormous, chaotic immigration in mid-century, advertisements such as this were common in his paper: "Julliana Fellerzerin, of Creutzenach, came to America ten years ago and was with Jacob Bauman; married a tailor named Wolff and they went to the Blue Mountains. Her brother, Johannes Feltzer, arrived last year, and awaits news about her at Bastian Neff's, the Crown Tavern, outside Germantown."[32]

On the other hand, very little information exists to indicate that Germantowners continued to have much interest in what was going on in their old homelands. Saur frequently printed articles in his newspaper concerning events in Europe, but these news reports usually served the editor's sec-

---

[31] *Pa.Berichte*, October 16, 1749.

[32] Ibid., April 1, 1751. Christopher Saur's importance as a printer (especially of the Bible) and disseminator of German opinion throughout Pennsylvania is well known. For an overall view of his life and works, see Harry A. Brandt, *Christopher Saur and Son: The Story of Two Pioneers in American Printing.* . . . , Glencoe, Ill., 1938, or Edward W. Hocker, "The Sower Printing House of Colonial Times," *Pa.Ger.*, LIII, Part 2 (1948), pp. 1-125. Other articles relating to Saur's religious views and quarrels as well as to the actual content of his paper and almanac can be found through the index of the *PMHB*. For his political activity, see Weber's *Charity Schools*. Much of the distortion about the Pennsylvania Germans has come from the use of Saur's works as typical of the thought and action of the Germans. As a sectarian and an atypical one at that, his ideas probably never represented those of more than a tiny minority, although he was widely known and read.

tarian interests rather than his readership's political curiosity. The progress of wars was slighted in favor of news such as the item that "several edicts have been issued in Europe against the Moravians, and the King of Great Britain has forbidden the circulation of Moravian books or the holding of Moravian services 'in our dominions.' "[33] Books purporting to be about current affairs in Germany had much the same flavor: "Just Published, Price four Pence or three shillings a dozen, A Most Remarkable Prophecy concerning the Wars and Political Events, especially the Glorious King of Prussia. Taken from an ancient Latin manuscript which is deposited in a famous Library in Europe, with an Essay of Explication."[34] The only other concrete indication of German sentiment is the changing of the name of an inn from the Sign of the Stag to the King of Prussia in 1757.[35]

Proving that the links with Germany became weak and disintegrated with time is not quite the same thing as showing how the Germantowner assimilated into the general English culture of the colonies, if, indeed, he did. Traditional belief on this subject has usually held that the Germans tended to cling to their language and their ways and to form, whenever possible, a separate society. This was a cause of consternation to people like Benjamin Franklin who saw, in failure to acculturate, a threat to the unity and the strength of Pennsylvania: "Why should the Palatine boors be suffered to swarm into our settlements, and, by herding together, establish their language and manners, to the exclusion of ours? Why should Pennsylvania, founded by the English, become a colony of aliens, who will shortly be so numerous as to Germanize us, instead of our Anglicizing them, and will never adopt our language or customs any

---

[33] Repeated December 20, 1750 in the *Pa.Gaz.*

[34] *Pennsylvania Journal*, November 27, 1760. Advertisement.

[35] See *Pa.Berichte*, October 29, 1757. Actually, this proves little about Germantown's continuing interest in Germany, as the new landlord was a recent immigrant.

more than they can acquire our complexion?"[36] Near the end of the century, Benjamin Rush, more of an admirer of the Pennsylvania Germans, looked at the situation more carefully and more objectively: "The intercourse of the Germans with each other is kept chiefly in their own language, but most of their men who visit the capital and trading or country towns of the state, speak the English language."[37]

As far as the situation in Germantown is concerned, Rush seems much closer to the mark than Franklin, and close analysis of such evidence as is available seems to show, contrary to long-held opinion, that there was little desire to maintain German identity. While this, of course, does not apply to isolated rural groups like the Amish, it may have widespread implications for an understanding of the early assimilation patterns of non-English speaking immigrants in urban and near-urban areas.

The kinds of records left in Germantown actually offer a unique, if indirect, opportunity for studying the spoken language of a prephonograph population. Pastorius, whose influence was so strong in the initial shaping of the community, indicated an understanding of the importance of language in the process of acculturation. In the preamble to the original code of laws for Germantown, he stated that "by no means shall anyone be pardoned by the excuse that he does not understand the English language and so did not know of such a law."[38] He further admonished his own chil-

---

[36] H. E. Jacobs, "The German Emigration to America, 1709–1740," *Narrative and Critical History*, Part III, *Pa.Ger.*, VIII (1897), pp. 148-149.

[37] Benjamin Rush, *An Account of the Manners of the German Inhabitants of Pennsylvania Written in 1789*, Daniel Rupp, ed., Philadelphia, 1875, p. 54.

[38] Gesetz, Ordnung und Statuta der Gemeinde Zu Germantown . . . , Pastorius Manuscripts, Vol. I, HSP manuscript collection. Dated 1691, in a bound journal book together with the Germantown Charter and the laws of Pennsylvania. (Hereafter cited as Gesetz Buch.)

dren: "Dear Children, John Samuel and Henry . . . Though you are of high Dutch Parents, yet remember that your father was Naturalized, and ye born in an English Colony, consequently each of you *Anglus Natus* an Englishman by Birth. Therefore, it would be a shame for you if you should be ignorant of the English Tongue, the Tongue of your Countrymen."[39]

When the General Court established a school in Germantown, which was run by Pastorius from 1701 to 1718, it would appear to have been conducted in English, judging by the textbooks written by the teacher himself and used by him in his classes. These included: *A New Primmer . . . 1698; Lingua Anglicana or Some Miscellaneous Remarks concerning the English Tongue; Lingua Latina or Grammatical Rudiments; Collection of English Rhymes Alphabetically Arranged; A Breviary of Arithmetic and Arithmetical Hotch-Potch; Formulae Solennes or Several Forms of Such Writings as are Vulgarly in Use, Whereunto an Epistolography is Annexed;* and *Vademecum or the Christian Scholar's Pocketbook.*[40] The text and explanations of all these books were in English and could not have been conveniently used in a classroom where German was the usual language of address.

Throughout the entire century there are indications of a mixture of English and German. The continued influence of German is most clearly seen, perhaps, in those written documents that give a clue to the pronunciation of words. In a will, written in English in 1744, it was directed that the money of the deceased be divided into *"tree* equal parts," a phonetic spelling that surely points to the way in which the words were spoken.[41] In the tax list of 1780, the name of Wynard Nice is spelled "Vinard," and Martin Beck is referred to as Martin "Peck." It is interesting to note that while many spelling changes of this nature are still in evi-

---

[39] Pennypacker, *Pa.Ger.*, IX, p. 113.
[40] This list appears in Learned, *Pastorius*, p. 165.
[41] Michael Wagner, WB G, p. 142, #112, September 8, 1744.

dence in the census of 1790, they have mainly disappeared by the Direct Tax of 1798. There are none at all by the tax list of 1809, and, in fact, many of the typically German names have been anglicized, such as "Showaker" for "Schauecker."[42]

Translations of family names such as "Holtz" and "Zimmermann" to "Wood" and "Carpenter" took place with increasing frequency during the century, and there are other examples of language in transition. Often the change was a simple anglicization, as when a baby baptized Johann Carl Möhr in 1745 was married thirty-eight years later as Charles Moore.[43] Some changes are more complex, however, as may be seen in the burial records of a man who died in 1793. A man named "Johann Gärtner" was listed among those buried by the minister of the Reformed Church in November, in the Lower Burying Ground. The records of the caretaker of that cemetery, however, listed no such interment, although a Johann Jardene was buried on the same date. A good bit of Huguenot influence in the lower part of town provides a possible explanation for the extra stage required for the "Gärtners" to become "Gardners."[44]

While babies were still baptized largely with the German form of their names throughout the century—"Maria" for "Mary," "Andreas" for "Andrew," "Jacob" for "James"— they habitually used the anglicized form by adulthood as indicated by the names on the census list of 1790. Among women, the "a" form of names like "Elisabetta" or "Dorothea" was quickly changed. English names such as "Sara" or "Hugh" became more common, while purely German ones like "Ulrich" and "Cunnigunda" tended to disappear.

---

[42] "1809 List of Inhabitants," *PMHB*, 15 and 16.

[43] St.M.Rec., Baptisms: vol. I, October 28, 1745; Marriages: vol. II, June 3, 1783. Dropping the "Johann" was common, since the name was frequently given to every male in a family and was undoubtedly seldom used.

[44] See burial records of both the Reformed Church and Hood Cemetery for November 27, 1793.

A puzzling entry in the birth records of St. Michael's involves a mother named "Pekki" Miller, wife of Andreas, who baptized a baby "Crasy." It is obvious that English names had become stylish in Germantown by the end of the century, although with a most peculiar pronunciation.[45]

The records kept by Germantown organizations also point to the continual anglicization of the written records of the community during the eighteenth century. Both the major churches kept their registers and minutes in German for most of the period, but this is understandable in view of the fact that their pastors were almost always newly arrived from Germany. During the 1790s, when the pastorate of the Reformed Church was continually changing hands and the records were kept by various members of the congregation, they were almost all written in English. When English names appear in St. Michael's records, they are painstakingly written in English script by the German minister even when the rest of the page is German in calligraphy. In addition, after 1750 the minutes of the Lower Burying Ground were kept in English; from the time of its founding in 1760, the Union School records were always in English in an apparently school-trained hand; and from 1781 the same was true of the records of the Upper Burying Ground.[46]

Fortunately, seventeenth- and eighteenth-century German calligraphy differed radically from the English style of the same time, which makes it possible to do a closer study of the way in which acculturation was taking place. By examining the signatures of Germantowners, one can sometimes tell what language they used as a matter of course.

[45] St.M.Rec., Baptisms: vol. II, October 12, 1794. The family name is given as "Miller" although two babies baptized in the same family are under the surname "Müller." St.M.Rec., Baptisms: vol. III, October 23, 1796; June 22, 1800. The given names appear to be "Peggy," short for "Margaret," as the mother's name and "Gracie" as the name of the child.

[46] Hood Cemetery Records; Minutes of the Union School; "Records of the Upper Burying Ground," *PMHB*, 8, p. 424.

There are two main sources for signatures. One is the will book collection, in which the signature from the original document was copied as nearly as possible by the clerk, so that one sees clearly whether or not the actual signature was in German. However, often the clerk was English, and the copying was purely mechanical, so that while it is apparent that the writing is in German script, it is less easy to be sure of what it says. In any case, of 308 Germantown wills entered in the books for Philadelphia County during the eighteenth century, the vast preponderance were signed in English (65 percent) while only 12 percent had Dutch or German handwriting, the remaining 23 percent having been signed with a mark. These proportions remain fairly stable throughout the century.

An even better source for Germantown signatures exists in the 1783 list of 439 signers to a Memorial that sought to have Germantown made the capital of the United States.[47] The writing is first hand, not through the offices of a clerk as in the case of the wills, and all names were written within a reasonably short period of time, illustrating the situation at a given moment rather than stretched out over the course of people's lives. Almost three-quarters of these men, 74 percent, signed in English, while 22 percent of the signatories used German, a rise in the percentage of German names used on wills, due to a smaller group of marks used by this sample.

It is interesting to find in the Memorial corroboration, if not proof, of the theory that the use of German as a common tongue was generational, that it died out rather quickly among the second and third generations. Of the 423 literate signatures on the petition, 203 involved individuals who were the only members of their families to sign, while there were 84 family groups represented by from 2 to 4 members. As a total, 72 percent of the individual signers wrote in

[47] Memorials to Make Germantown the Capital of the United States, 1783, 1787. NAMP microcopy 247, roll 60, pp. 117-121; pp. 137-139.

English, while 28 percent used German. In 65 percent of the family groups all of the members signed in English; in 28 percent of them, the signers were divided between the two languages; and in only 7 percent of the family units did all members sign in German. Table 12 combines this information with the tax lists, thus making possible statistical correlation between length of residence in Germantown and use of English as a written language.[48] The only area that does not follow the pattern of increased English usage with increased length of residence is that of the high percentage of all-English-signing families among those who do not appear on any Germantown tax or census list, but the figures on which they are based are too small to have any statistical relevance. Most of these families are not newcomers at all but from long-established families, such as the Leverings, whose actual residences were across the township line in Roxborough.

Specific families were then checked to see if the general results applied in a sampling of actual cases. In all cases where the signatory could be traced as a second- (or later-) generation Germantowner, he wrote in English. Even some of those who were clearly first-generation Americans signed their names in their adopted language, especially if they had been in the New World for a considerable period of time; for example, Christian Duy is known to have arrived in 1750, and his signature is English, while Caspar Windish, who arrived in 1752, signed in German, as was more typical of his generation. These men were of a similar economic standing. Many of those who arrived in the decades of the twenties and thirties were still living at the time of the petition, and it is they who account for the frequency of mixed-language families—the old grandfather who still used his native tongue, his sons and grandsons who had adopted the language of their own native land, America. Thus, Christo-

---

[48] This material is provided by checking the Memorial against Keyser's "List of Property Owners, 1766," *Germantown*, pp. 37-41 and the 1773 and 1780 tax lists.

TABLE 12

RELATIONSHIP OF LENGTH OF RESIDENCE IN GERMANTOWN TO USE OF GERMAN OR ENGLISH SIGNATURES, 1783

| | Individuals | | | | Family Groups | | | | | | |
| | English | | German | | All English | | Mixed E-G | | All German | |
	No.	%	No.	%	No.	%	No.	%	No.	%
Those known to have been in Germantown by 1766	20	87.0	3	13.0	30	75.0	9	22.5	1	2.5
Those not known to have been in Germantown until after 1773	50	72.5	19	27.5	17	53.1	13	40.6	2	6.3
Those appearing only on the Memorial	70	68.6	32	31.4	4	66.7	—	—	2	33.3

SOURCE: Memorial to Make Germantown the Capital of the United States, 1783; List of Germantown Property Holders, 1766; Philadelphia County tax lists, 1767, 1773, 1774, 1779, 1780; various church and land records.

pher Meng who immigrated in 1728 appears in German, while his son, Melchior, signed in English. No members of original Germantown families who remained, such as the Streepers, were writing in German. The few cases of marks made by illiterates among family members also seem to belong to the first generation elder, while the sons, in *all* cases, sign in English. Jean Bigonet, who was married in 1753 as a newcomer to Germantown, was among those who asked to have Germantown made the capital thirty years later. He signed with his mark, which the clerk transcribed as "Bikony," while his sons, who both signed "Bigony," used English. Another example of transitional stage and continuing German accent, is the man who wrote in English, but spelled his name "Shmith."[49]

The evidence would seem to make it rather clear, therefore, that in urbanizing communities, at least, the requirements of a heterogeneous society probably encouraged comparatively rapid acculturation. The reason for continuing German speech was primarily continuing German immigration rather than conscious effort to retain ethnicity among the second and succeeding generations. There is also some evidence that the older members of the community considered the use of their German signatures as something formal, although they had begun to employ English as their everyday language. Christian vanLaaschet wrote some of the minutes of the Lower Burying Ground in English, but when he signed his name to the audit, it was full of German flourishes.[50] The increasing influence of English is also found in the signatures of many old timers which change in the course of time from pure German to a kind of combination German-English script. Adam Haas who arrived in German-

---

[49] The information for this section comes from cross reference of Rupp, *30,000 Names*, the various Germantown tax lists, the baptism and burial registers of St. Michael's and the Reformed Church, the *U.S. Census*, 1790, and the Will Books.

[50] Hood Cemetery Records, March 11, 1782.

town sometime before 1748, was writing his name this way, twenty-six years later: *ₓₓₓₓₓₓ* : a hybrid mixture of the two styles.[51]

At the other end of the scale, young people and servants appear to have used English. The source material on this is less well defined, but it does exist. Of twelve runaway German or Dutch servants from Germantown listed in the newspapers in the second half of the eighteenth century, all but one spoke some sort of English, four of them rated as tolerable or good. How quickly this acculturation began may be indicated by the German woman, twenty-six years old, who had been in the country ten months and already knew "a little English."[52] The records of St. Michael's indicate that children were becoming increasingly unfamiliar with the language of their ancestors. Four of the thirty-three children who were confirmed there in 1784 could neither read nor speak any German at all and had to be examined in English.[53] From the time of the Court School run by Pastorius, there was usually some form of English education offered in the town, and by the end of the century the Union School served the lower end of town, the Concord School (which taught entirely in English) was open in Upper Germantown, and the Harmony School operated off and on in Chestnut Hill. Both the Reformed and the Lutheran churches occasionally offered services in English well before the end of the century "due to demand, especially among the young."[54]

The part played by the different religious groups in Germantown in the acculturation of the members of their congregations was an important factor in the speed with which Germantowners did, or did not, assimilate into the society

[51] St.M.Rec., Baptisms: vol. I, August 20, 1748; Burials: vol. II, December 23, 1781. Hood Cemetery Records, December 15, 1774.
[52] *Claypoole's Advertiser*, September 17, 1797.
[53] Richards, *St. Michael's*, p. 47.
[54] Ziegenfuss, *St. Michael's*, p. 25.

of the New World. There is no doubt that the Quakers lost their Dutch character the most quickly.[55] Of course, from the very beginning the Meeting in Germantown had a somewhat international flavor—reflecting seventeenth-century Quakerism at large—with Dutch, German, and English members.[56] In addition, it was closely attached to the other Meetings in Pennsylvania, all of which were English. The mutual aid aspects of Quakerism guaranteed that when "Derrick Isaacs [OpdenGraff] a Dutch friend of German Town" acquainted the Philadelphia Monthly Meeting of the poverty of some of the Dutch there, aid would be forthcoming. And since this aid required "Samuel Carpenter and Griffith Jones to pay their subscriptions unto one, or some of them, that are in most need of a present supply," it insured direct contact between the Germantowners and their English coreligionists. In 1705 Germantown sought, and received, aid in both money and kind from Philadelphia, Frankfort, Abington, and Byberry for erecting a new, stone meetinghouse.[57] These religious contacts encouraged facility in English and frequent interaction between the Dutch and English Quakers. The anglicizing of names took place almost at once, both in relation to the spelling of last names and the choice of a first name for the baby: "Tison" became "Tyson," and Aret Klincken named his first baby born in the colonies "Anthony."[58]

Two other interrelated factors operated to achieve the

[55] Frederick B. Tolles, *Meeting House and Counting House: The Quaker Merchants of Colonial Philadelphia, 1682-1763*, 1948, rpt. New York, 1963, p. 32.

[56] For a discussion of this point, see Oswald Seidensticker, "William Penn's Travels in Holland and Germany in 1677," *PMHB*, 2 (1878), pp. 237ff.

[57] Minutes of the Philadelphia Monthly Meeting, I, 14 (February 3, 1684), FrDR. Also see Horace M. Lippincott, *An Account of the People Called Quakers in Germantown, Philadelphia*, Burlington, N.J., 1923, p. 7.

[58] AbMMRec., pp. 17-18, Swarthmore microfilm.

result that, by the third generation, there was almost nothing left to connect the children of original Dutch Quaker settlers with their continental roots. The first of these is that there was no continuing stream of immigration from the continent to the Quaker meetings of Pennsylvania. Later sectarians came, of course, Mennonites, Dunkards, and others, but the Quaker migration had run its course. In fact, so unusual was the whole idea that there had ever been a real Dutch Quaker movement, that some nineteenth-century historians persisted in referring to the first community as "Mennonite."[59] Therefore, there was no renewal of old world culture to counteract the constant contact with the English among the Germantown Quakers.

Second, the pressure to marry within the Meeting was far stronger than the tendency to marry within the nationality. Almost every marriage that is recorded of Germantown Quakers took place either with other old family Dutch members of the Meeting or with English Quakers.[60] The family of Jan Lucken, while larger than most, was typical in its choice of marriage connections among the early German Quakers. Lucken was a Quaker from Crefeld, who was married to the sister of another of the original settlers. He and his wife arrived in America in October 1683 without children, and in the following year the first of their daughters was born. For the next twenty-one years the couple produced a child approximately every two years, having in all five girls and six boys. One of the girls died young, but the rest all married beginning in 1706; all had made first marriages by 1728, and after that several married a second time. The daughters married three sons of original Dutch

[59] For this presentation, see Daniel K. Cassel, *Mennonites*, chapter 2. A great many historians have used a great deal of paper refuting Cassel's contention that Pastorius and the original thirteen settlers were not Quakers, but Mennonites.

[60] AbMMRec., Marriages: 1685-1721; 1745-1841, Swarthmore microfilm.

or German Quakers from Germantown (one a son of Pastorius), one Englishman from the Germantown Meeting, and one Englishman from Abington township. The sons married five English Quaker girls from out of the township and three daughters of Germantown Quaker families. Two of these latter were left widows and remarried English members of the Germantown Meeting.[61] The combination of these three circumstances—close religious contacts with their English neighbors, lack of ongoing immigration, and marriage within the Meeting—meant that by the middle of the eighteenth century those original Quaker families left in Germantown, such as the Johnsons (formerly Jansens), are almost impossible to identify as Dutch and probably should be assigned, for the purposes of sociological study, to the English group.

The cultural assimilation of the Lutherans and Reformed Church members was not as rapid nor as complete as that of the Quakers, but there was no positive force working against it. The essential German nature of the religion, including the common use of the German language for the service, and the continual influx of new immigrants from the continent assured at least a minimum ongoing contact with cultural roots. On the other hand, these groups were not actively hostile to the environment and influence of their new homeland, nor do they appear to have been highly motivated to retain their ethnic legacy. The following was written by an English minister from Cheltenham township, in 1760: "I have an invitation from some of the English people in Germantown to preach for them, as there is no kind of English worship in the town, except a Quaker Meeting House. . . . The use of the Lutheran Church of the upper end of Germantown, and of the Calvinist of the middle of town, are both offered to me by their respective ministers and people, as they appear more willing to have a minister of the Church of England to preach to their people that understand English (as most of the young people

---

[61] Genealogy of the Luckens family.

do) than any other denomination."[62] By the end of the century, the school run by St. Michael's offered instruction in English as well as German. Both German churches had also become popular places to get married for young English couples. Over 200 of them married there between 1750 and 1800, including Benjamin Franklin's granddaughter, Elizabeth Franklin Bache.[63] It is interesting that there was no particular antagonism to the cultural integration of these churches with the surrounding culture during the eighteenth century. It was not until some generations later that controversy between English and German factions within each became so bitter that both congregations ended by splitting and forming separate institutions.

It was the Pennsylvania sectarians who made a conscious effort before the nineteenth century to retain the language and culture of the Old Country, and, in fact, to maintain a closed community in the midst of an open society. Those groups who migrated to the west immediately and settled in isolated regions often managed to achieve their goals. Those members of the sects who settled in Germantown were far less successful. The community was already too crowded to avoid continual contact with the outside world, and the lures of assimilation were many and seductive. Besides, in that bustling, business-oriented town, how attractive would a religion be whose central idea was expressed in this manner by its spiritual leader: "Know that when you are successful in the world, God has forsaken you; but when all misfortune comes upon you here, then know that God still loves you."[64]

The attempt by the sects to maintain cultural separatism in Germantown weakened their own positions, rather than

[62] Keyser, *Germantown*, p. 291. Quoted from a letter by the Reverend Mr. Neil, May 12, 1760. Note that the Quaker Meeting in Germantown is considered by him a wholly English institution.

[63] St.M.Rec., Marriages: vol. III, January 9, 1800. "Elizabeth Franklin Bache to John Edmund Narwood, both single; from Philadelphia."

[64] George N. Falkenstein, *History of the German Baptist Church*, Lancaster, Pennsylvania, 1901, quotation from Conrad Beissel, p. 57.

providing a bulwark of German identity in America. Since both Mennonites and Dunkards practiced adult baptism and relied heavily on conversion, their members were often culturally out of the German stream by the time they were baptized. Contacts also remained close with those in one's family who were not sectarians, and in many cases pressure was brought to bear on the convert to change his mind. John Gorgas, for example, left his daughter Mary only £20 by his will if she remained "in the Lancaster monastery" but £30 if she left.[65]

Again it was Christopher Saur who left later generations with the feeling that Germans, on the whole, were antiassimilation, through a well-publicized war waged in his press against the assimilating effects of the Charity Schools proposed by William Smith and others in the 1750s.[66] His arguments, while given a religious and cultural base, were largely political, however. While he may never have seen the letter written by Dr. Smith to the Bishop of Oxford in 1756 which stated that "till we can succeed in making our Germans speak English and become good Protestants, I doubt we shall never have a firm hold on them,"[67] Saur sensed the political threat behind the educational proposal. His response included a plea for German cultural separation and at one point indicated that parents in Germantown were afraid that if their children learned to speak English and associate with others, they would want to dress in English style.[68] Given the situation known to have existed in Germantown, the sentiment seems somewhat artificial and unrealistic. In fact, it is unlikely that the mere fact of learning English could have seemed like a threat to a man as fluent as Saur himself. His son, Christopher II, succeeded him in his business, and generally held much of the same view of life as his father. Yet he became one of the founders of the Union

---

[65] John Gorgas, WB F, June 2, 1741, #198, p. 221.

[66] The best and most complete source for the history of the Charity Schools controversy is still Weber's *Charity Schools*.

[67] Ibid., p. 61.   [68] Ibid., pp. 58-59.

School in 1759, which included an English, as well as a German, section.

The stated goals of the Charity Schools as set forth by William Smith were certainly not incompatible with the actions, if not the unconscious attitudes of the heterogeneous immigrants to eighteenth-century Germantown: "By a common education of English and German Youth at the same Schools, acquaintances and connexions will be form'd, and deeply impressed upon them. . . . The English language and a conformity of manners will be acquired, and they may be taught to feel the meaning and exult in the enjoyment of liberty, a home and social endearments . . . which will naturally follow from school acquaintance, and the acquisition of a common language, no arts of our enemies will be able to divide them in their affection."[69] The men of Germantown did not join the four special German Battalions organized by the Committee of Safety at the time of the Revolution, but were assigned to the general Battalion of Philadelphia County.[70] In general, life seems to have been conducted in a more-or-less English way, although with a definite German accent, and while the reasons involved pragmatism and the desire for a well ordered and prosperous society rather than idealism and a wish to jump into some kind of a democratic melting pot, the effects were much the same. What the Charity Schools never got a chance to accomplish by design was accomplished by accident in the urban atmosphere of a small, polyglot, industrial city, heavily influenced by scaled-down versions of the same causes and effects that operated in nearby colonial Philadelphia.

[69] Ibid., p. 27. A letter written to the Society for the Propagation of the Gospel, December 1, 1753.
[70] *Pennsylvania Archives*, 6th Series, Vol. I.

PART II

THE COMMUNITY

A TOWN IS a place in which people live their lives in continual contact with each other; a community is the dynamic of interaction created by that contact. The nature of a community is determined by the beliefs, habits, and expectations of its citizens and the way in which these intangibles are ordered to control the social processes within the town. A historian who intends to use the tools of the modern social scientist to examine the world of the past cannot be satisfied with the external portrait of the town, but must also attempt to explore the sources of the internal workings of the community.

In comparison with the sociologist who creates ideal types and analyzes existing societies by means of personal contact and scientifically controlled interviews, the historian is at the disadvantage of having to construct his models and find his ideas among data that exist without reference to his intentions or goals. As Peter Laslett has said about the materials used in historical demography, "[they were all] gathered by men who neither had our purposes in mind, nor could have been made to see their importance if someone had tried to explain them."[1] Still, by comparing the material that has been left with the general constructions of societies based on present-day research, it may be possible to understand something of the nature of past communities.

For general historical purposes, two kinds of community organization may be postulated. One occurs in the "communal society" where cultural and social change are very slow and where "folkways" take the place of formal contracts or rationalized institutions.[2] Methods of ordering com-

[1] Peter Laslett, "Introduction," *EHD*, p. 2.
[2] For a general discussion of the two types of society, see Logan Wilson and William Kolb, *Sociological Analysis, An Introductory*

mon life grow out of long and intimate association of men with each other; they rely on a law that is made up of the traditional conceptions of rights and obligations, and customary procedures are used for assuring them; legislation, codification, and jurisprudence do not enter into it.[3] The extreme form of communal society is the isolated rural village. The opposing pattern of community organization is the "associational society" in which culture is impersonal, individualized, and in a process of continuous change. This pattern occurs in the urban setting, where "the bonds of kinship, of neighborliness, and the sentiments arising out of living together for generations under a common folk tradition are likely to be absent or, at best, relatively weak in an aggregate the members of which have such diverse origins and backgrounds. Under such circumstances competition and formal control mechanisms furnish the substitutes for the bonds of solidarity that are relied upon to hold a folk society together."[4] Sociologists have usually recognized that the two patterns of community life just described are not completely identified with the difference between rural and urban, village and city life. They frequently describe a variation in which "a complex society can be just as tightly organized and inflexible as the organization of the simpler communal society."[5] In this model, of which the medieval city is an example, the rigidly unified, inflexible, unchanging, and all-powerful culture patterns of the communal society are applied to the urban situation. In eighteenth-century America,

---

Text and Case Book, New York, 1949, chapter 11, "Societies: Communal and Associational Types," pp. 344-392. The material on the communal or "folk society" is a reprint of Robert Redfield's classic article, "The Folk Society," *American Journal of Sociology*, 52 (January 1947). A more recent description of the closed society may be found in Eric Wolf, *Peasants*, Englewood Cliffs, N.J., 1966.

[3] Redfield, "Folk Society," *Sociological Analysis*, p. 356.

[4] Louis Wirth, "Urbanism as a Way of Life," *Cities and Society*, p. 53.

[5] Wilson and Kolb, "Societies," *Sociological Analysis*, p. 345.

and perhaps in many frontier situations, the antithetical variation is an equally significant development, although, for some reason, it seems to be rarely noticed or described. The requirement for group interaction among individuals of varying backgrounds in a wilderness situation imposed the necessity of forming associational societies within the confines of relatively isolated small towns or villages.

Despite the village size and rural location of most colonial towns, they could not become communal societies. The people who lived in them, particularly in the Middle Colonies, shared few common traditions or habits. They were all immigrants, and, in places like Germantown, from remarkably different backgrounds. They were continually moving in and out, and there was no firm base of population to insure the transmission of the culture. It was impossible, therefore, to develop a folk society in which "the patterns of conduct are clear and remain constant throughout the generations . . . [in which] the congruence of all parts of conventional behavior and social institutions with each other contributes to the sense of rightness which the member . . . feels to inhere in his traditional ways of action."[6] In New England, where the attempt was sometimes made to establish communities artificially by means of consciously constructed intellectual models, the results at best were mixed in relation to satisfaction or permanence.[7]

On the other hand, all but the largest metropolitan centers—Philadelphia, Boston, New York—lacked the numbers and diversity necessary for the growth of a flourishing associational society. There were just not enough people to assume leadership in the variety of tasks required by an impersonal and codified approach to community living. Too

[6] Redfield, "Folk Society," *Sociological Analysis*, p. 360.

[7] On the fact that New England villages attempted to accomplish the end of creating a folk society, see Lockridge, *A New England Town*, pp. 18ff. A contrasting opinion that New Englanders did, in fact, succeed in establishing "other-oriented communalism" as a prime value of public life is presented persuasively by Zuckerman, *Peaceable Kingdoms*, especially the preface and introduction.

many people actually knew each other or were related to each other or attended church together or served in the militia together to be entirely objective or impartial. How, for example, could one find a road jury in a township of less than 500 taxpayers whose members would have no stake in the placement of the new cartway? It is difficult to take a formal and legalistic approach to neglect of the community's fencing regulations when the culprit is one's own brother-in-law.

Unfortunately, there is one question the historian probably should not attempt to answer. Williams has pointed out, in the context of the modern village of Ashworthy, how difficult it is to examine the operation of social class or status in a "face-to-face" society where "a knowledge of personal characteristics and detailed individual histories influences status judgments and attitudes."[8] The only possible way for an outsider to arrive at an accurate understanding of the subtleties that underlie the status system is by assembling a great deal of personal material on subjective preferences. Lack of any contemporary evaluative material and the scarcity of even formal information on the importance of various community jobs make this topic liable to serious misinterpretation. It is far too easy to reason tautologically from the modern attitude that certain ethnic groups are of a "higher class," to arbitrary assignment of status to those of, say, English background, living in eighteenth-century Germantown. Even a knowledge that these were the people who mattered more in Philadelphia or the colony at large only obscures the very answer that is sought: did they, in fact, have higher status, more respect, or greater influence among their neighbors in the Germantown community? One might assume a close correlation between wealth and status, yet records of local organizations show that they were frequently led by men whose tax assessments were below the community average, while several very wealthy men played little part in the life of the town. In addition, leaders in

[8] Williams, *Ashworthy*, p. 7 fn.

church or local government endeavors were so frequently self-appointed rather than chosen by others, that it may speak more to a desire to raise one's status than to a position of community respect already obtained.

In any case, the internal workings of the class system in Germantown are best left alone, in the absence of any substantial body of subjective material. It is still possible and valuable in a sociological sense to consider external process, to deal with the ways in which the "inhabitants of the Germantownship," as they styled themselves, set about creating a community from a relatively small population pool of diversified background. In practice, what they did fell somewhere between the rigid internalization of the consciously created folk society of New England and the chaotic "privatism" of impersonal cities.[9] The mobile and heterogeneous population of Germantown, complicated by its superstructure of nonresident gentry, failed to develop the informal, traditional leadership patterns of village societies, while the face-to-face nature of daily life prevented the formation of a rationally articulated society of laws and formal institutions. This dual difficulty resulted in problem solving on a utilitarian basis and a lack of cohesion in community life, both secular and religious. In the course of colonial history, surely many places shared the dilemma that was Germantown's, and an understanding of community process in this case might be more useful in seeking "the American tradition" than the study of such atypical phenomena as small New England villages or large Eastern cities.

[9] Warner sees "privatism" as a method of group organization that was utilitarian and economic, with no foundation of moral consensus: "Psychologically, privatism meant that the individual should seek happiness in personal independence and in the search for wealth; socially, privatism meant that the individual should see his loyalty as his immediate family and that a community should be a union of such money making, accumulating families; politically, privatism meant that the community should keep the peace among individual money-makers, and, if possible, help create an open and thriving setting where each citizen would have some substantial opportunity to prosper." *Private City*, pp. 3-4.

CHAPTER 5

Render unto Caesar...:
The Secular Government

IN THE middle of the eighteenth century, a Professor Achenwall from the University of Göttingen made some observations on life in North America, based on a series of interviews with Benjamin Franklin. Among other things, he compared town building in New England and Pennsylvania: "In New England improvement of the land is made in a more regular way than in Pennsylvania, whole towns are laid out, and as soon as sixty families agree to build a church and support a minister and a schoolmaster, the provincial government gives them the required privilege, *carrying with it the right to elect two deputies to the legislature*, from the grant of six English square miles. Then the town or village is laid out in a square, with the church in the center. The land is divided ... *leaving however the forest in common*. ... Nothing of this kind is done in Pennsylvania, where the proprietor wants only to sell land and as much as any one wants and wherever he likes."[1] Although Franklin's propaganda is visible behind the partisan tone of these remarks, there is a good bit of significant material contained within them regarding the nature of town communities in the two regions.

From the very beginning, town government in New England stood at the center of the political machinery. Not only did it emerge as the locus of effective authority in the province of Massachusetts but its officials, the selectmen, fre-

[1] J. G. Rosengarten, "American History from German Archives With Reference to the German Soldiers in the Revolution and Franklin's Visit to Germany," *Narrative and Critical History*, Part XIII, *Pa.Ger.*, XIII (1904), p. 75. From Professor Achenwall's observations on North America, 1767. Emphasis supplied.

quently served as representatives to the General Court.[2] The towns dealt directly with the colonial government without any intervening political body; representatives of the towns rather than of counties sat in the General Court. Massachusetts had no counties at all until 1643 when four shires were set up to organize the town militias into larger units for the benefit of the United Colonies of New England.[3] The system developed slowly, however, and then only as an administrative unit; it acquired no political powers or control. Other New England colonies, such as Rhode Island and Connecticut, never found it necessary to form counties at all until well into the eighteenth century. By the time a group of Massachusetts freemen petitioned the General Court for the right to set up a town, they had already gained both experience and insight into government operation.

The Pennsylvania town was endowed with none of this political necessity. As Lemon noticed: "The lack of the political significance of boroughs and the open society rendered separate status for towns of lesser significance than in medieval England."[4] The reasons for settling people in groups rather than on individual farms had been stated by Penn in 1685: "I had in my view Society, Assistance, Busy Commerce, Instruction of Youth, Government of People's Manners, Conveniency of Religious Assembly, Encouragement of Mechanicks, distance and beaten roads."[5] In a heter-

[2] See, for example, Demos, *Little Commonwealth*, p. 7; Lockridge, *A New England Town*, p. 45. Chapter 1 of Zuckerman's *Peaceable Kingdoms* is especially useful in understanding the position of the eighteenth-century Massachusetts town.

[3] Powell, *Puritan Village*, pp. 148-149. For a brief description of the Massachusetts county system, see *Massachusetts State Government*, 1956: rpt. Cambridge, Mass., 1970, put out by the League of Women Voters of Massachusetts. Even today they find that "Massachusetts counties do not engage in many activities common to American counties elsewhere."

[4] Lemon, "Urbanization," *WMQ* (1967), p. 518 fn.

[5] William Penn's "Further Account," *PMHB*, 9, p. 68.

ogeneous society, however, most of these items were bound
to become private matters, and when it came to the general
politics of the colony, the towns were always second in importance to the counties. The freemen who attended the
Pennsylvania Assembly were representatives of the counties,
excepting those from the city of Philadelphia, which alone
among municipalities had the right to send legislators to the
colonial government.[6] Political activity, therefore, was directed throughout the eighteenth century at the county
level, and the potential either of local expression of political
thought or local control over governmental business was
seriously weakened. Despite a fairly liberal franchise requirement, a small townsman had much less opportunity to
become an officeholder in Pennsylvania than he did in New
England, since it required prominence not merely among
a few hundred close neighbors but among thousands of constituents over a widely scattered area.[7]

The second major point of difference, noticed by Professor Achenwall, was the basic control by the town, as a community, over the use and distribution of land. In Massachusetts, the grant from the General Court was to groups of
settlers who had deputies or spokesmen to represent them,
and who, according to Lockridge were "searching for the

[6] See the Frame of Government, 1696, *Pennsylvania Archives*, Colonial Records, I, p. xli; Charter of Privileges, Colonial Records,
Minutes of the Provincial Council of Pennsylvania, II, pp. 56ff. Lemon
discusses the importance of counties in Pennsylvania's system, *Best
Poor Man's Country*, p. 25.

[7] It would be interesting to know how much of the apparent disparity in the amount of democratic participation in one colony or
another is related, not so much to the franchise, but to the size and
availability of the political unit as a practical matter. Perhaps findings
of greater democratic tendencies in New England (for example
Grant, *Kent, Connecticut*) have a relationship to *town* participation
in colony affairs while Klein's findings that transportation difficulties,
political indifference, and illiteracy kept participation low in New
York relates to the use of the *county* system. Milton M. Klein,
"Democracy and Politics in Colonial New York," *New York History*, 40 (July 1959), pp. 221-246.

opportunity to create a communal life . . . to shape . . . their own versions of the good society."[8] In addition, it was a grant rather than a sale, which implied continued control if necessary to achieve the stated community goals. The towns were provided therefore with a chance to set aside *before private division* the choicest, most convenient locations for the village green, the common woods and pastures, and the church, as well as to order the distribution of private lands from a complex set of social criteria, rather than simply on the basis of ability to pay.[9] The town government's continued strength and control were assured by the presence of a "land bank"—land not yet distributed but available for private use at the discretion of the community—which survived in many Massachusetts towns for generations.

Land in Pennsylvania was not a community responsibility, but a private investment, and this method of distribution had a strong effect on the way in which the internal structure of the Germantown community developed.[10] Every piece of property required for community functions had to be bought and paid for, and since, except for the short-lived period of borough status (1691-1707), there was no true formal town government at all, the questions of who owned the community centers, who ran them, and who was entitled to use them, were continuing problems. Land for the most basic community needs—a cemetery and a market— was purchased from the holdings of one of the original owners. Although Pastorius had intended that an acre of public land be set aside before the distribution of actual sites to the members of the Frankfort Company and the Cre-

[8] See, for example, Powell, *Puritan Village*, pp. 97ff.; Lockridge, *A New England Town*, p. 3.

[9] Greven, *Four Generations*, chapter 3, especially pp. 41-51. This may have a good deal to do with Lemon's findings on the tremendously poor social and spatial definition of local institutions in Pennsylvania: *Best Poor Man's Country*, especially pp. 116-117.

[10] For the effect of this land investment in other places, see, for example, Wood, "Lancaster," *PMHB*, 96, pp. 346-368.

felders, there is no evidence that this was done.[11] Although a public site was chosen, by 1691, eight years after settlement, the acre had become so valuable that it was sold in exchange for two quarter-acre burying lots one at either end of the town and the money to buy one-half acre for a market near the cross street. Since religion was not a community matter as it was in Massachusetts, no land was set aside for a meetinghouse, which, in turn, meant that the town had no community-owned center.

The formation of a body politic was never an issue with the original Germantown land owner, the Frankfort Company. It is true that Pastorius thought in terms of the formation of a community and felt that his friends who made up the membership of this group had the same ends as he: "they purchased 15,000 Acres of land in this remote part of the world, some of 'em entirely resolv'd to transport themselves, families & all; this begat such a desire in my Soul to continue in their Society, and with them to lead a quiet, godly & honest life in a howling wilderness, (which I observed to be a heavy Task for any to perform among the bad examples & numberless Vanitates Vanitatum in Europe)."[12] Compared to some of the English land companies that settled other colonies, the Frankfort Company was more an aggregation of individuals than an organized group. It never sent any settlers nor did any of its members remove to Pennsylvania. The power of attorney which was granted to Pastorius by the company when he left Germany was purely for the financial management and administration of their estates: "said Pastorius in the Name of the Constituents shall receive & Conserve in the best form of Law the things themselves, the Possession thereof and other Rights; Order the Tillage of the ground & what belongs to husbandry there

[11] See Pastorius's introductory notes to the Grund und Lager Buch; Tinkcom, "Market Square," *Germantowne Crier*, 19 (September 1967), p. 69; Keyser, *Germantown*, pp. 170-171.

[12] Francis Daniel Pastorius, "The Beehive," HSP. Handwritten journal kept by Pastorius, p. 223.

according to his best diligence, hire labourers, grant part of the land to others, take the yearly Revenues or Rents; and shall & may do all what the Owners may do in Administration. . . . What will be reasonable will be assigned unto him out of the expected Incomes or Rents in Pennsilvania."[13] In other words, Pastorius was an estate agent; he had no specific political or governmental jurisdiction. Since the company had no legal relationship to Germantown, when its financial interest in the community dwindled, it passed entirely out of the history of the New World.[14]

The settlers who arrived from Holland with rights to Germantown land included some of the Quaker purchasers from Crefeld. This group had no definite ideas of community life nor any plan of settlement and was quick to accept Pastorius as its leader and spokesman, despite the fact that he was an outsider. He was an obvious choice: an educated man, personally acquainted with the proprietor, and possessing access to the greatest amount of land, since he controlled all of the Frankfort purchase or 50 percent of the total acreage of the Germantownship. Pastorius rapidly acquired political power on a colony-wide scale and was named in 1684 as one of the first three justices of the peace appointed for Philadelphia County. He was also chosen as a member of the Assembly in 1687.[15]

In 1689, six years after the colony had been settled, William Penn finally granted a charter for the formation of a government in Germantown, which was approved in England in 1691. Although this charter government lasted only seventeen years, it formed the basis for the practical handling of day-to-day affairs for the rest of the century. While officially Germantown operated under control of the county government after 1707, in many ways the community appears to have been run by a series of unofficial

---

[13] Learned, *Pastorius*, p. 121. Power of attorney granted to Pastorius, April 2, 1683. Trans. by Pastorius.

[14] See Pennypacker, *Pa.Ger.*, IX, pp. 95-102.

[15] Hocker, *Germantown*, p. 24.

associations whose workings had been shaped by the corporational approach of the first charter. The original Penn document set up "one body politique and corporate by the name of the Bailiff, Burgesses and Commonality of German Towne, in the County of Philadelphia."[16] The form was that of the most conservative of English boroughs, a completely closed corporation: Pastorius was designated bailiff or chief officer; there were four burgesses and six committee men. The corporation had the power to make ordinances, impose fines, levy and collect taxes, hold a court and a market, and admit others to membership. The bailiff and the two oldest burgesses were to serve as justices of the peace, the bailiff and the three oldest burgesses formed a Court of Record, and other officers were to be elected from within the corporation once a year.[17] The only clue to the possibility that there was any political organization in Germantown before enactment of the charter, was that one of the signers designated himself "towne president." The other signatories used their occupations as title—merchant, linen maker, or yeoman—except for Pastorius who had the curious appellation, "civilian." Failure to mention any other official title may indicate the possibility that the leaders of the township selected OpdenGraff as "towne president" to act as spokesman on this one occasion.

This experiment in borough government made by Penn at Germantown rested on a completely different basis from the borough governments of the New England towns. In Sudbury, for example, "every major issue was discussed in open town meetings and over 132 meetings were held in the first fifteen years."[18] Even in places like Dedham where candidates for admission had to undergo examination before

---

[16] *Pennsylvania Archives*, 1st Series, I, pp. 111-115.

[17] For a brief discussion of Germantown borough government and a comparison of it with other Pennsylvania boroughs—Chester, 1701, Bristol, 1720; Lancaster, 1742—see Frank Worthington Melvin, "The Political Beginnings of Germantown," *Germantowne Crier*, 9 (September 1957).

[18] Powell, *Puritan Village*, p. 119.

they could either buy or rent land on a long-term basis, each member of the community, once accepted, shared in all decisions involving the town, and even, in many cases, those concerned with private affairs.[19] Pastorius himself recognized that the form of local government in Germantown was unique for Pennsylvania. In 1698 he wrote to his father in Germany: "concerning the ordering of the civil government . . . at Philadelphia . . . each year certain persons are elected from the whole people, who make the necessary laws and ordinances for that year . . . they help to care for the common weal, by and with the governor of the province . . . justices . . . decide all disputes occurring according to the laws thus made, after the facts have been investigated by twelve neighbors. And all this is done in open court, so that everyone, great and small may enter and listen. In my German city, Germantown, there is an entirely different condition of things, for, by virtue of the franchise obtained from William Penn, this town has its own court, its own burgomaster and council, together with the necessary officials and well-regulated town laws, council regulations and a town seal."[20]

What Pastorius and his fellow Germantowners created was an English government based on German traditions.[21] Participation in the decision-making process so marked in the New England town meeting was missing altogether, but citizens were expected to know the laws that "all may live manfully according to them and no one may plead ignorance as an excuse for his disobedience," including ignorance of the English language.[22] The General Court, as the

[19] Lockridge, *A New England Town*, p. 8.

[20] *Germantowne Crier*, 8 (September 1956), letter from Francis Daniel Pastorius to his father, May 30, 1698.

[21] See Learned, *Pastorius*, pp. 225ff., for a comparison of the laws and regulations of Germantown with those of Frankfurt am Main, the home town of Pastorius, and other towns of the Lower Rhine in Holland and Germany.

[22] Preamble to the "Laws" *Pa.Ger.*, IX, p. 320, p. 322. While the original Gesetz Buch still exists, a careful check determined that the

corporation sitting in deliberation termed itself, considered that it had the responsibility to "make and establish as many good and reasonable laws, ordinances and statutes as for the salutary government of this community and its affairs as may be necessary and advantageous, and may . . . bring such into effect and perfect them, and also may, when changing circumstances make it necessary, alter their laws, or withdraw them, and establish new ones."[23] The consent of the governed was no more solicited than their participation. The tone of the relationship was established in this paragraph: "Wherefore, we, the present first Bailiff and Burgesses of the place, do hereby in friendly manner inform each and every citizen, inhabitant and tenant under Germantown jurisdiction that we . . . by virtue of the powers given to us . . . have in several General Courts . . . drawn up the following laws and ordinances, and also unanimously determined that they shall be published and made known to the community by public reading. . . . And as we now earnestly wish and desire that, towards those who henceforth shall serve in the Magistrate's office here, all citizens and subjects under our jurisdiction may with just zeal and conscientious obedience, submit to and support such laws and statutes."[24] The requirement that the people assemble in a public place once a year to have the laws and ordinances read aloud to them, was reiterated in the law book when the nineteenth of March was chosen as the yearly date of this event.[25] A cold choice when one considers that this meeting must have taken place out of doors, there being no public building large enough to accommodate a gathering of this size.

If the active participation of each citizen had been expected in the governing of the community, it would have

---

Pennypacker translation is accurate enough to serve as an easy reference and will be cited rather than the original, except where there is a difference.

[23] "Laws," *Pa.Ger.*, IX, pp. 319-320.

[24] Ibid., pp. 320-321.

[25] Ibid., p. 332. Law #40 was passed 17d 1mo 1696.

been necessary to screen new members in the manner described by Lockridge for Dedham. Since such consensus was
not required under the projected form of government, homogeneity of individual belief was not essential. Decisions of
the court were by majority vote, and the secret ballot was
used.[26] Admission to the corporation, therefore, was a purely
financial matter, with a usual fee of six shillings, occasionally
waived for poor or elderly souls who wandered into the
township.[27] Membership in the corporation, or at least the
permission of the General Court, was required for residence: "Each and every one who shall hereafter wish to buy
or rent land in the township . . . or to settle within it, shall
first procure from the General Court of his fellow citizens
the right or privilege of living here, and without such permission no one shall participate in our privileges."[28] The
privileges included such favors as obtaining a liquor license
from the Court of Records or tieing one's "horse or mare
or any other cattle upon the fence lands of the corporation
either by day or by night."[29]

Privileges also included the right, or obligation, of officeholding. In addition to the bailiff, the four burgesses, and
the six committeemen stipulated by the charter, the small
community was also expected to provide a recorder, a town
clerk, a treasurer, a sheriff, a coroner, a messenger, and a
constable (two after 1696).[30] In the seventeen years covered by the Charter, 283 offices actually were filled, out of
a possible 306. This was an enormous number of positions
for a population that never reached much higher than 200
people or about 60 families at any one time. Given movement in and out of the township, which was always con-

---

[26] Raths-Buch, 6ᵈ 6ᵐᵒ 1691.

[27] For fee, see Raths-Buch, 24ᵈ 2ᵐᵒ 1692; for waiving of the fee,
ibid., 25ᵈ 10ᵐᵒ 1694, or 25ᵈ 11ᵐᵒ 1694/5.

[28] "Laws," *Pa.Ger.*, IX, #32, p. 328.

[29] The Records of the Court of Record, 3 November 1702 [*sic*];
3ᵈ 4ᵐᵒ 1704.

[30] The information on offices and officeholders comes from the
Raths-Buch, where the election returns were officially entered.

siderable, 101 individual adult males can be traced as having
lived in Germantown during the borough period, of whom
28 are known only through the lists of officeholders and
the rest appear on the list of original land owners of 1689,
the tax list of 1693, the list of lot holders in 1714, or any
combination of these. Seventy-three percent of the identified owners held office at least once, while only 31 percent
never participated in government at all. The actual percentage of involvement is undoubtedly lower since there were
many who lived in the township for a short while and never
appeared on any of the lists. This is indicated by the decline
in the percentage of officeholders whose names appear on the
lists: 54 percent of the 1689 list, 50 percent of the added
names in 1693, and 45 percent of the new arrivals on the
1714 list.[31] Still, even these corrected figures argue for a certain practical, if not theoretical, level of democracy in the
running of the township.

Had the offices been held on a completely equal basis,
each inhabitant on the list would have served approximately
three times. Of course, the actual distribution in no way re-
sembled this ideal (table 13).

Seventy percent of those who held jobs can be seen to
have held the average or less, while those who held more
were as likely to hold more than ten positions as they were
to hold between four and ten. Nine of the eleven men who
held ten jobs or more were landowners in 1698; none was
unlisted among the property holders. Large numbers of
jobs held by a single man often indicated continued reelection to the same position: Peter Schumacher was a burgess
ten times; Peter Keurlis, a constable six times. Committee-
man was the office to which men were most frequently re-
elected; 75 percent of those who held the post did so more
than once. The Potts family made something of a specialty
of being sheriff, four members serving in that capacity between 1700 and 1707.

---

[31] Based on table 5, together with the lists of officeholders, Raths-
Buch; and lot holders, Keyser, *Germantown*.

Length of residence had an important part to play in election to office under the charter, less in relation to the number of men chosen than to the importance of the jobs they held and the percentage of the time that they occupied them. Table 14 divides all the available jobs into categories according to their significance, in order to make some useful conclusions. The first rank includes the bailiff, the burgesses, and the committeemen; the second rank contains recorder, clerk, treasurer, and sheriff; and third rank has the least prestigious jobs of coroner, messenger, and constable. The men are divided by whether they first appeared on Germantown lists in 1689, 1693, or 1714 as property owners or only on the officeholding lists themselves, thereby indicating rental status and a short stay in the township. Of course, many of the earlier arrivals were present for a short time and had disappeared by the next listing, so that appearance in 1689 does not guarantee long-term settlement. As a matter of fact, four of the officeholders who were present on the first lot-list and were elected in the first years of the charter no longer appear by 1693. Landowners from 1689 not only held a disproportionate number of all places, but were even more heavily represented in the jobs of first rank. Conversely, those who never held land in the township, although most numerous among the officeholders, held the smallest percentage of least important jobs in relation to their representation. The relatively high percentage of men who owned no land until 1714 and took jobs of the third rank (almost twice their percentage of officeholding in general) may indicate the way in which younger men gained needed experience for becoming community leaders later in the century.

The community at large was opposed to the idea that there was any special status attached to officeholding that could excuse an official from doing his share of the common work. The first set of laws read and published 28^d 6mo 1691 had held that "the members of the General Court, together with the town clerk and messengers, in consideration of the

TABLE 13

DISTRIBUTION OF OFFICEHOLDING IN GERMANTOWN
UNDER THE CHARTER, 1691-1707

Office-holders	No. of Offices															Total
	1	2	3	4	5	6	7	8	9	10	11	12	13	14	Over 14	
No.	29	17	5	2	1	4	2	1	1	4	2	1	2	1	1a	73
%	40.0	23.0	7.0	2.7	1.4	5.5	2.7	1.4	1.4	5.5	2.7	1.4	2.7	1.4	1.4	100.2

SOURCE: Raths-Buch.
a Pastorius held twenty-one jobs during the seventeen-year period.

TABLE 14

DATE OF SETTLEMENT RELATED TO OFFICEHOLDING
UNDER THE CHARTER, 1691-1707

Known Date of Property Ownership	Officeholders (N-73) No.	%	First-rank Opportunities (N-168) %	Second-rank Opportunities (N-65) %	Third-rank Opportunities (N-45) %	Total Opportunities (N-278) No.	%
1689	28	38.5	67.8	52.3	35.6	164	59.0
1693	9	12.0	10.1	15.3	13.3	33	11.9
1714	7	9.5	5.9	6.1	11.1	19	6.8
None	29	40.0	16.1	26.3	40.0	62	22.3

SOURCE: Raths-Buch; Keyser's lists of property-holders 1689, 1714, 1693; tax list.

length of time which they spend in consultation and the arrangement of the common business and affairs, shall, so long as they are performing such duties, be excused and free from the common compulsory labor." In a different hand immediately following, however, was added: "N.B. This law, after repeated opposition and final solicitation of the community, has been by the General Court repealed and abolished."[32] There are no other attempts to set any member of the community apart through legal privilege, especially since membership in the corporation was intended to be universal.

The laws as they were published fell into several categories. Most numerous were those regarding public regulation of roads, fences, buildings, taverns, fire codes, and common rights of passage, which accounted for over half of the laws and ordinances formally inscribed during the charter period.[33] Perhaps the thorniest problem was fencing, since it involved conflict between common and private responsibility. The obligations of the private citizen in regard to taking care of his livestock and trees accounted for another 25 percent of the laws.[34] The rest of the code concerned itself with a miscellany of issues, including blue laws against Sunday shooting, racing, and liquor and the responsibilities of the General Court in relation to leases, contracts, and sales agreements, care of the poor, reading of the laws, and granting of incorporation. Finally, the requirements for public service were spelled out. "The common service must be done equally by all who have families. But whoever has one or more properties in addition at any time, must do extra service for each one, when his turn comes." This law was superseded in 1696 by a more explicit one, which, however,

[32] Gesetz Buch, #19.

[33] Covered in this category are those laws in the Gesetz Buch numbered: 1-13, 18, 22, 27, 33-39, 40[b], 42, 44, 45, 49, 50, and several amendments at the end.

[34] Ibid., nos. 14-17, 20, 21, 23-25, 47, 48, 51, 51[b], and several amendments thereto.

no longer penalized the larger property holder: "The road master, as often as common service is needed to be done, shall the day before call upon as many persons as he considers necessary for the present work, and those persons are bound to be upon hand and to work. Whoever does not come himself or send some capable person in his stead, shall have to pay six shillings fine for each day, but if he is so sick that he cannot do his own work, or if he has a wife in childbed in his house, in this case he is not compelled to serve. The aforesaid road master must always keep just and accurate reckoning with all of those who remain in arrears."[35]

The formal laws and ordinances found in the Gesetz Buch do not exhaust the issues on which the General Court found itself obliged to act. Although the condition of the Raths-Buch prevents any close analysis of the sessions of this body, it shows that, without making its situation legally binding, the court also touched upon education, the holding of fairs, care of the poor, the regulation and conduct of elections and, most particularly, the business of the Frankfort Company.[36]

Relations between the company and the town grew more confused during the borough period. The absentee owners had become dissatisfied with Pastorius as land agent and had sent Daniel Falckner to take his place. Falckner, however, not only made himself unpopular in the neighborhood by trying to collect long-lapsed company rents, but also became embroiled in the Keithian controversy which raged among Quakers throughout the colonies.[37] Nevertheless, the company still exerted so much influence in the township by virtue of its enormous land holdings that when Pastorius resigned as attorney for the company in 1700, he also lost most

[35] This is law #30, which replaced #18, above.

[36] See, for example, Raths-Buch, sixth session, 1692; 13^d 6mo 1694; 27^d 4mo 1698; 30^d 10mo 1701; and the election polls for each year.

[37] For a more or less concise account of these affairs, see "The Sprogell Trouble," Keyser, *Germantown*, pp. 93-100. The other side of the story is told in Schmauk, *Pa.Ger.*, XI, pp. 122-125.

of his local political power. While he served as clerk or recorder several times, he never held the post of bailiff after 1697, nor did he sit on the General Court.[38] This left no one in the township with the requisite legal interest or ability for ordering community affairs. Falckner, who should have taken over as prime mover in Germantown, expressed his idea of what was required in the manner of local authority in *Curieuse Nachricht*: "for outward affairs let one or two Justices of the Peace be installed according to the English law, as careful supervisors and trusty regulators. Then a case would rarely occur which would have to be appealed to the supreme authority."[39] His thoughts on a Utopian community included no provision for government at all![40]

After Pastorius retired from the public life of Germantown, the duties of the General Court were frequently confused with those of the Court of Record, due to a lack of legal training on the part of the remaining officials. There was a tendency to handle matters such as fence or road surveys at either level interchangeably, and while the law stated that contracts, land sales, and leases were assigned to the General Court, they were almost always dealt with by the Court of Record. In 1701 David Lloyd prepared a general reform of the law of Pennsylvania and of its courts which tightened the whole judicial system considerably. The new codification made the Germantown practice of using the General Court as appellate, without reference to provincial or county courts, even more questionable.[41]

At just the wrong moment Germantowners were begin-

<hr/>

[38] Raths-Buch, lists of officeholders.

[39] *Falckner's Curieuse Nachricht*, p. 187.

[40] "Daniel Falckner's Project for Founding A Community in Pennsylvania and for Making Profit with Capital," *Pa.Ger.*, XIV (1903), pp. 231-245.

[41] For a good summary of the reformed court system of Pennsylvania see chapter 9, "Reforms of 1701," in Roy Lokken, *David Lloyd: Colonial Lawmaker*, Seattle, 1959. Misuse of the General Court by the Court of Record in Germantown as an appeals court occurs several times in the Records of the Court of Records; e.g.: 7^d 11mo 1700/1.

ning to think of themselves as part of an articulated and independent community. While Pennsylvania was centralizing its control over its increasing population, the Germantown Corporation was petitioning the Governor's Council that it should be exempt from the taxes, levies, and jurisdiction of the County Court of Philadelphia because as a corporation, its own Court of Records and magistrates were empowered to take care of all its own charges without help from the county.[42] The Council tabled this petition, but the government began quietly to build a case against the illegalities of the borough government, and on February 11, 1707, the Queen's Attorney, George Lowther, permanently adjourned the Germantown court, thus ending the life of the borough and the experiment in this form of local control. Specific charges against Germantown included the unauthorized laying of taxes by the General Court, appointing unqualified men as justices, binding over within its own jurisdiction rather than to the Philadelphia courts, and "that Johannes Kuster married a couple without the limits of the Corporation."[43] The real issue seems to have been that the corporation status of Germantown was too ambiguous to exist within Lloyd's new system and that its offices overlapped too much with those of the county government.

There can be little doubt that loss of the charter and demotion to township status permanently crippled any attempt by the Germantown community to develop government control of its own affairs and to defy the Pennsylvania drift toward county dominance. Yet, it is very probable that there was little local regret. As early as 1696, it had been necessary to pass a law under the charter levying a £3 fine for anyone who refused to accept government service for reasons other than religion or age.[44] Unlike their New England counterparts of an earlier generation, Ger-

42 *Pennsylvania Archives*, Colonial Records, II, Minutes in Council, 5ᵈ 1ᵐᵒ 1700/1, pp. 13-14.
43 Records of the Court of Records, 11ᵈ 12ᵐᵒ 1706/7.
44 "Laws," *Pa.Ger.*, IX, p. 332, #43.

mantown's first settlers had participated little in governmental affairs at home and were not really anxious to do so in the New World.[45] They may, in fact, have been rather relieved to get rid of a charter that demanded such an incredible number of officials and required them to spend so much of the time needed to seek private financial success on unremunerative public affairs. The goals of the Holy Experiment were, for them, largely negative ones—to avoid service and be left alone. In this respect, Warner's concept of the private city can be applied to Germantown as well as Philadelphia: "Both in its form and function, the town's government advertised the lack of concern for public management of the community."[46]

It is difficult for the twentieth-century urbanite, even with intense exercise of historical imagination, to realize that when there is little record of government in a given area, the possibility exists that there was actually very little government. Somehow it seems that the dearth of information must be due to missing sources. In some cases this may be true, but for the most part, in the townships of Philadelphia County, at least, it would seem that there was a bare minimum of local control. After all, what was there for government to do? The largest single responsibility was the distribution of land, and this was being handled on the provincial level. There were housekeeping duties to attend to: the opening and maintenance of roads, the building of bridges, the licensing of taverns and peddlers, the capture and punishment of criminals, the settlement of local quarrels and disputes, the assessment of property, and the collection of taxes to pay for these chores. The poor and the orphaned had to be provided for, and the orderly passage of property from one generation to another through the registration of wills and

[45] Compare, for example, the background of the leaders of Powell's *Puritan Village* with the Germans described in Wertenbaker, *Middle Colonies*, pp. 218ff., or by Schmauk, *Pa.Ger.*, XI, pp. 169-170.

[46] Warner, *Private City*, p. 9. Lemon makes the same point several times in *Best Poor Man's Country*. For example, see p. xv; pp. 218-219.

the administration of estates had to be accomplished.⁴⁷ The county took care of these tasks, and beyond them, people were expected to manage for themselves.

The system seems to have suited the Germantowners. As long as they were not burdened by the onerous worries of formal government, they were more than willing, for the rest of the century, to handle the affairs of their own community without outside interference. As late as 1797 a number of inhabitants of Germantownship petitioned the state legislature, stating that since they had purchased their own poorhouse, they would like to be allowed to deal with the problem of poverty in their usual way.⁴⁸ Not only were they eager to be left alone, they tended to view the local community for which they were willing to be repsonsible in the very narrowest sense. In 1750 the managers of the semipublic Lower Burying Ground complained that "Whereas Numbers of Strangers or Persons not residing in and living out of Germantown Limits, by frequently bringing and burying their dead . . . unto such of our Burying Ground in Germantown as have formerly been purchased and granted for the only use of the inhabitants of Germantown will in all appearances very soon render our said Burying Ground . . . insufficient to contain our own Dead and having taken into consideration, that such Strangers or Persons, living in other places or townships have no just right to bury any of their dead into our said Burying Grounds."⁴⁹ This sounds very much as if strangers from distant colonies were stealing into Lower Germantown to bury their dead under cover of dark-

---

⁴⁷ The exact handling of these areas is cloudy and changed in Philadelphia County during the course of the century. The Minutes of the County Commissioners for Philadelphia County, 1718-1751 (Phila.Arch. microfilm) are quite complete and show little evidence of dealing with anything save roads, bridges, taxes, the county workhouse, and prison. The Quarter Sessions Court, established in the 1682 Frame of Government, gradually assumed more of these duties in the second half of the century.

⁴⁸ *Claypoole's Advertiser*, March 31, 1797.

⁴⁹ Hood Cemetery Records, p. 10, February 28, 1750/1.

ness, whereas what was actually being considered was use of the ground by neighbors who lived just across the boundary in Bristol or Northern Liberties, and who were frequently active civic or religious leaders in the township itself.

On the other hand, there is no particular indication that the members of the Germantown community had any interest in becoming involved in politics outside the township. This conclusion must remain tentative, however, since careful investigation meets with failure to turn up much record of individuals running for office, serving on county boards of one sort or another, or attracting attention for participation in colonial affairs in general. Germantowners, for example, are mentioned in the court records most frequently for failing to appear for service on the juries for which they were called.[50] The records of the Philadelphia area during the Revolution might be used for a more complete analysis.[51] When the Council of Safety for the county of Philadelphia was named, no one from Germantown was selected, although it was the most populous district outside of the City itself. When committees were chosen by districts to drive off cattle in preparation for the British approach, Germantown was not mentioned at all. There are almost no records of the Revolutionary Government contracting for goods and services with Germantown businessmen, although Germantown was obviously the largest industrial area in the entire state.[52] Nor was there a single Germantown woman who served on the committee for Ladies Donations for the Revolutionary Army, run by the wife of General Joseph

[50] This is true of Grand Juries and Travers Juries, Quarter Sessions and Oyez and Terminer Courts. See, for example, a list of six in the Oyez and Terminer Records, Phila.Arch., June 1784 (p. 227), or QS Rec., December 1767; September 1778; September 1779.

[51] *Pennsylvania Archives*, Colonial Records, XI, May 21, 1777 and following.

[52] An exception to this was George Losh who supplied the army with gunpowder. Christopher Ludwig, famous as a baker for the Continental Army, did not work out of Germantown at that time.

Reed, and including a district made up of "Germantown and Bettelhausen."[53] This was not because the township was to any large extent embued with Tory sympathy. There was only one prominent Loyalist, Christopher Saur, whose estate was attainted, and those who refused the loyalty oath (most of whom were Quakers) amounted to no more than 11 percent of the total taxpayers in 1779.[54] The British were not under any illusion that the area was friendly to them: "I saw Major Balfour, one of General Howe's Aide de camps [*sic*], who is very much enraged with the people around Germantown for not giving them intelligence of the advancing of Washington's army, and that he should not be surprised if General Howe was to order the country for twelve miles round Germantown to be destroyed, as the People would not run any risque to give them intelligence when they were fighting to preserve the liberties and properties of the peaceable inhabitants."[55]

The dawn of independence brought only the faintest vitalization of political spirit to Germantown. There was a brief flurry of activity in the mid-eighties when the question of the funding bill and the readmission of Tories to public life caused a mild amount of factionalism among the Germantowners, but of the ten men prominently mentioned in the newspaper for being involved, only three were regular residents of the township, the rest being summer people.[56] There were no Germantown citizens among the Pennsyl-

[53] *Pa.Gaz.*, July 12, 1780. "Bettelhausen" was the name frequently used for the area between the Roxborough to Abington Road and Cresheim Creek. (See figure 1.)

[54] See Hocker, *Germantown*, p. 119 for a record of Christopher Saur's affairs. The 1779 tax list is the basis used to figure the percentage of nonjurors.

[55] "Diary of Robert Morton, October 5, 1777," *PMHB*, 1 (1877), p. 15.

[56] See, for example, articles in the *Pennsylvania Journal*, June 21, 1783 and January 8, 1785; *Pa.Gaz.*, February 16, 1785 and March 2, 1785.

vania Delegation to the Federal Constitution in 1787, and only a modest number under the chairmanship of Charles Bensell, who signed a petition to approve the constitution later that year. The only time interest in governmental activity heightened was when the issue was somehow related to the pocketbook: a petition to the assembly against the Militia Bill (293 signatures), one against the taxes that had been levied on Germantown properties (200 names),[57] and the petition to make Germantown the capital of the United States which included over 450 names. While this last has a fine patriotic ring to it, the wording of the petition itself, which reads like a clever real estate advertisement makes it clear that economic considerations were uppermost in the minds of the signatories: "The subscribers would consider themselves greatly deficient in Duty and Respect, should they fail to make a tender of Germantown. . . . Every sentiment of Esteem *as well as Regard to their own Interest* forbids their Silence. . . . The beautiful situation, salubrious Air, excellent Water, plentiful Market, extensive Pastures, fertile Soil and Contiguity to one of the most flourishing commercial Cities in the union . . . there is a commodious public Building which contains ample rooms for their meetings and convenient Apartments for the Public Offices . . . a considerable number of Houses, some of them not inelegant, are ready for the reception of the members, and many Families who will do all in their power to supply any Deficiency that may arise from the want of entire Houses."[58]

Closely related to the lack of interest in political activity was a Germantown attitude toward the law and its courts that ranged from indifference through suspicion to actual hostility. The community had begun with the early Quaker

[57] William Henry Engle, "Pennsylvania Delegates to the Federal Constitution," *PMHB*, 10 (1886), pp. 446-460; *Pennsylvania Packet*, September 22, 1787 and February 9, 1789; *Pa.Gaz.*, April 18, 1787.

[58] Memorial to Make Germantown the Capital, September 4, 1783. Emphasis supplied.

prejudice against the profession,[59] and, in common with most of Pennsylvania, had consistently ignored the registration of deeds, land titles, and wills. The reaction had persisted, however, long after the rest of the colony had changed its point of view and Philadelphia had become famous for its clever, subtle brand of lawyer. It has already been mentioned that from the time that Pastorius died until the end of the eighteenth century, not one single permanent resident of the township classified himself as a member of the profession, despite the large number of summer people who were prominent figures in the field. The fact that Germantown was not a county seat, and that there was no courthouse in the township can only partially account for the situation. The amount of business transacted in this industrial center should have made a legal career profitable, even if the papers had to be finally taken to Philadelphia for endorsement. Surely, too, it seems somewhat strange that of the five busy justices of the peace in this rather urban environment—far from being a village where one dealt only with stray cows and missing chickens—three were tanners, one was an innkeeper, and one a doctor. A clue to the long-standing nature of the dislike of the legal system is found in a resolution passed by the "inhabitants of Germantown" in 1787: "we know not a more exalted act of charity and benevolence than that of presenting a shield against the rapacity of law, which in the increase of costs, and delay of justice in our courts has become such an enormous and oppressive evil, that it is the duty of every real friend to the community to prevent the people from wasting their property by the chicane of law, or corruption of our courts. . . . Therefore resolved: 1) That in all cases of altercation or dispute among ourselves or any of our neighbors, we will use our utmost influence to have the same settled by an amicable reference to men, equally elected by each party. 2) We will acquire a perfect knowledge of the fundamental principles of our constitution, and will carefully prevent any violation of

[59] See Tolles, *Meeting House*, pp. 50-51.

them by our servants, who may be intrusted with the different offices of government."[60]

Considering these sentiments, it is small wonder that Germantowners had few affairs that they were willing to air in court. During the twelve years of the charter period that are covered in the book of the Court of Records,[61] there were 111 sessions called: at 55 of them no business was conducted, half the time because there was nothing to do, the other half because the bailiff, the sheriff, or some other essential court officer was unable to attend. When the latter was the case, proceedings were almost never so important as to require rescheduling in less than the usual six-week interval. The paucity of the record indicates that Germantown did not face the problems of Plymouth Colony where Demos found "an enormous quantity of actions between neighbors."[62] There were, in fact, no really serious court actions entered at all. The total lack of robbery leads one to believe that perhaps this was handled by the justices of the peace, who kept no records. Perhaps the same is true of other criminal matters, for certainly there must have been some, or the General Court would not have ordered the building of a jail and the erection of stocks in 1704.[63]

Of the 260-odd cases that came before the Court of Records, nearly 45 percent were concerned with the transfer of land, either through lease or sale. There were 9 money bonds or contracts validated by the judges and an equal number of cases tried for failure of contract. As in the laws and the records of the General Court, there was a tremendous amount of trouble with fences; no less than 59 matters

[60] *Pennsylvania Evening Herald*, March 10, 1787.

[61] Although the Records of the Court of Records covers the entire seventeen-year span of the charter's existence, there is a four-year gap from 1696 to 1700 and another interval of almost a year in 1705, when no records were kept.

[62] Demos, *Little Commonwealth*, p. 49. The court records for Bucks and Chester counties in Pennsylvania exhibit a pattern closer to Plymouth than to Germantown.

[63] Raths-Buch, 6d 11mo 1703/4.

involved insufficient fences, fence surveys, or livestock straying because of improper fencing. Beyond this, there was a scattering of cases dealing with vandalism, juvenile delinquency, violation of liquor licenses, suits for gossip or slander, failure to comply with various blue laws, and failure to do the common work or appear for court duty. There were 7 apprentice indentures between neighbors and their sons, 7 cases of assault either by males or females, and 1 case of a man who "beat and abused" his neighbor's hog and was fined four shillings.[64] Part of the reluctance to bring action may have been due to the fact that in the earliest deliberations of the General Court, it was decided that the plaintiff in a civil action was to bear the court costs.[65] This was the reason why one case, at least, never came to anything; when the jury found David Sherkes not guilty of slandering Abraham OpdenGraff, the latter wanted to appeal, but on being reminded that "he must pay the costs, he went away."[66]

The decision in this case is open to some question, perhaps, as OpdenGraff was an extremely unpopular man. Although one of the original settlers, he held office only once and was frequently before the court for abusive behavior, first toward his neighbors, and then toward the bailiff and the court itself. It is quite obvious that those who were not liked were apt to be in frequent trouble; the court, in fact, seems to have been used as a final agent of social discipline. As soon as Daniel Falckner began to collect the Frankfort Company's rents, he found himself in continual conflict with the court over his fences, and eventually his horses were taken from him until he should pay a huge fine.[67] It is likely that the combination of this sort of legal harassment and informal social ostracism was extremely effective: of four men who appeared before the court on several occasions for

[64] Records of the Court of Records, 2^d 8mo 1694.
[65] Raths-Buch, 6^d 6mo 1691.
[66] Records of the Court of Records, 3 Oct [*sic*] 1704.
[67] Ibid., 11^d 3mo 1703; 28 Nov [*sic*] 1704.

breaches of social restraint, none remained in the township by 1714.

The personal quality of justice in a small community like Germantown therefore made it extremely difficult to obtain an impartial hearing. Judgments were bound to be made largely on the basis of irrelevant factors, such as general community feeling about an individual. This came to the notice of the Queen's Attorney when a man was cleared in the local court of deadly assault because the man he injured (evidently in a duel) had recovered. The more objective legal opinion was that the victim's recovery should not have diminished the guilt of the defendant.[68] There was also some feeling that to serve the court in some areas might be to do damage to one's friends. Thus Lenert Arets had to be appointed as fence surveyor from out of his district when "Jacob Gaetschalck and John Lensen say they will not betray their neighbors [by viewing fences] especially John Lensen."[69]

After the affairs of Germantown were merged with those of the county and handled by the Philadelphia courts, it becomes impossible to follow the records with a high degree of accuracy. The condition of the records of the Common Pleas allows for no investigation of land or business disputes that may have reached the courts, and local justices handled most cases of neighborly irritation that had previously appeared before the Germantown Court of Record, without making any permanent note of it. Still, by carefully searching the records of the Court of Quarter Sessions for Philadelphia County, it is possible to gather a good bit of information concerning Germantown.

Assault was the one crime that continued to be directed against neighbors and that often grew severe enough to be taken up to the county court. Investigating these cases more closely, one turns up several high-spirited young blades of

[68] Ibid., 8ᵈ 6ᵐᵒ 1704; 3 Oct [*sic*] 1704.
[69] Ibid., 13ᵈ 4ᵐᵒ 1704.

the local gentry who had overindulged, a few political arguments between patriots and Tories that got out of hand, and one case that seems to have involved antagonism between the permanent residents and the summer people.[70] Although the rate of assault never reached as high as 1.0 per 1,000, it rose during periods of faster population growth. For the 1750s and 1770s the rate was 0.3 per 1,000; for the sixties it was 0.4 per 1,000; and for the 1790s, it ran as high as 0.9 per 1,000. (This compares with a modern rate in Philadelphia in 1970, for example, of 1.23 per 1,000.)[71] These figures do not include the one really big quarrel that took place in Germantown during the fifties and sixties over the internal control of St. Michael's Lutheran Church. In 1762 and 1763 alone, relating to this issue there were seven assaults, eleven outstanding citizens required to give bond for good behavior, nine men charged with riot, seven others with forcible entry and detaining of property, and the Rector with a misdemeanor, his wife having been one of those accused of assault.[72] It is easy to see why polite society

[70] QS Rec. For example, Edward Shippen paid the fine for his son, Joseph, convicted of assault, September 1763; December 1763. Charles Bensell, Jr., fined for the same offense, £300, September 1780. (He must have been something of a black sheep as he was also found guilty of fornication, September 1774.) For political argument, see Matthias Lucken and Griffith Jones, September 1780. In December 1799 two local "German" boys were tried for beating up several members of the Morris family.

[71] The rates are figured on the population as represented in table 2 and the number of assault cases that can be identified in QS Rec. as relating to Germantown. The 1780-1790 QS Rec. are missing, so no rates can be compared for that period. One problem in using any of the court records for this study is that the locale of the crime and the criminal's home address are never mentioned. Therefore, one must count on recognizing Germantown names. This is also true of the lists of jurors, justices, witnesses, and all other material relating to Philadelphia County. The figures for 1970 are from the 1972 Book of the Year, *Encyclopedia Britannica*, p. 765.

[72] QS Rec., September 1762, December 1762, June 1763, December 1763, March 1764.

often imposed a ban on the discussion of politics and religion.

No other crimes occurred in Germantown frequently enough during the forty years covered by the county record to be quantified. There were no murders and only one rape; there were twelve accusations of men running "tippling houses" and two of "disorderly houses," presumably then, as now, a euphemism for whore houses; there were four cases of felony and fourteen of robbery or larceny. All but two of these were in the 1790s and seem to indicate, as do the figures on assault, that patterns of behavior in respect to crime were beginning to change with the large influx of new people in that decade. There were two cases of riot in the 1770s that seem to have been related to Revolutionary fervor. There was a small number of family-oriented problems: ten men were charged with fornication and ordered to support illegitimate children; there were six cases of apprentice abuse (significantly enough, five of these were in the nineties); there was one case of wife beating and three of divorce; and there were two cases of refusal to support indigent relatives. There was some concern over Germantown roads and bridges both in the Commissioners' Minutes for the first half of the century and the Quarter Sessions Court Records for the second half. In the twenty-two-year record of the Court of Oyez and Terminer, the only Germantowners to appear were witnesses in the treason trial of Jacob Ming, whose family lived in the township; Andrew Heath, an innkeeper in Germantown, also accused of treason and also found not guilty; and Anthony Gilbert, a local strongman, who was found not guilty of manslaughter in 1792.[73]

County offices held by local men within the township included tax collector under the supervision of the county commissioners, overseers of the poor and of the highways, and constables, all appointed by the Quarter Sessions Court.

[73] Oyez and Terminer Court Records, Phila.Arch. (microfilm), September 26, 1778; December 4, 1778; February 1792.

Tax assessors (as opposed to collectors) appear to have been elected, since there are two cases of Germantown men refusing reelection in the late 1750s,[74] but none appears to have been chosen from the township before 1750 when Derick Keyser was mentioned in the Commissioner's Records.[75] Germantown tax collectors do not appear to have had any particular problems and for many years, in fact, never even had to request abatements for complaining citizens.

The most common practice in appointing men to look after the roads, the poor, and the keeping of the peace was to choose three men for the township—one from lower Germantown, one from Cresheim, and one from Sommerhausen. The constables usually lived in the districts for which they were appointed; this was less often true of the highway supervisors and least often of those in charge of the poor. Men chosen for this last responsibility tended to be among the more substantial, better-known citizens, and therefore from central Germantown. After 1795 the law was changed in respect to the constables, and only one was selected by the court; he was expected to find his own assistants.[76] During the period of British occupation at the time of the Revolution, this was evidently a very difficult job to perform, caught, as it were, between two legal (or illegal) governments. In 1778 four men tried to refuse the office of constable and in 1779, it was "Ordered—that an attachment issue against the Constables of Germantown . . . for their contempt in not attending this Court—which having accordingly issued—the said constables were taken by the sheriff and brought before the court—and upon the reasons rendered by them were discharged by the Court upon payment of costs."[77] The job of highway supervisor was a par-

[74] See *Pa.Gaz.*, September 7, 1758; September 20, 1759.

[75] Minutes of the County Commissioners, November 17, 1750.

[76] *Pa.Gaz.*, March 23, 1796. Bill signed by the Governor, February 13, 1796.

[77] QS Rec., September 1778; Oyez and Terminer Records, April 5, 1779, p. 357.

ticularly thankless and difficult task, taking up a great deal of time and likely to make one unpopular with one's neighbors into the bargain. There were several instances throughout the century of men fined for neglecting this particular assignment.[78]

While the overseers of the poor were appointed by the County Court of Quarter Sessions, the way in which they went about their work was largely left to the community, including the funding for the care of their charges. Tradition has it that before the poorhouse was purchased in 1775,[79] needy residents were placed in the homes of volunteers and that later a fee was paid by the town for their support, so that they were, in effect, auctioned off to the lowest bidder. Children were usually apprenticed to a trade.[80] There may have been direct money payments in some cases, although the only evidence is a single will in which money was left to those poor who "were not on the public dole."[81] The problem was never terribly large; in 1790, from a population of 2,764, there were only 12 residents of the poorhouse, 10 women and 2 men.[82] In the days of the charter, the money to support them came officially from taxes, fines for certain offenses such as drunkenness, and the sale of stray cattle, horses, or sheep impounded by the constable.[83] There is no reason to suppose that this manner of handling the matter changed. The government also lent indirect assistance in the form of tax abatements. In the four years from 1795 through 1798, for which records exist, 29 Germantown men were

[78] See, for example QS Rec., March 1758 or March 1765.

[79] Sheriffs' Deeds, Vol. B, November 23, 1775. A house and lot on the corner of Rittenhouse Street and Main Street: lender, Christopher Ludwig; debtor, J. Adams Hogermoed; buyer, overseers of Germantown. Price: £128.

[80] I have found no real authority for this information. It appears in Hocker, *Germantown*, pp. 94-95, and in Richard S. Fuller, "Anti-Poverty in Early Germantown," *Germantowne Crier*, 18 (January 1966), p. 15.

[81] George Berkman, WB O, #26, p. 34, October 18, 1766.

[82] *U.S. Census*, 1790, p. 196.   [83] Hocker, *Germantown*, p. 95.

helped in this way. Ten of them were abated twice, while 5 left the township after being rated poor.[84]

There were also private sources of help for the indigent. Thirty-seven bequests were made in Germantown wills for community projects during the course of the eighteenth century and of these, twenty-one involved sums left to "the poor." Who was to administer or distribute these funds was never made clear—either the money was to be handed out directly by the executors or it was given to the overseers of the poor to handle with the general community funds. Occasionally the gift was somewhat more specific: "for schooling for the poor"; "for the poor at the Upper end of Germantown"; "for the poor, especially the widows"; or for the poor of some particular religion, "the Dunkard poor," for example.[85] In the case of special problems, a local collection was usually taken.[86] When the county or the colony had a particular charitable outlay to make, they chose neighborhood men of standing and substance to handle the affair. Yet, it could hardly be considered to be handled in the manner of a communal society. The lack of small-town, face-to-face communication in Germantown is shown in the formality of a notice that appeared in a Philadelphia paper in 1776: "To the Poor. Whereas we, the subscribers, are entrusted with 200 bushels of coarse salt, to be distributed gratis, for the benefit of the Poor in general, according to their several necessities; they are desired to apply on the 28th and 29th of June instant, at the house of Paul Engle,

[84] Tax Allowance and Abatement Ledger.

[85] Catharine Reif, WB P, #361, p. 519, January 1774; J. G. Bogert, WB L, #88, p. 151, September 9, 1758; John Johnson, WB X, #33, p. 45, March 17, 1794; Henry Weaver, WB N, #161, p. 299, February 4, 1765.

[86] See, for example, *Federal Gazette*, August 8, 1792. After the powder mill was blown up and the family of one of the men killed was in desperate circumstances, three prominent men raised money to meet the situation. It is interesting, however, that only one of the three was a permanent Germantown resident, and he was a newly arrived "country gentleman."

at the upper end of Germantown, where due attention will be given by Ludwig Englehart, Jacob Engle, Christian Schneider, Jacob Hall and Peter Keyser."[87]

The community also accepted a certain share of responsibility for the education of the young, again in a mixed system of public and private concern for social service. Unfortunately, it is almost impossible to obtain a clear picture of the educational situation since, while there are many unsubstantiated legends about Germantown schools and schoolmasters, the actual records are scanty. Under the charter the General Court of Germantown had appointed three men as supervisors of a community school on December 30, 1701. Their duty was to collect contributions from the local citizens and to arrange for a teacher.[88] As the most learned man in the area, and one who by his own admission was little suited to the pioneer ways of earning a living, Pastorius became the master of the community school. Regular classes were held for eight hours a day during the week and a half-day on Saturday. As this would have been a real hardship for those who were needed to work at home, a night school was also kept by the court and taught by Pastorius.[89] Although these schools are said to have existed from 1701 to 1719 (long after the demise of the court itself), it is unclear how much of the time they were actually in operation, especially since Pastorius spent long periods during the early years of the eighteenth century working for the Yearly Meeting of Friends in Philadelphia.

The court school would appear to have been well sup-

---

[87] *Pa.Gaz.*, June 19, 1776. The men listed are all in the top 10 percent tax bracket for both 1773 and 1780. Ludwig Englehard does not appear on the 1780 list, having died in the meantime, but the rating of his estate shows that he, too, was one of the financial leaders of the community.

[88] Raths-Buch, December 30, 1701.

[89] See his estimate of the usefulness of his own education in his *Beschreibung*, pp. 72-73, HSP. The information that exists on the court school is found both in Keyser, *Germantown*, p. 77, and Hocker, *Germantown*, p. 46.

ported in the neighborhood.[90] Sixty-one patrons can be identified over the eighteen-year span of the school's existence.
Of these 70.5 percent owned land or paid taxes in the Germantownship between 1693 and 1715, while most of the remaining 29.5 percent are known to have been residents of
either Roxborough or Bristol, just beyond the township
boundaries. Thus the Rittenhouses who ran the mill on the
Wissahickon sent at least three boys to the Germantown
school. A few of the others were probably renters, with
children, who were never recorded on any of the land lists.
Checked from the other point of view, 63 percent of those
who are known to have held land in Germantown between
1693 and 1714 contributed to the fund at least once. This is
apt to be a fair indication of the number of those who provided an education for their school-age children; such
people as Joseph Shippen who obviously sent his boys elsewhere to school felt no community responsibility to contribute. On the other hand, Christopher Witt, who had no
children, may be found on the list of patrons.

After the court school came to an end, apparently with
the death of Pastorius in 1719, there was no local government to establish a school with the kind of community
sanction it had enjoyed. Throughout the years that followed,
there were three kinds of educational institutions attempted
in Germantown: those run by religious organizations,[91]
those run by private masters on an individual basis without
community involvement in management, and those that
were undertaken by groups of Germantown leaders to fulfill the needs of a secular society for an educated citizenry.
None was public in any legal sense, although the last type
aimed at performing a community service. None achieved
the kind of institutional stability the twentieth century has

---

[90] A combination of lists from Learned, *Pastorius*, p. 182, and Keyser, *Germantown*, p. 78, provided information on the school's patrons,
while a cross check of these with the 1693 tax list and 1714 List of
Property holders allowed a comparison with total families.

[91] Education in relation to the church will be discussed in chapter 6.

demanded until very recently—all were frequently closed for local crises or lack of proper teachers. Even the Union School, which eventually became Germantown Academy, and, in retrospect, may be said to have a remarkable record for longevity, had several periods when one or more of its branches failed to operate, and one stretch of over six years when no minutes were kept nor trustees elected.[92]

Basically education was still a family responsibility,[93] even though there were those who regarded it as an opportunity that should be made available (though not required) by the community. There was, for example, no general public recognition of a duty to educate the children of the poor. All the community schools did this from time to time, however, using money left to them directly or to the "poor children of any denomination" in the wills of local citizens.[94] One public-spirited schoolmaster who undertook to run a grammar school for the teaching of Latin and Greek in Germantown in 1761 really thought in terms of the social obligations of the educator: "Although this school is primarily for boarders, the Inhabitants of the Country (who are not able to bear the Expense of a City Education) may have their Children taught at an easy rate; the Intention of the Subscriber being to open a door for the Instruction of the Poor as well as the Rich, without any Distinction as to Sect or Persuasion. The Subscriber will teach five poor Boys gratis, upon their producing Testimonials of their real Poverty, promising Genius, and moral Character."[95]

[92] For the general history of Germantown Academy, see Harold E. Gillingham, "Germantown Academy: A List of the Contributors, Trustees, and Officers to the 'Public School of Germantown,' Founded 1760, Chartered September 15, 1784." Typescript, GHS.

[93] For example, Men's Minutes of the Germantown Preparative Meeting, 1756-1895, 3 vols., manuscript, FrDR. (Hereafter cited as Men's Minutes.) 25ᵈ 7ᵐᵒ 1764. "We fear there is not a due care taken for education by some heads of families."

[94] For example: Sarah Paris, WB X, #409, p. 608, July 27, 1797; Benjamin Engle, WB M, #261, p. 458, December 31, 1762.

[95] *Pa.Gaz.*, December 12, 1761.

There are a few mild hints in the records that survive that there was even a small amount of coeducation practiced in Germantown, or at least that some provisions were occasionally made for the training of girls. Two of the children who attended the evening sessions of the court school in 1702 were female,[96] and the application blank for admission to the Union School originally read, "the son or daughter of, or belonging to (as the case may require)."[97] The idea of educating older girls with boys must have been too far in advance of its time, however, for two years later a number of Germantowners requested that the trustees provide the school with a mistress to teach their "daughters and young children" reading and writing.[98] Mention is made in 1767 of a girls' school being started on the second floor of the Union School, but as the exact same note appears again in 1776, these classes must have operated only sporadically.[99] Only one benefactor left money to poor girls as well as boys to be educated in English and arithmetic without regard to religion.[100] It was not until the time of the yellow fever epidemics at the very end of the century that there were any fashionable schools for girls in Germantown, such as Mrs. Capron's where young ladies could learn "French and English languages, writing, history, Geography, Music, Drawing, Fillegree [*sic*], Embroidery, landscapes, as well as flowers and all kinds of needlework."[101]

The way in which the Union School was started tells much about the forming of community associations gener-

[96] Learned, *Pastorius*, p. 182.

[97] Minutes of the Union School, March 16, 1761. This also seems to indicate that it was intended that people should arrange for the education of their apprentices or indentures along with their own children.

[98] Ibid., May 10, 1763.

[99] Ibid., additional minutes inserted as a last page in the journal, in what appear to be nineteenth-century penmanship and style.

[100] Paul Engle, WB W, #200, p. 333, December 18, 1792.

[101] *Aurora*, August 18, 1798.

ally in eighteenth-century Germantown. When there was enough feeling in town that there was need for a school in the community, a meeting was called in a local inn by "several of the inhabitants of Germantown and places adjacent." Here a plan was "unanimously" agreed upon, for "a large and commodius School House to be erected in said town, near the center thereof, two rooms on the lower floor whereof should be for the use of an English and High Dutch or German Schools; . . . and that there should be convenient dwellings built for the School Masters to reside."[102] This could hardly be the plan of a moment, yet nowhere is there any indication of exactly who was the moving spirit behind the idea. It is possible, taking into consideration the closeness of the date to the time of the Charity Schools controversy, that the Union School was intended as Germantown's answer to the idea of English schools for German children. In this case the fact that Christopher Saur II (the father was dead by 1759) was one of those chosen to take subscriptions for the new enterprise and became one of its first trustees is significant. There is also a remarkable similarity between the setup of the school and that of the University of Pennsylvania in respect to the "Fundamental Articles, Concessions and Agreements for the well Regulating and Government of the Schoolhouse and the Schools therein to be kept" which speaks, perhaps, of the early interest of Joseph Galloway in the affair.

It is almost impossible, however, to pick out the real leaders behind the school and, by and large, this kind of joint or anonymous leadership was the rule in most Germantown associations of the eighteenth century. It seems to have been a private use of the style of government followed by the public sector in the New England town meeting. Decisions were made, according to the minutes of such organizations as the Upper and Lower Burying Grounds, by unanimous consent or simply by "those present" and carried out by

[102] Minutes of the Union School, December 6, 1759.

committees of members.[103] Even when there was less than four pounds in the treasury of the Lower Burying Ground, it required three men to settle the accounts.[104] Although little is known about the Library Company, which appears to have been started in 1745, the newspaper advertisements for its annual meetings between 1753 and 1771 mark it as something of an exception; in addition to three directors, it also listed a treasurer and secretary who served definite terms and performed continuing functions.[105] The Lower Burying Ground, whose records are among the most complete, did not differentiate among officers, with the exception of treasurer, until 1794, although there was one man hired as gravedigger before that time.[106]

In general the community was controlled by a fairly complete cross section of its population. The nineteen original trustees of the Union School not only included members of every one of the five major denominations in Germantown but also a spread of backgrounds from purely English to two who still signed their names in German. There were two who were strictly summer people and three who were local residents but lived outside the boundaries of the township; the rest included representatives from the entire length of Main Street itself. The occupational range extended from doctor and gentleman to craftsman and farmer to miller and printer. The only area in which the trustees varied from the community at large was in relation to wealth. The median assessed valuation of those who were still living in Germantown when the 1773 tax was taken was £17 or over twice the £8 of the general population; the average was also more

103 Warner has a similar thesis on the handling of government by committee in Philadelphia, not only during the colonial period, but as a basic feature of institutional life in that city throughout its entire history. See *Private City*, especially pp. 9-10.

104 Hood Cemetery Records, September 3, 1767.

105 E. V. Lamberton, "Colonial Libraries of Pennsylvania," *PMHB*, 42 (1918), pp. 193-234. The notices for the Germantown Company appear in the *Pa.Gaz.* each April for these years.

106 Hood Cemetery Records, March 11, 1782; January 1, 1794.

than double, £30/6 as opposed to £12/16.[107] This kind of balanced leadership was true of other organizations with the exception of the Lower Burying Ground which excluded nonresidents.[108]

The same nonselective pattern seems to have characterized the membership of the various civic organizations. Since the groups were privately financed, anyone who could pay his way was welcome, with the exception that strangers, Negroes, and mulattoes could not be buried in the cemeteries. Even here, the Upper Ground was willing to compromise in the case of strangers, though not in the case of Blacks.[109] Subscriptions were solicited and conveyed certain rights, usually independent of the amount contributed. This is particularly worth noting; at least in the early years of the community, a man who donated two shillings, or a wagonload of stones or a day's work, was on an equal footing within the organization with one who gave two pounds. Membership in the cemeteries carried the right to be buried in the lot or to have the members of one's family buried. After 1760 the Upper Ground offered this only to those who paid over two shillings, while, in addition to a membership fee, there was a burial fee for the Lower Ground after 1776.[110] Those "well affected and generous persons as were willing to contribute to and to assist in the funding of [the Union School]"[111] were entitled to sit on the board of trustees which was elected annually. Those who joined the volunteer fire company, which was established in 1764, by paying what they felt they could afford, rather than a fixed

[107] Based on the 1773 tax list, which includes occupations, and the trustee lists for Germantown Academy, printed by Gillingham, "Germantown Academy," pp. 39-50. For averages of community wealth, see table 11.

[108] Hood Cemetery Records, February 28, 1750/1.

[109] "Records of the Upper Burying Ground," *PMHB*, 8, March 24, 1766, p. 419.

[110] Ibid., p. 415 (1724); p. 418 (1760); and Hood Cemetery Records, February 3, 1737/8; March 8, 1777.

[111] Minutes of the Union School, December 6, 1759.

fee, not only had help in putting out their fires, but were assured of four comembers who would "watch suspicious persons and salvage threatened goods."[112]

There seems to have been little pressure on an individual to join any of the community organizations, although inducements, such as lottery prizes, might be held out when funds were badly needed.[113] Once a man had agreed to serve as trustee or other leader of any of the community associations, however, he was expected to take an active part in affairs; figureheads were severely discouraged. Virtually every organization had within its bylaws some rule regarding the fining of those leaders who failed to attend meetings or otherwise fulfill their functions. This had been true as far back as the time of the borough charter: "Each and all who are chosen by the General Court, for any kind of commission or service, shall be compelled to enter on such duties and fulfill them faithfully under penalty of three pounds fine. But the person so chosen may state truthfully with yea or no, if he for conscience sake cannot take upon himself such duties, or if he is under sixteen or over sixty years old, or if the preceding year he held any commission in the general or open court."[114]

For the voluntary organizations that replaced the charter in running the town, the fine was much smaller, usually two shillings, which must have answered the need, for most of the surviving attendance records of community meetings are excellent, considering the problems of weather and roads and the general difficulty of running life on a schedule in those days. Insistence on participation and attendance may have done much to keep control of the town out of the hands of its part-time upperclass, the Philadelphia residents, who could not be expected to be available regularly. The Library Company, set up in imitation of the one in Phila-

[112] Hocker, *Germantown*, p. 85.

[113] For example, *Pa.Gaz.*, August 30, 1753, on lottery for St. Michael's School.

[114] Gesetz Buch, 17[d] 1[mo] 1696; "Laws," *Pa.Ger.*, IX, p. 332.

delphia in 1745, was active for twenty-six years, and with one exception, all its chief officers were local residents.[115] The only group that failed to enforce its rules in this respect was the Union School, which was frequently forced to suspend business for lack of a quorum. The problem of part-time leadership by "big names" from the city, such as Joseph Galloway or Henry Hill, is shown by the number of times the minutes of the school recorded that "the severity of the weather prevented the Philadelphia members . . . from attending" or that business had to be "adjourned to the first of April next or when the Trustees from Philadelphia can give their attendance."[116]

Community patterns of aid and association became more formal in Germantown, predictably enough, with the large rise of population around the middle of the century. Increasing numbers of strangers made it more and more difficult to conduct business on an informal and neighborly basis. New organizations, such as the Library Company, the Union School, and the fire company date from this middle period, and groups that had long existed first kept regular minutes and set themselves up on a structured basis at this time. It can hardly be coincidence that the church registers of St. Michael's and the Reformed Church both date from this period, although for the Lutherans there are a few scattered records of earlier times in the papers of individual ministers. The minutes of the Men's Meeting of the Germantown Friends commence in 1756, second day, seventh month, with the entry: "It being Recommended and advised to, by those from our Quaker Meeting of Philadelphia, that our Several preparative Meetings should minuit [*sic*] and keep a Record of Several Matters and things which may be transacted thereat; this Meeting therefore falling in aggreeing [*sic*] therewith Do appoint Thomas Rose to prepare a Book for that purpose at the Charge of this Meeting."[117]

---

[115] Lamberton, "Colonial Libraries," *PMHB*, 42.
[116] Minutes of the Union School, December 1761; March 23, 1762.
[117] Men's Minutes, opening paragraph.

Rules and orders of procedure were laid down for the Lower Burying Ground in 1750-51, and the Upper Burying Ground started a minute book and burial record in 1756 when the caretaker who had been in charge since 1724 finally resigned because of old age and feebleness. The informal nature of Germantown associations before this time is highlighted by the fact that he had been in charge of the records and minute book of the association for the first thirty-two years of its existence although he was unable to write![118]

There were continual physical manifestations of the increased formalization of community patterns of culture after the early period. A market was erected in 1741, a fact that had great significance in terms of unconscious feelings of the community about itself. While there is evidence that there had been a good bit of informal roadside selling earlier, and, for that matter, later in the century, and while there were a number of private retail outlets within the township, the market house represented a physical commitment to the idea of Germantown as a public entity.[119] The community saw itself as an established unit, probably still with borough importance, for, technically, towns could not have markets and fairs unless they possessed borough status.[120] Most of the churches built either additions or new buildings during this period, including the Reformed Church and the Dunkards, who had formerly worshipped in the homes of members. The Union School was undoubtedly the most elaborate piece of public architecture attempted in the township and came

[118] Hood Cemetery Records, February 28, 1750/1, pp. 10ff; "Records of the Upper Burying Ground," *PMHB*, 8, p. 416. During the period 1724 to 1756, while J. F. Ax was in charge, those accounts that were kept were written in his presence and attested to by three other members of the committee. No record of the burials was kept. It is known that Ax could not write from checking his will: WB O, #155, p. 206, March 5, 1768.

[119] Tinkcom, "Market Square," *Germantowne Crier*, 19 September 1967), pp. 69-75.

[120] Lemon, "Urbanization," *WMQ* (1967), p. 518.

to serve as a public meeting place for the larger group gatherings that could no longer adapt to the informal rooms of one of the taverns. Still, no real public building of a strictly governmental nature took place, since the actual functions of the town remained private and administrative rather than public and political.

The ultimate confusion, therefore, over what the Germantown community actually was, whom it included, and where its legal standing rested was never solved. While the New England towns found ways to develop early governments of consensus into later governments by majority, the unstructured, extralegal status of Germantown organizations made this transition impossible to accomplish.[121] Reliance continued to be placed on business conducted by an undefined group styled "the Inhabitants of Germantown," which usually meant any of those people who lived within or nearby the township and had a private concern in the matter at hand. Most affairs actually involved a relatively small percentage of the population at large, and when the issue was of a controversial nature, both sides would usually purport to represent the whole of the citizenry.[122] Every petition, every newspaper item, every organizational foundation continued to be attributed to "the Inhabitants of Germantown" even in the face of increasingly legalistic government at both the state and local level by the end of the century. The extralegal nature of this setup was bound to create problems. Charters of incorporation, which became desirable after the Revolution, were sometimes difficult to obtain because it was uncertain with whom the government was officially dealing. The confusion left some strange lega-

---

[121] Lockridge, *A New England Town*, especially chapter 7, where the change in importance of town meeting and selectman is discussed in terms of how an expanding population allowed less opportunity for sharing leadership after 1685.

[122] See, for example, continuing news articles in the *Pa.Gaz.* in the late nineties relating to the turnpike controversy. These are abbreviated in Jenkins, "News," GHS.

cies, which continued to cause problems right into the twentieth century. In 1755 a potter's field was purchased by "the Inhabitants of Germantown," more specifically, probably, by the membership of the Lower Burying Ground, to provide for strangers, Negroes, and mulattoes. Almost two hundred years later this piece of property, long since unused as a cemetery, became attractive as a site for development, but the prospective buyer had a difficult time finding out who was the owner and from whom it could be purchased. By deed it still belonged to "the Inhabitants of Germantown,"[123] a ghostly group whose legal standing, always flimsy, had disappeared entirely in the modern world of association.

[123] Hocker, *Germantown*, p. 79.

CHAPTER 6

...And unto God...:
The Church

It is easy enough to "render unto Caesar the things which are Caesar's and unto God the things which are God's" in a community where there is general agreement on which are whose. In those places where consensus has proven impossible, such as most parts of seventeenth-century Europe, the state may still tacitly invest an established church with the power to make spiritual and moral decisions. Philosophically, this legitimatizing of the government's right to supervise morality is a vital function of a state religion, even when a large part of the population may dissent, openly or covertly, from the specific forms of the church itself. James Harrington, author of *Oceana*, and political theoretician of a Utopian bent, recognized the importance of a national religion even while maintaining the principle of religious freedom.[1]

The American experience made possible various types of "holy experiment" in the relationship of church and state that could never have taken place in European communities where centuries of past tradition and practice laid a heavy hand on the ability to change. It is ironic that in New England, where close identification of church and government was attempted, the final effect was not much different from Pennsylvania, where the experiment took the form of total disestablishment. Perhaps it is true that the "primacy of religion cannot sustain itself against the solvents of cheap land and private opportunity,"[2] but in any case the surface

[1] For a discussion of Harrington's views as expressed in *Oceana* and a comparison of them with William Penn's ideas, see Dunn, *Politics and Conscience*, pp. 81-88, especially pp. 87-88.

[2] Warner, *Private City*, p. 3.

picture in both places was one in which Caesar came to control the things which had been God's.

While the Puritans required complete conformity of belief as well as behavior and aimed at exclusion of all who were not of a like religious and community mind, they could not be said to have created a theocracy.[3] As Lockridge points out, the clergy in the colony were, in fact, prohibited by law from becoming civil officers.[4] It might be more accurate to say, rather, that the town had captured the church and its functions: "No longer did Brown [the minister] call vestry meetings [as he had in England] and sign vestry orders. The town ran its own meetings, granted Brown land and meadow, and elected its own officers independently. No longer did Brown visit each farmer to collect his tithes . . . he was paid a salary from the town treasury, just as the town clerk and the constable were; and the town invoice takers gathered the tax for these salaries. Brown's new church did not even have glebe land; the only perambulation was the one around the town plot. No sexton rang the bell or recorded births and deaths. A town drummer drummed for a meeting and the town clerk was ordered to record all births, deaths, and marriages."[5]

William Penn, on the other hand, in his new colony engaged himself in the practical work of setting up a community on the principle of inclusiveness. The nature of Pennsylvania and of the Quaker philosophy was such that there was no dominant tradition that could be used as the basic moral presupposition behind which the government would operate. Only the most general kind of protestant-Christian ethic would be broad enough to take in the many backgrounds from which the new colonists would come. Penn solved the problem by disestablishing the church entirely in his charter for Pennsylvania. Although he exclud-

[3] See Zuckerman, *Peaceable Kingdoms*, pp. 6ff. and Lockridge, *A New England Town*, pp. 5-6.

[4] Lockridge, *A New England Town*, p. 23.

[5] Powell, *Puritan Village*, p. 137.

ed non-Christians from government and atheists and heathens from political equality, he insisted that none "be molested or prejudiced for their religious persuasion or practice in matters of faith and worship, nor shall they be compelled at any time to frequent or maintain any religious worship, place or ministry whatever."[6] The moral functions of the community were to rest with the government rather than the church and the purely denominational justification for "being good" was to be eliminated. The government assumed the right to legitimate action in the field of morality on the rather rationalist grounds that "moral uniformity is barely requisite to preserve the peace."[7] What was being attempted, therefore, was a new kind of multi-religious community in which not even the last line of defense could be justification by faith.

For this aspect of the so-called "holy experiment," Germantown served as a test case. A certain amount of confusion, a legacy from the European background, plagues a modern understanding of the early setup: the German word, "Gemeinde," translates both as "community" in the civil sense and "congregation" in the religious sense. Thus Pastorius wrote not only of setting up "Gesetz, Ordnung und Statuta des Gemeinde" but also of having built a "Kirchlein für Gemeinde."[8] The preamble to the laws makes it perfectly clear, however, that there was no intention of establishing a state religion in Germantown. Pastorius inserted a copy of Penn's charter for Pennsylvania as well as the charter for Germantown at the beginning of the Gesetz Buch, and included a rephrasing of the right to liberty of conscience in his preamble to the Germantown laws: "all the citizens, inhabitants and under tenants under Germantown jurisdiction . . . [recognize] with thankful hearts the special providence of the Almighty, as well as the gracious kindness

[6] Dunn, *Politics and Conscience*, p. 99.

[7] Ibid., p. 67.

[8] See the Gesetz Buch, and Namaan Keyser, "Old Germantown," *Pa.Ger.*, XV (1904), p. 61.

of our King and Governor, by virtue of which every one
may without the least constraint or oppression, serve God
unrestrainedly according to the best of his knowledge and
conscience, and may worship him more freely than is possible in most other lands at this time."[9]

The laws for Germantown were based on "the firm
foundation of reason and daily experience" as well as on the
Holy Scripture, and the list of those actions considered
secular crimes shows how completely morality was assumed
to be under the overall care of the state: "[Germantowners]
shall keep themselves from all sin and evil . . . such as these:
cursing and swearing by his Holy name, blasphemy against
his divine majesty, unchaste babbling talk . . . the dice, cards,
and other plays, lying, false witness, slander, libelling, in-
surrection, fighting, duelling, murder, incendiarism, reviling,
scolding, especially against parents, magistrates, masters and
women, stealing, robbery, fornication, adultery, blood or
Sodomitical crime, drunkenness, forgery of a manuscript,
or seal, debasement of coin, or false representation of boundary lines."[10]

With the secular government caring for those moral
lapses that were apt to disrupt the life of the townspeople,
with no pressure to conform and no persecution against
which to dissent, with no common bond of tradition or belief to encourage religious activity, it is little wonder that
church organization was slow to develop in Germantown.
Despite the fact that the Crefelders arrived in Germantown
as a group, their reasons for leaving their homes were individual and personal rather than communal or religious,
which meant that there was no ready-made sect or body
with which latecomers could identify.[11] The religious be-

[9] "Laws," *Pa.Ger.*, IX, p. 321; somewhat retranslated by reference
to the Gesetz Buch.

[10] Ibid., p. 321.

[11] For a discussion of the importance of group migration to early
church organization among the Germans, see Schmauk, *Pa.Ger.*, XI,
especially p. 3, pp. 169-170.

liefs of most of the early settlers, whether Quaker, Mennonite, or Pietist, put stress on the inner light, on the necessity of individual solutions to religious problems rather than reliance on group experience and ritual.[12] Those sects, like the Dunkards, that placed great emphasis on communal life, failed to implement this aspect of their tenets in the highly mobile and heterogeneous atmosphere of Germantown.

The Quakers were the first to establish a congregation; they began meeting at the homes of members on a regular basis within a year of their arrival in the New World and had built a log meetinghouse, the *Kirchlein* referred to by Pastorius, by 1686.[13] They were, of course, aided and encouraged by the presence of a colony-wide organization to which they could attach themselves, and by the end of the first year (1684), Germantown Meeting had become an affiliate of the Philadelphia Monthly Meeting. Within a few years, it was part of the Abington Monthly Meeting, under which it operated until the very end of the eighteenth century, only becoming part of the Frankfort Monthly Meeting in 1798.[14] Despite its early foundation and its use as the meeting of attendance by such prominent Pennsylvanians as James Logan and Isaac Norris, the Germantown Meeting

[12] Pietists are best defined by Dubbs, *Pa.Ger.*, XI, p. 20, as those who remained attached to the Lutheran and Reformed churches while seeking reforms (similar to English Puritans) in contrast to the Sectarians who broke away to form separate groups. Dietmar Rothermund, *The Layman's Progress: Religious and Political Experience in Colonial Pennsylvania, 1740-1770*, Philadelphia, 1961, has an interesting discussion of the difference between communal and individual religious experiences and their implications in colonial politics in Pennsylvania. He also comments on the important distinction in the Great Awakening between revivalism as a form of religious experience and as a revolt in matters of denominational organization.

[13] Keyser, *Pa.Ger.*, XV, p. 72.

[14] Most of this information is inferential—the Germans applied to Philadelphia for aid in 1684 (Tolles, *Meeting House*, p. 69), but their Protest Against Slavery was delivered to the Abington Monthly Meeting in 1688 and was forwarded from there to the Philadelphia Yearly Meeting.

never became large or powerful, nor was it particularly influential within the township. The original membership was quickly decimated both by bitter participation in the Keithian controversy during the 1690s and by the early removal of most of the original settlers to larger homesteads out of the area. As early as 1705, when the first stone meetinghouse was built, none of the trustees for the property was from the original Crefeld group, nor, for that matter, did any of them actually live within the boundaries of the German-township.[15] It is also true that throughout all of the eighteenth century most of the active families, with the exception of the Johnsons, the Joneses, and the Deavses, came from the surrounding townships, often being millers or farmers in Roxborough and Bristol townships respectively.

The total membership of the Germantown Meeting was never large, except among the original thirteen Crefelders, twelve of whom were Quakers. Hocker mentions seventeen Germans whose names appear in the Abington Monthly Meeting records between 1683 and 1690, while Lippincott mentions twelve others who were prominent in the first fifty years of the Meeting.[16] During the 1730s subscriptions to the Yearly Meeting from Germantown rose from fifteen in 1731 to a high of twenty-six in 1734, but fell off to twenty-three by the end of the decade.[17] While there are no other lists of members throughout the century, the signatories to wedding certificates (particularly of those marriages that took place at the regular Sunday worship between two members of the local Meeting) give a rough estimate of the size of the congregation. In 1746 when Thomas Nedrow, who later became one of the weighty members of the Meeting, married Ann Luckens, daughter of

[15] Comparison of the list of trustees from Lippincott, *Quakers*, pp. 7-8; 1693 tax list; 1714 List of Property holders; and a map of the area, 1700, photostat, PHC.

[16] Hocker, *Germantown*, p. 27; Lippincott, *Quakers*, p. 9.

[17] Germantown Friends' Meeting, Accounts, 1731-1738, Collections of the Genealogical Society, HSP (unprinted).

a prominent member of the congregation from Bristol Township, there were thirty-nine people present, of whom twenty-two were males. About twenty-five years later, at the wedding of John Johnson, Jr. (descendant of Dirck Janson, one of the early German settlers) and Rachel Livezey (whose father was an important miller in Roxborough), there were sixty-eight persons present, thirty-six of them men and only eleven actually residents of Germantown, although all belonged to the congregation.[18] The local prominence of the families involved makes it likely that most of the members were present. A list of members of the Germantown Meeting, drawn up in 1807 and taking into account the population boom of the nineties, provides the following information: there were a total of seventeen families represented by more than one member and ten single persons, of whom seven were women. Eight of the families had at least one branch living within the township. There were in all eighty-two male members, of whom forty-nine are known to have been adults and seventy-eight females, forty-three of them adult. The Johnson family was the largest, having eight men, nine boys, five women, and five girls. Six of the surnames represented a single nuclear family unit of mother, father, and young children. As a percentage of the town's total population, the size of the Quaker group in Germantown had followed the decline of the sect throughout Pennsylvania at large.[19]

The other two organized sects that appeared in Germantown before 1800 never acquired the importance of the Quakers, either in regard to numbers or to status. Although the Mennonites were meeting for worship in the home of a member before 1690 and were responsible for the second religious structure in the township—a log meetinghouse, planned in 1703, completed in 1708—they never represented

[18] AbMMRec., Marriage Certificates: Thomas Nedrow to Ann Luckens, 3d 10mo 1746; John Johnson, Jr., to Rachel Livezey, 16d 11mo 1770.
[19] Germantown Preparative Meeting, List of Members, 1807, FrDR.

more than 15 percent of the population. By 1770 when their permanent stone meetinghouse was finally built, the congregation numbered only twenty-five souls.[20] A rush of members in the eighties brought the total to fifty-two, although only thirty are known to have taken communion in that year.[21] The Dunkards fared little better. Arriving in America in 1719 in a disunited state (having quarreled on the ship coming over), only a part of the group came to Germantown. The first congregation there was formed in 1722, but throughout the century constant strife and numerous removals kept their number small, and there were but fifty members in forty families by 1770 when their meetinghouse was built.[22] The significance of this sect to the township has been overstated by local historians, perhaps because Christopher Saur was one of the elders.

As the eighteenth century progressed, the Lutheran and the German Reformed churches became the largest and most important of the religious institutions in Germantown. Initially, this was very simply because these groups made up the largest part of the German immigration to Pennsylvania and thus to Germantown. Estimates vary so widely that no figures can be safely presented; for example, the guesses of earlier historians of Reformed Church immigration for one period range from 386 to 15,000 members. A reliable Lutheran historian has explained this by stating: "The fact is that the communicant membership, the baptized membership and the merely hereditary or sympathetic membership are such very different entities that in the lack of figures based on any common understanding, results are almost sure to be unreliable. But it is safe to say that . . . the majority of the German population was affiliated with the

[20] Cassel, *Mennonites*, p. 108.

[21] Ibid., p. 108.

[22] H. R. Holsinger, *History of the Tunkers [sic] and the Brethren Church* . . . , Lathrop, California, 1901, pp. 122-126, p. 140, privately printed, available at the Lutheran Theological Seminary.

two great Protestant Churches of the German Reformation."[23]

The eventual predominance of these groups in the Germantown area was not immediately apparent. For one thing, despite their numbers, a total lack of common background gave many who lived within the same town in America very little basis on which to form a united church beyond the formal designation of "Lutheran" or "Reformed." Each province or territory in Germany had developed its own peculiar forms, based on the Church Order of each ruler. Henry Melchior Mühlenberg, organizer of the Lutheran Synod in America, outlined the problem in his journal: "On the 28th of April [1748] we conferred in Providence regarding a proper liturgy to be established in our congregations here. . . . To adopt the Swedish liturgy was neither expedient, nor necessary, inasmuch as most of the members of congregations in this district are natives of the Rhine and the Main, and they regard the singing of the collects as popish. *Nor could we select the liturgy to which each person had been accustomed from youth, because nearly every land, or town, or village possessed its own.*"[24] Moreover, until the late 1740s, when Mühlenberg had set up the Lutheran Ministerium and Michael Schlatter had arrived from the Classis in Holland to organize the Reformed Church Coetus, there was no real united effort to serve the vast body of German churchmen who had come to the New World.[25] Not being separatist by nature and requiring ordained leadership, they frequently identified themselves with the most congenial of the English churches—Anglican for the Lutherans, Presbyterian for the Reformed—and had thus hastened their own assimilation. Justus Falckner, who, with his brother, Daniel,

[23] Schmauk, *Pa.Ger.*, XI, pp. 228-229.

[24] Henry Melchior Mühlenberg, *Hallesche Nachrichten*, I, pp. 436-437, T. E. Schmauk, trans., *Pa.Ger.*, XI, p. 266. Emphasis supplied.

[25] The best general history of the Reformed Church is the one already mentioned by Dubbs, *Pa.Ger.*, XI.

lived in Germantown for several years around 1700, saw the development of this situation, even at that early date: "The local Protestants . . . are either of the Evangelican Lutheran or the Presbyterian and Calvinist Church. . . . And as the Protestant Church is here also divided into three nations, so there are here an English Protestant Church and a Swedish Protestant Lutheran Church; and also persons of the German nation of the Evangelican Lutheran and Reformed Churches. The Germans, however, I have spoken of not without cause as merely several [persons] and not the . . . Church: those who are destitute of altar and priest forsooth roam about in this desert: a deplorable condition indeed. Moreover, there is here a large number of Germans who . . . have crawled in among the different sects who use the English tongue."[26]

Although there is a tradition that regular church services were held in Germantown for 40 newly arrived families beginning in 1694, it is questionable whether these services conformed to any established ritual. Most of the participants belonged to a strange Pietistic group known as the "Hermits of the Wissahickon" or the "Society of the Woman of the Wilderness," which flourished briefly before 1700 near Germantown, and whose members were eventually absorbed into the Lutheran congregation, of which group they were nominally members all along.[27] More reliable records do not begin until after the first third of the eighteenth century. In 1732 a deed was conveyed to the Reformed Congregation of Germantown for an eighth of an acre on the Market Square on which to build a church, and

[26] Letter from Julius Falckner to Germany, "Concerning the Condition of the Church in America," written c. 1700, Schmauk, *Pa.Ger.*, XI, pp. 128-130.

[27] See Oswald Seidensticker, "The Hermits of the Wissahickon," *PMHB*, 11 (1887), pp. 427-441; also Theodore E. Schmauk, *A History of the Lutheran Church in Pennsylvania, 1638-1820*, Philadelphia, 1903, pp. 83-120.

reference was made to actual construction work in a letter to the Classis of Holland in 1734.[28] The vital statistics and minutes of the Church Consistory begin in 1750 and the accounts a year later. While there are no membership lists available, a letter from the elders of the Church in 1735 put the number of male members at 30,[29] roughly comparable to the number of Quakers at the same period. Communion lists for Easter 1750 show 170 participants, men and women.[30]

The Lutherans were organizing at approximately the same time. Title for their church land was conveyed in April 1738,[31] and even before that time Lieutenant Governor Thomas had issued a permit for the collection of religious funds to liquidate a debt for the land as well as for a church and school building. Forty-seven men are listed as contributors from the congregation, indicating that St. Michael's began with a larger membership than either the Quakers or the Reformed Church.[32] By 1746 there were said to be about 70 families. Complete registration of vital statistics began in 1746, and although there are many gaps, this is the period from which permanent organization may be said to have been in effect. Financial records do not begin until 1766, after the church had been shaken by a ten-year period of schism and dissension. Rebuilding membership was a slow process even after the internal disorder was resolved, but by

[28] Hinke, "Address," in Keyser, Germantown, pp. 381-402.

[29] J. I. Good and William J. Hinke, eds., *Minutes and Letters of the Coetus of the German Reformed Congregations in Pennsylvania, 1747-1792,* Philadelphia, 1903, p. 1.

[30] Ref.Ch.Consis.Rec., p. 4.

[31] A copy of this title is reproduced by Richards, *St. Michael's,* p. 9.

[32] Little Book I, St. Michael's Archives. The 1739 collection from building fund contributors listed here gives the names of the persons who subscribed, along with the amounts, in money or in kind. Fortunately, members are listed separately from contributors like Benjamin Franklin who were not members.

the 1780s approximately 300 people a year were receiving communion at St. Michael's.[33]

While there is no way to get an exact count of church membership, it is possible to determine something about the relative size of the two major denominations. The only nearly overlapping communion lists for Reformed and Lutheran churches are from the early 1750s. In 1750 there were, as already reported, 170 communicants for the Reformed Church; in the following year, the first in which such records were kept for St. Michael's, the total there was 265. There is a more complete comparison available, however, in the children's records. For the decades of the 1770s and 1790s, the confirmation records of both congregations are quite complete. They show a total of 349 Lutheran children confirmed in the seventies to 141 Reformed children, and 203 Lutherans to 104 Reformed during the nineties. The same ratio of about two to one is observed in the baptisms for the second half of the eighteenth century, the period for which the best of such records exist. The fifty-year average for St. Michael's is just over 62 babies baptized per year, while the forty-seven-year average of the Reformed Church, whose baptismal record began in 1753, is just 33. The Lutherans had three peak years, 1756, 1757, and 1799, when over 100 baptisms were recorded, while the Reformed Church had only one year as high as 70, and that was during the early period, in 1754. The large number of baptisms in both groups in the early fifties is probably a reflection of the enthusiasms of the Great Awakening in general, and zeal for newly founded organizations in particular. A steadily widening gap between the two groups is evident since the ratio was only four to three in the fifties, and it was not until the nineties that it rose to better than two to one, on a group of over 1,000 children. By com-

[33] St.M.Rec., communion lists. The number decreases somewhat in the nineties, reflecting the formation of Lutheran churches in neighboring townships, as well as the beginning of more regular English services in Germantown.

parison, it is interesting to note that there are only 25 Quaker children definitely known to have been born within the township during the 1790s.[34]

Of course, the membership of the congregations of the Germantown churches included those from the more rural surrounding townships, as well as residents of Germantown itself. To isolate as far as possible the religious habits of true Germantowners, the surnames of steady attenders appearing in all available church records and membership lists of the five major denominations were checked against the tax lists of 1773, 1780, 1798, and the census of 1790. Given all the shortcomings of this method of analysis (incomplete lists, more than one family per surname, etc.), the profile that emerges is still a significant one.

TABLE 15

CHURCHGOING HABITS OF GERMANTOWN RESIDENTS, 1770-1800

	Known Attenders					Non-Attenders	Total Surnames
	Lutheran	Reformed	Quaker	Other	Total		
No. of Surnames	118	64	29	18	229	177	406

Not only does table 15 bear out the general information concerning relative sizes of the religious groups within Germantown, it also confirms the often stated but rarely proved

[34] The figures are all based on the baptism registers of St.M.Rec. and the Ref.Ch.Rec. The Quaker figure is from those children born between 1790 and 1800 who are listed in the membership book of 1807. This is probably unfair, since it compares a gross number of infants with a list of children who must have survived past infant mortality. Since both St. Michael's and the Reformed Church have a confirmation rate of about 35 percent of baptism, it would be reasonable to multiply the Quaker figure by almost three. This would conform to other facts known about the relative sizes of the various religious groups in Germantown.

thesis that close to half of the American colonial population was unchurched.[35]

Church membership was not a necessary adjunct to status. Several of the most influential families in the township were unchurched, including the Bringhursts and the Ashmeads who lived almost next door to the Reformed Church and just around the corner from the Quaker Meeting. Those who were unaffiliated were often the most anglicized of the local residents. Also frequently missing from the church lists were those who first came to Germantown as summer visitors, then as year-round gentry, and those local English single persons, widows or unmarried men, who remained in the township for only a short period of time. Perhaps this was for lack of an English Church within the limits of the town: while there were occasional Methodist services held at the Union Schoolhouse after 1794, the congregation was not formed until after 1800; there was no Anglican Church until St. Luke's was organized in 1811, and even then it was composed of only twelve families.[36]

There were many problems created by the laissez-faire attitude toward religion and the lack of pressure to conformity, as well as by the mobility of the population in the new colonial community. One of the most obvious effects was a growing lack of interest in the church as a vital center of life. As the study of numbers indicates, the growth of church attendance in no way paralleled the population growth of the township, except in the first burst of organizational development that accompanied the population boom of the 1750s. In fact, the average number of members taking communion at St. Michael's declined from 346 per year between 1770 and 1775 to 210 per year between 1795 and 1800, while the total population during the same period increased 44.2 percent.

[35] See, for example, Richard Hofstadter, William Miller, and Daniel Aaron, *The American Republic*, Englewood Cliffs, N.J., 1959, vol. I, pp. 108-110. It is also curious to note that only 22 percent of the Germantown estate inventories mentioned Bibles.

[36] Keyser, *Pa.Ger.*, XV, pp. 288-290.

While men still ran the church affairs, handling the business matters, the account books, and the lotteries, religion seemed to become much more the province of women, another indication in such a patriarchal society that it was somehow deemed less important. There were frequently many more women than men who took communion,[37] and in total confirmations for both the Lutheran and Reformed churches from 1747 to 1799, girls outnumbered boys by eight to six. Among the Quakers, a Women's Meeting for Business was mentioned as early as 1779, although there are no minutes before 1784. From then on, the women seem to have assumed a larger and larger responsibility for many of the housekeeping duties of the Meeting, granting certificates for removal, examining prospective new members (female or juvenile), and censuring for fornication or marriage outside the Meeting.[38] Even the scanty records of the Dunkards show fifty-five women baptized between 1748 and 1788, while only forty-nine men are listed for the same period.[39]

Another serious problem for the amorphous, mobile, religious community was that of determining membership. Who was entitled to belong to the church, who was entitled to participate in its religious observances, who was to speak for it, and, finally, who was to make its decisions? The sects, Dunkards and Mennonites, had the least trouble with these questions: those adults who had been baptized into the faith and were willing workers were the members of its meeting. Their identification is shown by the greater frequency with which they left money in their wills for others of their order than did members of the regular

[37] See, for example, St.M.Rec., communion lists for 1769, when, in October and December of that year, sixty-nine women and fifty-one men were present at communion.

[38] Women's Minutes of the Germantown Preparative Meeting, 1784-1802, FrDR. (Hereafter cited as Women's Minutes.) The first mention that there is a Meeting for Women occurs in the Men's Minutes, 28d 2mo 1779.

[39] Falkenstein, *Baptists*, p. 139.

churches.[40] The Quakers had no basic ambiguity regarding membership either. Those who came from other places were required to present a certificate of removal for acceptance into the Germantown Meeting. Those who married were expected to choose a fellow Quaker and have the ceremony performed within the Society. The most frequent cause for censure and potential disownment recorded in the minutes of the Germantown Meeting was "marriage by a hireling priest to one outside our Society."[41] Those who had problems, either moral such as drinking or gambling, or strictly legal such as contract disputes, were expected to lay them before the Meeting and abide by the decision there made. It was possible, although not easy, to join the Society after adulthood, but most members of the Germantown Meeting were birthright members—that is, Quakers by virtue of the fact that their parents were Quaker.

It is interesting to note, however, that even with such theoretically clear-cut boundaries, the Quakers occasionally had difficulty in assigning membership. There was, for example, the case of Abraham and Samuel Pastorius, great grandchildren of the founder. Their parents, long dead, had been disowned by the Meeting during the minority of "said Children." Were these sons to be regarded as members or were they not? The Monthly Meeting to whom the problem was passed ruled in favor of acceptance of the two young men, but the practical aspects of the case finally required that it be decided otherwise: "[Abraham] took a loose latitude in his Conversation such as Swearing and behaving rudely, unbecoming a person professing our religious principles, was treated with thereon and admonished by the overseers, but continues as usual, and it being also observed

---

[40] In the 308 registered Germantown wills, there are 9 bequests to St. Michael's, 4 to the Reformed Church and 3 to the Quakers. Despite the small percentage of sectarians in the township, there were also 9 bequests to them.

[41] See, for example, Men's Minutes, 10,11,12^{mo}, 1771; and Women's Minutes, 1794, 1796.

that they both wholly neglect attending our Religious Mgs and rather chuse when they go to any place of worship, to go elsewhere, and has Signified to some ffrds (who were appointed to enquire of them whether they look upon themselves as members amongst us or were desirous to be looked upon as Such by us) that they chuse not to be deemed members."[42]

The regular churches, Lutheran and Reformed, found it most difficult to make distinctions between members and nonmembers. As already mentioned, there was confusion concerning communicant membership, baptized membership, and hereditary membership. People moved about so often that any definition in terms of traditional family participation was impossible. In 1748 the Coetus of the Reformed Church attempted to clarify the situation by ruling, first, that no person was to be recognized as a member of a church who did not contribute annually to its support and, second, that members of one congregation were not to be permitted to receive communion in another without presenting a certificate of removal, a device obviously borrowed from the Quakers.[43] The attempt was made to regularize the membership of the Germantown Reformed Church in 1764, when new rules were passed stating that "those who wish to be considered members of the congregation, shall hand in their names, in order to enter them into this record book, in order that we may know who are members and that they want to contribute to the support of the church and the minister and that they pay every half year the half of their subscription."[44] No list was ever entered, however, and there is no evidence that the rule was ever enforced. The Germantown Church continued pretty generally to regard as members those who thought of themselves as belonging and who attended the church, assigning to it the vital events in their lives of baptism, confirmation, communion, marriage, and

[42] Men's Minutes, 6,7,8mo, 1766; 24d 12mo 1766.
[43] Dubbs, *Pa.Ger.*, XI, p. 175, p. 176.
[44] Ref.Ch.Consis.Rec., January 19, 1764.

burial. The only hint that any kind of old community pattern still operated is in a reference in the Consistory records to the fact that voting for church officers was done by family heads.[45]

A rare listing of members for St. Michael's in 1786 and 1787 shows that the problem of mobility was an acute one at that institution also. Out of a total of 311 names, only 41.5 percent appear on both lists.[46] The conservative faction of the Lutheran Church had made an early attempt to define its membership, when it had held that only those who were in good moral standing according to the elders could be members of the congregation, that no one outside of the membership could be an elder or vestryman, and that only long-standing members of good reputation could aspire to these offices. Most significantly of all, the conservatives showed their real anxiety in the face of an unfamiliar and sometimes frightening world of mobility and heterogeneity. They expressed a desire to create some sense of community in the old, village pattern when they stated in their manifesto: "Newcomers without enough experience have no right to speak. Those who move around a great deal have no real interest in the community, like those who have been here four years or more and have contributed their riches, etc."[47] The opposition group, which was much the larger, set forth the doctrine that everyone who desired should be able to be a member and have the sacraments and that the pastor had no right to withhold them from anyone.[48] Although the conservatives eventually regained control of St.

45 Ibid., May 1, 1775.

46 St.M.Rec., vol. II, "Register of Souls of the Honorable Members of the Evangelical Lutheran Congregation in Germantown," September 4, 1786; September 4, 1787.

47 This is taken from a document in St. Michael's Archives, dated January 1753, which accompanies a list of those leaving the Germantown Church with Pastor Handschuh in order to support Mühlenberg and the Pennsylvania Ministerium.

48 Also in St. Michael's Archives, under the same date, appended to a list of those who refused to follow Mühlenberg.

Michael's, the membership policy continued to be an inclusive one, as shown by the fact that the sacraments were regularly administered to a number of Germantown residents who were publicly part of the Schwenkfelder sect, but who built no church of their own in the area until the 1790s.[49]

In general, there was little dissension and a good bit of cooperation among the various religious groups in eighteenth-century Germantown.[50] Both the Lutheran and Reformed churches had made their facilities available to the Anglican minister, the Reverend Mr. Neill, during the 1760s,[51] and English services were held regularly in the latter for summer visitors during the yellow fever epidemics at the end of the century.[52] When the Reformed Church formed a building fund in 1794, 32.5 percent of the donors were from outside its membership, 25 percent from St. Michael's alone.[53] In an emergency, when the minister of one church was absent, his place might be taken by the representative of the other denomination. The baby of Elias and Catherina Hestler was baptized on "Dominum XVIII post trinitum, in my absence by the Reformed minister," according to the St. Michael's register[54]—a matter-of-fact entry, which would hardly be found in a place where religious

[49] For the history of the Schwenkfelders and specific information on those members who settled in Germantown, see the *Schwenkfelder Genealogy*. For a shorter discussion and summary, see Howard W. Kriebel, "The Schwenkfelders in Pennsylvania," *Narrative and Critical History*, Part XII, *Pa.Ger.*, XIII (1902), pp. 76ff.

[50] This is not unique. Lemon points out that "the denominational attitude, that is, mutual toleration among groups which was so clear in Pennsylvania, had already developed in Europe by the late seventeenth century," *Best Poor Man's Country*, p. 112.

[51] Keyser, *Germantown*, p. 291.

[52] Ref.Ch.Consis.Rec., May 1, 1797.

[53] Ref.Ch.Rec., Accounts, Building Fund, 1794. There were 141 subscribers.

[54] St.M.Rec., Baptism: vol. I, September 3, 1758, born; Dom xviii pt, baptized. In the Lutheran calendar this would be the last Sunday before Advent.

tolerance was less the rule. An occasional baby was even baptized into both churches although this was very rare.[55] The ease with which one could move back and forth from one church to another was frequently used to advantage by those inhabitants within the community who wished to avoid scandal. When, for example, Caspar and Magdalena Spies were married in St. Michael's on January 8, 1771, there is no doubt that the bride was pregnant, for a baby, Maria, was born to the couple less than three months later. The parents avoided the moral issue by having the baby baptized in the Reformed Church, so that there was no record of just how soon after marriage she was born.[56] Still, one who practiced complete religious impartiality, such as Ulrich Hagerman who left a sum in his will "to the use of the poor without minding any religion," was apt to be considered "eccentric."[57]

Religious quarrels, when they did take place in Germantown, were usually between factions of the same church or sect. The Quakers fell apart over the Keithian controversy as early as 1692, when the two OpdenGraff brothers, Dirck and Abraham, took opposing sides in the issue, one signing the paper of a "pretended" Meeting to the Philadelphia Yearly Meeting, the other becoming one of the signatories

[55] For example, Anna Sorber, daughter of Henrich and Catherina: born, June 1, 1800; Baptized, July 8, 1801 in both St. Michael's (vol. III) and the Reformed Church. The other children of this couple had all been baptized in the Reformed Church, as was the father; the mother had been raised in St. Michael's.

[56] St.M.Rec., Marriage: vol. II, January 8, 1771. Ref.Ch.Rec., Baptisms: May 19, 1771. The records of many other families show similar evasions. Another common method of evasion was to refrain from baptizing an early baby until the next child in the family was born. At that time, the older child was also brought to church, probably on the theory that the minister and congregation were less likely to remember the date of the marriage. When marriage and baptism certificates are compared, there is a high correlation of early baby to late baptism.

[57] Ulrich Hagerman, WB K, #155, p. 242, January 2, 1755. Also see *Pa.Berichte*, January 16, 1755.

on a petition to the Yearly Meeting in London, asking for settlement of the matter.[58] It is very likely that continuing unpleasantness in the Meeting hastened the removal of many of the early settlers from the township; five of the six who signed the testimony in favor of Keith were gone before 1714. At the time of the Revolution there was another split in the Meeting over the question of military service and the war in general. The Streepers family, part of the original Crefelder group, was disowned for allowing its sons to be "engaged in training and exercising in the military way."[59] The Meeting refused to allow itself to be disturbed by outside events at all, being the only one of the Germantown churches whose records were not disrupted during the time of the occupation and the only group to find that none of its members was in want after the difficult winter of 1780.[60]

Intragroup wrangling among the Germantown Dunkards received a great deal more publicity than it was worth, because of the public quarrel between Christopher Saur and Conrad Beissel, head of the Cloister at Ephrata.[61] Nevertheless, the effect on a small group cannot be overrated, when over twenty of its members marched publicly out of Germantown and off to Ephrata in 1739. The Moravians, who withdrew from the Reformed Church in the late 1740s, headed by the former lay pastor, John Bechtel, removed to Bethlehem, causing a similar flurry in that congregation,

[58] "Minutes of the Philadelphia Monthly Meeting," *Publications of the Genealogical Society*, IV, #2, p. 165. Pennypacker, *Pa.Ger.*, IX, p. 186.

[59] Men's Meeting, 21d 2mo 1776.

[60] Ibid., in answer to a query from the Yearly Meeting, May 24, 1780.

[61] For a full account of this, see Samuel Pennypacker, "The Quarrel Between Christopher Saur, The Germantown Printer and Conrad Beissel, Founder and *Vorsteher* of the Cloister at Ephrata," *PMHB*, 12 (1888). Also, George Falkenstein, "The German Baptist Brethren or Dunkers," *Narrative and Critical History*, Part VIII, *Pa.Ger.*, X (1899), pp. 69ff.

though the proportion of the split, and therefore its importance, was far smaller. It did lead to new regulations regarding the elders, newly elected members, and the duties of the Consistory, which were passed in 1750. These were put into effect in the following year when one of the deacons and one of the elders resigned over a split in policy within the Consistory. The records of the fifties in this church are filled with uneasy reports of resignations and removals: "At this occasion [January 10, 1755] an attempt was made to reunite the members who had left the congregation for some time, but as they would not accept the admonition, which I addressed to the congregation from Isaiah, Chap. 55, they continued in their separation. May the Lord open their eyes and bring them on their right way, where they find rest for their souls."[62]

A period of quiet and good will was broken by the Revolution, which evidently had a particularly disastrous effect on the Reformed Church. No records at all were kept from 1776 until 1790, when the congregation received a new minister and was put on a more regular institutional footing, both financially and organizationally. The minister who tried to preside over the hectic years did leave a summary of events that is worth quoting at length, as a first hand account of how enormously the national situation was capable of affecting the local one: "The congregation secured indeed another minister, but there was lacking the necessary unity and mutual love on both sides. . . . To this was added the unrest and sad consequences of the war, in that the British took possession of Philadelphia and neighboring districts, by which the church fell into complete decay. From the account presented in 1776 before my departure, it appears that the balance in the treasury at that time was £115.4.4, all of which was reduced to nothing in the following way . . . because there was no unanimity in the congregation and many members, because of the distur-

[62] See Ref.Ch.Consis.Rec., for the 1750s in general, especially January 14, 1754, January 10, 1755.

bances of the war, moved to other places, no salary could be collected for the preacher. He, however, had to live and what else could the elders of the congregation do but take from time to time from the surplus and pay the minister. . . . In addition it must be noted, that at first this small capital consisted of silver and gold pieces as well as good paper money, and whatever else was paid in was in Continental paper money, and it would have been lost any way . . . the financial condition was very bad for a number of years."[63]

The Lutherans also suffered from the war as reflected in the interruption of their services and register during the period of British occupation in the fall and winter of 1777-78, in the destruction of their church organ and decay of their facility, and in the wildly fluctuating state of their finances caused by unsuccessful attempts to cope with the general inflation.[64] The congregation as a religious body was not shaken, however. St. Michael's had already weathered its divisive upheaval long before, from 1756 to 1765. The trouble had begun, as it had in the Quaker, Dunkard, and Reformed congregations, as a local reaction to a more general situation, in this case increasing pressure to organize an American church with close connections to Halle, but with its own governing body or ministerium. Dissension arose among those who refused to follow Mühlenberg in this effort. Somewhat affected by sectarianism, they desired to choose their own ministers without any sort of ordination requirements at all. At first there were only 20 members of the Germantown church who remained in the traditional mold as represented by Mühlenberg. They were forced to withdraw from the church property and lost control of the register as well to the 135 radical members. As a brief sum-

[63] Ibid., deposition by the Reverend Mr. Helffenstein, between the entries for May 1, 1776 and the call to the new pastor, October 27, 1790.

[64] Church Book B, Treasurer's Accounts and Some Minutes from A.D. 1766, St. Michael's Archives. Also includes lists of elected elders and rules for the reunification of the church after the schism.

mary of the types involved in each group, it might be noted
that of those who can be traced, all but one of the conservatives were over forty years old, while among the larger
number of radicals, all but one were *under* forty, and one
was in his twenties. Moreover, the Mühlenberg faction had
only one in twenty who was illiterate, while 13 percent of
the larger group signed with a mark, and another 8 percent
wrote so badly as to make their names illegible. Finally,
there were 5 women in the more liberal group, none in the
traditional.[65] The men who ministered to the rump were
considered unordained by the Ministerium, and as Mühlenberg and his organization gained strength throughout Pennsylvania in general, the Germantown separatists, even though
they had possession of the church building, proved unable
to hold on to their membership. By 1762 100 Lutheran
families of Germantown and its vicinity petitioned the
Ministerium for a pastor and regular services, and when an
election was held between this new candidate and the pre-
siding radical minister, the latter did not receive a single
vote.[66] The final years of the schism were not without vio-
lence, however, as both groups began to look on the church
property as their own, and the largest number of court
actions related to a single issue in Germantown appears in
the Quarter Sessions Records in relation to the Lutheran
split.[67]

[65] Lists of members leaving St. Michael's or staying there, January
1753, St. Michael's Archives. Ages were determined by checking
burial records where possible. Further evidence appears available in
the fact that there were no babies recorded among the conservatives
even after the split was healed and they had rejoined the congregation, while the other group continued to produce children well into
the seventies and occasionally in the eighties.

[66] The most succinct account of this period is found in Ziegenfuss,
St. Michael's, pp. 18-21. An earlier description is in Richards, *St.
Michael's*, vol. II, pp. 35-40.

[67] See, for example, QS Rec., from January 1762 to December 1764,
when the Reverend Mr. Rapp of the radical faction evidently left
town.

Unlike any of the other religions whose splits may be traced through the changing allegiances of ex-members in other town records, the Lutheran church managed to heal its division so successfully that the registers continue to record marriages and babies in a smooth, reintegrated line, and very few of the parishioners (except for those who had the traditional wandering feet of the Germantowner) left St. Michael's. This must have been due, in no small measure, to the way in which reunification was achieved, revealed in a brief set of minutes from July 28, 1766.[68] It was signed by twelve men, two from the Mühlenberg faction, one who had been a member of the radical group, and ten others who either had taken no active part in the controversy or who had joined the church since that time. All were from families prominent in the community. The new church rules that were established show that these men had learned a great deal about getting along and running an organization under conditions of quite considerable freedom. First of all, a quorum was to consist of two-thirds of the Consistory members and the pastor; topics to be discussed were to be submitted before the meeting, in writing, if possible. Each member, in order from the oldest to the youngest, was to be given a chance to speak to the subject, with a fine for anyone who tried to interrupt another. At the end of debate, there was to be a vote, recorded in writing by the secretary, with majority rule in effect; however, all disagreement would be noted as to person and cause so that there would be no future misunderstanding among the members. Finally, "so as no member shall have the feeling of being restricted in their [*sic*] freedom of speech there will be a time set to talk to his brother. This will be before the Vestry board sits down and opens the meeting, and thereafter." The document is, all in all, an interesting mixture of Quaker attention to the importance of integrating everyone's point of view, the habitual use in the New World

[68] Church Book B, St. Michael's Archives.

of majority decision, and the traditional concept of the
village elder, shown in the directive to yield the floor in
order of age. Permanent sectarian influence can be seen
also in a rule that was added three years later: "Every three
months, fourteen days before communion, a day of repen-
tance and prayer shall be set aside, which will be announced
beforehand at the Church service. After the service the
members of the vestry will stand and speak up to any evil
or hostile feelings concerning a neighbor, or anyone else he
does not think worthy of the Last Supper. But beware of
false accusations or charges, so that you will not accumulate
new sins but may worship God in good conscience."[69]

Except during the periods of dispute within the various
churches, people tended to remain quite faithful to their
denominations. While there are almost no Quaker or sectarian families that do not have at least one branch extending into the two main churches by the end of the century,
very few names appear in all five records. One exception is
the Engle family, but this was an unusually extended family
with far more branches than most other Germantown kinship groups.[70] On the other hand, there are only a few really
large families, like the Johnsons (Quakers) or the Bockiuses
(Reformed) who remained faithful in all branches for the
entire period to the religion of their earliest Germantown
kin. In a study made of 300 families—150 nuclear, 150 extended—who appeared in the registers of St. Michael's and
the Reformed Church, this thesis on loyalty was borne out.
Among the nuclear families, 83 percent remained completely
within one or another of the congregations for all vital
events, while only 17 percent either switched or entered
one or more events in the other church. Of these, most were
single burials, and the probable reason involved the necessity of immediate action—burial never followed death by

[69] Ibid., August 3, 1769.
[70] There are more "Millers" or "Müllers" and "Keysers," but both
of these names represent several unrelated families rather than a
single stem.

more than two days—and the absence of the families' regular pastor.[71] Among the extended families there was a good bit more variation. Even here, however, a healthy minority, slightly more than 43 percent, remained, with all collateral branches, within a single institution.

If they remained. In addition to the totally unchurched, who accounted for almost half of Germantown's population, many families gradually fell away from formal religious practice in the course of time. Even when the whole family did not leave the church, many branches of it might be lost in successive generations. As in the case of acculturation, the community appearance did not reflect this condition on the surface, although declining church membership in times of rising population is a vital clue. Growing indifference among the second and third generations was masked by the continual arrival of first-generation settlers who quickly joined the church as a way to integrate themselves into the new neighborhood. Yet, it often appears from the church records that a family has moved out of the township because it no longer has its babies baptized or its weddings performed, when a check of the tax or census records shows that it is still in residence but has fallen away from regular religious practice.

The Germantown churches, in fact, seem to have played a very small role in the overall life of the community, even after they were organized and running in a fairly smooth and continuous way. By and large they had little influence on neighborhood development throughout the township. Unlike Germany, where the parishioners clustered around the village church and turned out at the sound of the bells,

---

[71] For example, the Dannenhower family was fully registered in St. Michael's for over fifty years, with the exception of the burial of widow Maria Elizabetta, who is found in the Reformed Church burial register, January 14, 1799. As her husband was buried five years earlier by the pastor of St. Michael's (St.M.Rec., Burial: vol. III, February 4, 1795), it is unlikely that anything but an emergency would have caused such a change. The family, therefore, really belongs in the faithful affiliation category.

in Germantown the church bells were heard more frequently by members of another congregation. Careful study of
the residence patterns of Germantown citizens matched with
their church affiliation shows an almost completely random
result. Those who attended St. Michael's were as apt to live
in Lower Germantown as up near Cresheim, while several
residents of Chestnut Hill were loyal members of the Reformed Church in Market Square. While this latter church
had a slight tendency to attract those who were transient
in Germantown, this was largely because its central location
in the most built-up part of town was closest to the places
where temporary inhabitants were apt to stop. The sects
and the Quakers also drew their members from quite considerable distances, often entirely outside the boundaries of
the township. Nor did the frequent availability of property
nearby attract members to resettle closer to their churches.
Thus, even over time the pattern remained scattered.[72]

The ministers of the traditional churches and the preachers or weightiest members of the sects almost never became
the most influential voices within the community. Some of
the leading Quaker families were among the most prominent
residents of the area, but, as most members of the Germantown Meeting lived outside the township proper, it was
much more difficult for them to become too involved in
affairs. The leaders of the other religious groups were all
far too impermanent. Before the middle of the century, no
regular minister was charged solely with a Germantown
congregation of his own denomination. The sectarian
preachers were characteristically wanderers, like Jacob
Gaetschalck who was commuting regularly between Skippack and Germantown as early as 1714. Alexander Mack,
who arrived with the Dunkards in 1729 and settled his
family in Germantown, set up and preached to six other
widely scattered churches (including one in New Jersey),
leaving him very little time to be a force in his home com-

[72] Based on a comparison of the location of families in the Deeds
in Brief and the records of the various churches and meetings.

munity. The Reformed Church was set up in conjunction
with the church in Philadelphia, and for many years the
same minister tended both. The Lutherans included Germantown on a traveling circuit, which took in not only
Philadelphia but places as far away as Trappe and New
Hanover. There is no evidence that the pastor of St. Michael's actually settled his family in Germantown until
Frederick David Schaeffer arrived in 1790.[73]

There were other problems faced by disestablished ministers in a new and heterogeneous community. As is evident
from the minutes of both churches, the method of raising
money for the minister's salary continually caused acrimo-
nious debate. Depending on the background of the immigrants involved, some churchgoers were used to a system
where a definite tithe was made and others to one where
each gave according to his own impulses. In established
churches it was possible to pay the minister out of the town
treasury as was done, for example, in Sudbury, Massachusetts.[74] This was, of course, impossible in multi-religious
Germantown. This issue became one of the most bitterly
disputed points in the schism at St. Michael's, one which
kept the pastorate at the Reformed Church empty for many
years.[75] The pastor, poor and mendicant much of the time,
was patronized rather than respected by his parishioners,
who tended to regard him as an object of charity rather
than authority. Only one, the Reverend Mr. Helffenstein,
rated a newspaper obituary when he died, and this may

[73] Cassel, *Mennonites*, p. 105; Falkenstein, *Pa.Ger.*, X, p. 63; Dubbs,
Pa.Ger., XI, p. 153; Ziegenfuss, *St. Michael's*.

[74] Powell, *Puritan Village*, p. 137.

[75] The question of the minister's salary is mentioned in the documents of both factions in 1753 (St. Michael's Archives). Minutes after
1765 continually contain suggestions for augmenting his salary. For
similar problems in the Reformed Church, see Ref.Ch.Consis.Rec.,
for example for January 7, 1760 and February 10, 1767, as well as the
Call to the Rev. Frederick Hermann by the Congregation, October
27, 1790. Also note the subscription raised in 1796 for paying the
salary of the minister.

have been because his wife was a member of a well-known Philadelphia family.[76] Being the pastor of a single church in a town that possessed at least five active religious societies also tended to dilute a minister's authority to speak on civic matters, since he would face a good deal of competition and have no special status or ready-made podium. Finally, since both of the regular churches, which offered the most influential situations in town by virtue of the size of their memberships, imported their ministers from Europe until near the end of the century, they were manned by pastors who were immigrants, who had, in a sense, less ability to understand affairs in the New World and how to handle them than the unlettered, second-generation son of a farmer or craftsman.

Since community leadership did not come from the church, the tendency to secularization was intensified. The place for town gathering was not the church as in New England towns, but the tavern as in the large, heterogeneous cities.[77] Later in the century the Union Schoolhouse became the focal point of many community activities, largely because it was standing empty and its trustees were men of considerable pull who wanted the building to be taken over by the public to solve their own financial problems. The custom of performing marriages in the home began early in Germantown; occasionally the ceremony was performed by a secular clerk with a state license, rather than by a minister.[78] Even more significantly, the first and most popular burial grounds in the town were public and nonsectarian. One, in fact, was begun in 1724 for the stated purpose of providing burial in a regular graveyard for those members

[76] *Germantown Zeitung*, May 17, 1790. His marriage had been in both the *Pa.Gaz.*, February 17, 1773, and the *Pennsylvania Chronicle*, February 15-22, 1773.

[77] Compare Lockridge, *A New England Town*, chapter 2, with announcements of Germantown meetings in the local newspapers.

[78] For example, St.M.Rec., vol. I, April 1751.

of the community who were not eligible for the Quaker or Mennonite cemeteries (the only available facilities at the time).[79] Although St. Michael's and the Reformed Church both established their own "God's acre" later in the century, the Dunkards never bothered until a drastic shortage of burial space developed during the boom of yellow fever refugees at the very end of the nineties. Even after each church had a burial ground, convenience superseded religious sentiment, and the public cemeteries continued to be widely used. It was, after all, easier for a Lutheran family who lived in Lower Germantown to bury its dead in the Lower Burying Ground than it was to transport the body all the way up the Main Street to Bettelhausen, the area where St. Michael's was located. By the same token, members of the Reformed Church who lived in Cresheim or north tended to make use of the Upper Ground, since it was closer than the churchyard.

More and more concessions were made to the everyday world by the organized religions. Both churches were forced to recognize fairly early that Caesar's work came before God's. Even Sunday communion took second place to the needs of property protection. Thus the Lutheran Ministerium had passed the following resolution in 1751: "In the future, Holy Communion shall be held before the tenth of April and the tenth of September, on account of naturalization, yet, if possible, always on Sunday."[80] In Germantown the Consistory of the Reformed Church laid down in its rules that it should not be called to meet on a market day "without the most urgent reasons."[81] There was even a most unusual reference in the Reformed Church accounts to taxes

---

[79] "Records of the Upper Burying Ground," *PMHB*, 8, p. 415.

[80] *Documentary History of the Evangelical Lutheran Ministerium of Pennsylvania and Adjacent States: Proceedings of the Annual Conventions from 1748 to 1821*, Philadelphia, 1898, "Transactions and Resolutions of the United Preachers," May 13, 1751, p. 34. (Hereafter cited as *Lutheran Ministerium*.)

[81] Ref.Ch.Consis.Rec., January 10, 1771.

paid by the church as an institution to the county for roads and the poor.[82]

Although the state reserved for itself the right to regulate morality according to some generalized nonsectarian formula, the churches still saw it as their responsibility to pass judgment in this area. St. Michael's entered in the register any moral infraction occurring within the parish, although no attempt was made to adjudicate differences. It would appear that the only sanction imposed for bad behavior was refusal of a proper burial: "Jacob Losch, the fornicator, was buried at the back of the churchyard, after he and his unhappy bastard came to their end."[83] The Reformed Church passed a resolution at the very first meeting of the Consistory that elders were to have oversight of the married people and their families in their districts, and if anything offensive occurred, were if possible to correct it. If not, it should be brought to the attention of the minister or the Consistory.[84] Thenceforth, however, there were no records of any actions taken under the resolution.

The Quakers went much further in their attempts to regulate the morality of members of their Society. Although the only punishment available to them was disownment from the Meeting, they worked hard at making members see the error of their ways. Committees from the Meeting, men or women, depending on the sex of the culprit, regularly visited wrongdoers and reasoned with them to make them repent. Moral delinquency most frequently involved fornication, drinking, gambling, swearing, or attending the Playhouse in Philadelphia. There was one case of clearly criminal import that was handled by the Meeting, although euphemisms were employed to describe the situation: "One of the Oversere's Informed this Mee[g] that their was found In the

[82] Reformed Church Account Book, Presbyterian Historical Society, October 24, 1791; the amount was £1/11/9.

[83] St.M.Rec., Vol. II, November 24, 1792 (burials). The translation is approximate; the language is very vague.

[84] Ref.Ch.Consis.Rec., July 6, 1750.

Possession of Jacob Dilworth a horse that was Suspected to be Clandestienly Taken out of his Neighbour's Stable which he Refused to Deliver up to the Owner till he was Compeld to it: which with divers other Circumstances Appearing, gives Room to Suspect he Either took the Horse or was Confederate with them that Did [*sic*]."[85] The failure of institutionalized religion to carve out a meaningful niche for itself in the new secular world, even in the area of morality, is shown by its powerlessness to affect the lives of its members through its judgments. Horse thievery and bastardy, in the last analysis had to be dealt with by the courts, and it was here that real control of the community lay.

Finally, it is interesting to observe that in this new kind of secular society, where the church had lost its position as moral arbiter, it had also loosened its control in two fields of social service—charity and education. Concerning the care of the poor, the exceptions were once again the Quakers, and, to a lesser extent, the Dunkards. Generally speaking, the Quaker Meeting appropriated about £3 per half year as its contribution to the needy. As this was funneled through the Monthly Meeting in Abington, it was not really a community enterprise, except in the significant sense that Quakers looked upon their true community as a religious, rather than a neighborhood affair.[86] The schooling of poor children was handled in the same manner, and the only time that the Germantown community itself appears to have become the focus of Quaker charity was during the Revolution, the mention of which was, however, studiously avoided: "It appears Necessary under the present circumstances of the Times to appoint some Members of this Meeting to inspect into the Necessities of poor ffriends within the compass thereof and to acquaint ffriends thereof seasonably, in order that Such who stand in need of relief may be ad-

[85] Men's Minutes, 26ᵈ 11ᵐᵒ 1790. Although the hand in which the Quaker records are kept is well educated, the spelling exceeds all bounds, even for eighteenth-century license.
[86] Germantown Friends' Meeting Accounts, 1739-1800, FrDR.

ministered to as speedily as may be."[87] The Dunkards also attempted to provide support for their own poor, and in 1747 they set up two donation boxes, a required one for the support of the church, the other for voluntary gifts to a special poor fund to be administered by one of the deacons. When a new church was built in 1770, the old meetinghouse became a kind of home for the aged of the congregation, where they were sheltered, clothed, and fed by the other members of the sect.[88]

The largest of the religious institutions, St. Michael's Lutheran and the Reformed churches, were the least involved in charity work. There are no specific accounts in St. Michael's record for aid to the poor before 1792, although it is extremely likely that the minister helped individual parishioners where necessary from the small balance maintained by the church.[89] The collections of the Reformed Church, which began to be recorded in 1752, are termed "alms" although they were spent for all church necessities.[90] In the original resolutions of the church elders, it was obvious that some of this money was intended for the poor, since it was written: "Alms shall be counted every three months and whoever is in need may then apply."[91] When the rector of the Philadelphia Episcopal Church gave a series of three sermons at the Reformed Church in Germantown in September 1797, asking for relief for the poor victims of yellow fever in the city, not only did several hundred individuals respond, but four business firms gave as institutions. None of the Germantown churches laid out

[87] Men's Minutes, 25^d 5mo 1779.

[88] Unfortunately, the Poor Book of the Brethren of Germantown seems to have disappeared. This information comes from excerpts in Martin Brumbaugh, *A History of the German Baptist Brethren in Europe and America*, Elgin, Ill., 1899, pp. 170ff.

[89] Church Book B, St. Michael's Archives.

[90] Ref.Ch.Consis.Rec., Treasurer's Accounts, January 11, 1752 and following. As with all the records of the Reformed Church, these were not kept between 1776 and 1790.

[91] Ref.Ch.Consis.Rec., July 6, 1750.

funds, nor, as far as can be told from the minutes, did they even consider doing so.[92]

As in the case of care for the poor, the religious organizations of Germantown took very little responsibility for the education of the young, except for training in the catechism by the two churches that practiced confirmation and accepted the sacrament of communion. Neither the Quakers nor the Dunkards appears to have run any schools attached to their Meetings during the eighteenth century, although it is probable that the school run by Anthony Benezet as a private endeavor between 1739 and 1742 was Quaker oriented. Tradition relates that a school was begun in the Mennonite Church building in 1708, and that it was in this institution that Christopher Dock worked after he arrived in Pennsylvania in 1714. Within four years, however, he is known to have been teaching in Skippack on a regular basis and only occasionally during the summer in Germantown. In 1741 he devoted three days a week to Skippack and three to Germantown, a strenuous schedule in view of the distance and the condition of the roads.[93]

The Reformed Church records reveal no expenses for either a schoolmaster or a schoolhouse, nor for any supplies. In the Consistory records of 1750, it is stated that the schoolmaster is to be paid two pounds per year for leading the singing, but the accounts regularly report payment to a "songleader" rather than to a teacher.[94] The closest approach to a church school in the vicinity of central Germantown was the Moravian School which was operated by John Bechtel, the lay pastor of the Reformed Church, from his own house in the 1740s. When the Moravians and their leader removed to Bethlehem, the school went with them.

[92] *Claypoole's Advertiser*, September 19, 1797; *Pa.Gaz.*, September 26, 1797. Results appeared in the *Pa.Gaz.*, November 1, 1797.

[93] The most complete work on Dock, including translations of his pamphlets is Gerald C. Studer's *Christopher Dock: Colonial Schoolmaster: The Biography and Writings of Christopher Dock*, Scottdale, Pa., 1967.

[94] Ref.Ch.Consis.Rec., Treasurer's Accounts.

St. Michael's Lutheran Church was the only Germantown religious organization that made continued efforts toward the education of its young parishioners over the course of the century. As early as 1748, Mühlenberg wrote in his *Hallesche Nachrichten*: "In Germantown [there are] now two [Church affiliated] schoolmasters. The one is Mr. Döling, a theological student, who formerly was among the Moravians, but left them several years ago. He keeps school in the heart of Germantown and has many children, but not all are evangelical. At the end of Germantown, there has been a school for almost three years. Near Germantown, there has also been a school of some twenty children. But it is now broken up, because of the lack of support and a schoolmaster."[95] In 1753 a lottery was held to raise money for a house and lot to use as a school and home for the Lutheran pastor,[96] but the first expenses in the account book do not appear until 1770; and they relate only to the salary of the master, not to the upkeep of a building. Accounts of St. Michael's for January 1771 show that the school was finally built with regular church donations and a matching fund from Lutheran friends in Germany. Expenses for the school appear again in 1773, 1774, and 1777, then not again until 1785, and after that not until 1797. It is probable that the school operated only fitfully during this time: the annual report to the Ministerium in Philadelphia for 1795 mentioned that "In Mr. Schäfer's congregations, the school at Germantown is at present vacant; but that at Barren Hill [part of Roxborough township] is in operation."[97] In 1797 a schoolmaster was hired again, and in the last year of the century contributions were once more being taken for the erection of a new school.[98]

In general, the adaptation of nonsectarian morality to a

---

[95] *Lutheran Ministerium*, p. 10.

[96] See *Pa.Gaz.*, August 30, 1753; *Pa.Berichte*, August 16, 1754; and other news items in both papers during 1753 and 1754.

[97] *Lutheran Ministerium*, p. 279.

[98] Church Book B, Treasurer's Reports, St. Michael's Archives.

multi-denominational world applied to education as much as it did to government. The preamble to the laws of the General Court in the original Germantown charter had set up a standard of right and wrong that was considered basic and acceptable to all "good people," regardless of religious persuasion, a necessity in the kind of colony that was developing in Pennsylvania. The application of this principle to the teaching of the young is clearly illustrated in whatever information remains concerning the schools of Germantown. While there can be no doubt that the material used to teach young children to read was heavily moralistic in tone and Protestant-Christian in outlook, the advertisements and prospectuses of the various Germantown schools rarely alluded to religious training. Even the news article for the lottery for St. Michael's school stresses how important it was for the community that the next generation be literate, while playing down any hint of sectarian advantage for the Lutherans: "We hope a design of this kind will meet with encouragement, as the only motive that induced the society to enter on such a scheme, was their being thoroughly sensible of the disadvantages they labor under, and the great necessity there is of a house in Germantown for their minister to instruct those children in reading and writing, whose parents are unable to give them such education; and as the society amongst themselves are unable to accomplish such an undertaking, were importuned to have recourse to a lottery, in order to enable them to carry on the same, as it will tend to the publick good."[99]

There were members of every one of the five established Germantown churches involved in the founding of the Union School in 1761. The Lutherans had the smallest representation, with no members among the planners in 1759 and 1760, and only one trustee when the institution actually opened. Connections were perhaps most closely maintained with the Reformed Church whose early ministers were always on the board and whose minister in the 1790s was one

[99] *Pa.Gaz.*, August 30, 1753.

of the two principal teachers. He did not teach religion, however, although he paid due attention to "morals and health." The subjects offered to "young gentlemen" were Latin, Greek, Hebrew, German, French, Spanish, and Italian; English grammar, geography, and mathematics; "improvement of the young gentlemen in every branch of useful and ornamental literature."[100] This was quite an ambitious program compared to the first intentions of the school, which were to teach reading and spelling for thirty shillings per year while writing and arithmetic could be added for an extra ten shillings.[101]

Nowhere, however, was the teaching of religion mentioned. This holds true in the plans of the simplest schools in the earlier part of the century, like the one run by a German schoolmaster in 1754 which offered reading and reckoning, summer, winter, and in the evenings,[102] or in those of the more elaborate academies of the nineties, like that of an ex-French master at the Union School, who hoped to offer in his own establishment Latin, German, Italian, French, English, penmanship, drawing, music, and mathematics.[103] The location of the Germantown schools was held to be guardian enough of the boys' moral development: "the Place, without Exaggeration, may be justly termed the Montpelier of Pennsylvania. The Opportunities and Examples of Vice and Immorality, which ever prevail in large Cities here will seldom present themselves, to decay the youthful mind from its natural Inclination of Virtue. Its Retirement, for want of Objects to divert the attention, will fix the mind to application and Study."[104]

The question of which school a child attended was determined far more by neighborhood than by religion: the

[100] *Pa.Gaz.*, November 1, 1794 and November 12, 1794.
[101] Minutes of the Union School, December 16, 1761.
[102] Hocker, *Germantown*, p. 80, from an advertisement in *Pa.-Berichte.*
[103] *Courrier Français*, October 12, 1796; May 25, 1796.
[104] *Pa.Gaz.*, March 5, 1761.

neighborhood school as an American institution might be said to have made its first appearance in eighteenth-century Germantown. The Union School, which was intended to fill a community need, specifically stated its nonsectarian admission policies in its charter. Even in the church-run school of the Lutherans, some of the pupils were not from the congregation.[105] The public school, which ran sporadically in Chestnut Hill from 1745 on, was called the Harmony School, according to tradition because it was intended for children who lived nearby, even if they came from across the township line.[106] The last of the community-run schools, the Concord School, was established on a corner of the Upper Burying Ground in 1775 because the Union School was deemed too far to walk in winter for the children who lived in Upper Germantown. It was a much less ambitious undertaking; the building was small, lessons were offered only in English (which is interesting in relation to the progress of assimilation), subscriptions were fewer and smaller.[107] It was conceived as an addition to the educational possibilities of the community rather than as a competitor of the Union School. Fourteen trustees of the latter contributed substantial sums to the building of the former, and two of its building managers served in the same capacity for the younger institution. If the active membership of the Concord School had more of a Dunkard cast (17 percent can be identified as Dunkards), it is probably because so many of them lived in the neighborhood; the same applies to the fact that the more centrally located Union School had a higher proportion of upper-class local citizens involved in its running. The summer gentry appears to have contributed gifts to whichever school was located in its neighborhood. The Neglees who lived just below Lower Germantown are found in the records of the Union School, while Blair McClanichan who bought the Chew mansion after the Revolu-

[105] *Lutheran Ministerium*, p. 10.
[106] Keyser, *Germantown*, p. 86.
[107] Record Book of the Concord School, Microfilm, HSP.

tion is on the list of donors to the Concord School.[108] As in the case of the cemeteries, the pragmatic problem of location created a utilitarian solution unrelated to religious conviction or practice.

By the end of the eighteenth century, Germantown's religious institutions were operating pretty much in the manner of organizations within an associational society; the earlier chaos and dissension had shown that communal tradition was not sufficient to a multi-faceted colonial town which lacked a basis for consensus. At the same time, it can now be seen from the vantage point of historical distance, that, where the impulses of both establishment and persecution are missing, the strength of the religious association tends to be weakened. The thirteenth convention of the Lutheran Ministerium, held in 1760, recognized the potential dangers that the heterogeneous, open society posed for the church: "since our church members dwell among all kinds of parties and unfriendly sects, polemics must also be treated, yet without mentioning names. . . . As many parties dwell together, intermarry and have relations of business and life one with another, a dangerous indifferentism is easily occasioned; therefore it is necessary at times to point out the differences, as otherwise the suspicion of indifference may also fall upon the preacher."[109] The dilemma of maintaining religious conviction where each church has an equal share of "the truth" and of maintaining power where each religion must compete in the open market for public support was seriously raised, perhaps for the first time, in colonial America, and was never really solved within the development of the new community framework.

[108] This information is compiled from the records of both the Concord School and the Union School.
[109] *Lutheran Ministerium*, p. 54.

PART III

PRIVATE LIVES

AT THE foundation of any sociological study of a community, past or present, lie the most tantalizing questions of all: how do its people conduct their private lives—what general factors can be extracted from their personal biographies, from their family structures and processes? Historians generally have undertaken investigation into these basic areas from a relatively superficial point of view: the social historian has examined the manners, mores, and appurtenances of daily life; the biographer has presented, in more or less intimate detail, narratives of the famous and infamous. Until recently, understanding and analysis of the workings of personal relationships among typical members of society were ignored, not only because of lack of interest on the part of the scholar, but also because these events seemed to be so completely unrecorded that retrieving them was held to be almost impossible.

Yet, in trying to plot the social curve of history to match the economic and political diagrams that have been developed, it may be far more important to know how many children were produced by the typical colonist and his wife than to know the number and sex of Benjamin Franklin's offspring. In fact, the latter fact, as social history, may be significant only insofar as it actually tends to bear out the ideas, for example, that extreme fertility was not necessarily the rule in the eighteenth century, that most families had at least one child who died young, and that illegitimacy was neither uncommon nor universally concealed. Obviously, it is absurd to try to generalize about the typical life in colonial Pennsylvania from the experiences of Franklin. On the other hand, it is almost impossible to deal with colonial family life from the papers of more commonplace people, since the more typical a person was, in this sense, the less likely he was to leave any private records behind.

Ironically, the best sources available to the historian for the study of the intimate factors of the life cycle of the individual and the family come from the most impersonal of documents, the public records. Census lists and other collections of vital statistics compiled by the government are rarely available to the historical demographer as they are to the student of contemporary population trends, but other sources may be exploited to provide unexpected insights into the facts of life of past populations. The most important of these have been, for European communities, the records of the established churches which registered the baptisms, marriages, and burials of a town.[1] Two main methods of using these materials to build a demographic model have been employed: family reconstitution, in which the whole community is charted in terms of the vital facts concerning specific families who lived there; and aggregative analysis, for those cases where there was too much mobility or nonconformity for the records to be all-inclusive in a specific way, but where general facts could be abstracted without reference to the individual.[2]

For New England communities, as Greven shows so beautifully in his work on Andover, family reconstitution may be richly rewarding, since the church was established, and the town kept vital statistics.[3] For most of the rest of colonial America, sadly enough, high mobility, disestablishment, and the general disorder of frontier conditions make

[1] For a discussion of the development of historical demography, see D. V. Glass, "Introduction," pp. 1-19, and Louis Chevalier, "Toward A History of Population," pp. 70-78, both in *Population in History*. See also, Hollingsworth, chapter 2, *Historical Demography*, pp. 37-61.

[2] Description of the two methods are found in chapters 3 and 4 of *EHD*, "Exploitation of Anglican Parish Registers by Aggregative Analysis," Eversley, pp. 44-95; "Family Reconstitution," Wrigley, pp. 96-159.

[3] See Introduction, supra.

the registers spotty and unreliable; great gaps make the results of their use at best what Laslett describes as "a matter of approximation . . . an exercise of the historical imagination."[4] Still, any results are better than none, and even where the church membership is so small that it is impossible to make any statement about the simplest rates of birth and death, there is much of value to be recovered from careful analysis of the church registers: "It is often possible to estimate some of the more complex demographic rates to a fair degree of accuracy without knowing the actual size of the population itself especially well."[5] General characteristics, such as age at marriage, life expectancy, birth intervals, and the like, are all possible to establish, at least tentatively.

In addition to the church registers, the work of the genealogist often has been relied upon to provide basic demographic information on such topics as the size of families and the amount of widowhood and remarriage. There is, however, a grave danger of distortion in placing too much emphasis on this material. Genealogies are usually made for families whose descendants have survived to a point distant enough in time to inspire investigation into their pasts. But what about families that were not successful—that failed to provide sufficient male members to ensure continuation of the line and that died out within a couple of generations? It is perfectly possible and, in fact, highly probable that most families of the past may have been unsuccessful in terms of survival. May it not also be possible that the generally accepted picture of the colonial family—a large unit created by the marriage of a man to a succession of wives, each of whom died in childbirth after producing several offspring, with enough of these surviving to make up a household of half-brothers and half-sisters—is a fallacy based on the genealogies of successful families? Would not the use of these same genealogies create a selective bias in favor of early marriage and special longevity of the male, as well as of large

[4] Laslett, "The Numerical Study of English Society," *EHD*, p. 4.
[5] Hollingsworth, *Demography*, p. 303, p. 37.

245

families and maternal loss?[6] For some topics, the spacing of births within a family, for example, the genealogy may be a useful tool, particularly as a check on other sources. It should never be used, however, to generalize about the overall shape of the colonial families within an entire community. The records of churches whose membership formed a cross section of the community in terms of wealth, occupation, and class (not those groups like the Quakers who were apt to be especially homogeneous) make a better statistical sample, even where seriously incomplete, than the most finished genealogy, which deals with an atypically successful family.

When the study of the population is widened from the strictly demographic to the more general sociological concepts of family process, the use of genealogies as well as many other sorts of source material becomes more valuable. The whole gamut of materials—tax lists, wills, inventories, deeds, newspaper items, contributor lists, and the like—is required to help provide tentative answers to such questions about family structure as patterns of kinship, inheritance, training, and control. These and other aspects of family life and the position of the family as an institution may not be amenable to strict statistical analysis, but study of them offers fruitful possibilities for understanding the social structure of the past.

Sociologists have long postulated, for example, a close relationship between communal societies and extended families, whether kinship groups scattered throughout the community or multi-generational, consanguine families living under a single roof.[7] The corollary to this idea is that asso-

[6] The question of the selective bias of genealogies is mentioned, though not explained in J. Hajnal, "European Marriage Patterns in Perspective," *Population in History*, p. 112, p. 115.

[7] The basic sociological concepts for defining the family are found in a great variety of textbooks. Those that seemed most pertinent to these purposes were the older *Sociological Analysis*, Part V, section 17, pp. 588-620; and the more recent Clifford Kirkpatrick, *The Family as Process and Institution*, 2nd ed., New York, 1963. There is also an

ciational societies will tend to require increasing emphasis on nuclear families and a weakening of the functions that the family as an institution is prepared to fulfill. Family structure and operation in eighteenth-century Germantown should be pertinent to this point.

It is also vital to the understanding of the colonial experience to consider the ways in which mobility and heterogeneity may be related to the development of the family as an institution. The family should be particularly vulnerable to those conditions that tend to restructure the traditional workings of other institutions, since, unlike government or religion, the family is not generally in a position to solidify its position by exchanging associational relationships for the more intensely personal ties of communalism. The family is, in fact, dependent on the support of the other institutions in the community. Where these become either weak, as in the case of religion, or expansive, as in the case of government, the strength of the family pattern tends to break down. The results of this are stated by Kirkpatrick in general sociological terms: "As a consequence [of the weakening and expanding of other institutions] there tends to be increased variability of familial behavior. This has a weakening effect, since an institution implies a pattern of expectations in regard to the behavior of others. The culture controlling family life tends to be the common culture of the family group, rather than the common culture of the community. Families therefore differ increasingly one from another with this restriction of a common culture to the familial group. . . . Variability engenders variability. Once

---

interesting chapter on "The Natural History of the Family" by Ralph Linton in *The Family: Its Function and Destiny*, Ruth Nanda Anshen, ed., Science of Culture Series, 5, New York, 1949, pp. 18-38. The idea of an extended family with close relationships, but not living under one roof, is developed by Greven in *Four Generations* and is an interesting one. Its lack of relevance to the Germantown situation would seem to point up the possibility of significant differences between New England and other parts of the colonies.

the great institutional uniformities crumble, the consequent variability in family behavior makes further variation inconspicuous and respectable."[8] The study of Germantown, may, therefore, illuminate, not the beginning of a new framework on which an "American Way" was built, but rather the idea that the American way consisted of having no framework at all.

[8] Kirkpatrick, *The Family*, pp. 142-143.

CHAPTER 7

From Cradle to Grave:
Demographic Notes

THIS chapter is a speculative exercise. The warning is especially necessary, as things that are put in mathematical form have a tendency to acquire a veracity and accuracy that is frequently undeserved. Yet, even speculation about the demographic facts of a society can be valuable in describing the human condition, if approached with proper respect for the pitfalls of overconfidence. Reflections on this topic, after all, are not the sole possession of the scientific era or the computer generation. One of the earliest arrivals in Germantown, Daniel Falckner, included several demographic questions about the Indians in his *Curieuse Nachricht*. These involved what might be called the fertility and life expectancy of the native population and attempted to explain changes in these factors as a result of European settlement.[1] In the middle of the eighteenth century, two European visitors to Pennsylvania, Peter Kalm and Gottlieb Mittelberger, described what they observed to be some of the demographic changes among the Europeans who had settled in the New World. Kalm, the more scientific of the two, is worth quoting and remembering on several points, not because he was always accurate, but because it is interesting

[1] *Falckner's Curieuse Nachricht*, p. 135, #40, for example, states that the Indians became subjected to disease and death as well as to a loss of fertility by virtue of adoption of a European diet. In answer to the question, "To what age do the Savages attain?" (p. 163, #56), Falckner presented no graphs, charts, or tables, but answered confidently, "There are but few of them known to us who are sixty to seventy years old. Formerly they lived to the age of a hundred." This again he attributed to the arrival and customs of the settlers.

to compare the first-hand observations of a contemporary with the reconstructed data of the historian.[2]

On family size: "It does not seem difficult to find out the reasons why the people multiply faster here than in Europe. As soon as a person is old enough, he may marry in these provinces without any fear of poverty. There is such an amount of good land yet uncultivated that a newly married man can, without difficulty, get a spot of ground where he may comfortably subsist with his wife and children."[3] This not only postulates the demographic hypothesis of earlier marriage as a cause of larger families, but also pinpoints the role of mobility as a contributing factor. On the other hand, Kalm noticed another, contrary, phenomenon: "The women cease bearing children sooner than in Europe. They seldom or never have children after they are forty or forty-five years old, and some leave off in their thirties. I inquired into the causes of this but none could give me a good answer. Some said it was owing to the affluence in which the people live here. . . . Some ascribed it to the inconstancy and changeableness of the weather."[4] This is interesting because of what it implies about the age at last birth among European women as well as what it says of Americans (borne out by the Germantown statistics). The theory that people who are better off tend to have smaller families is also suggested by Kalm.

On physical changes: Kalm ascribed most of the variations in this area, both favorable and unfavorable, to changes in diet. He found that children appeared to be much brighter and mature more quickly (although they also grew old sooner) than did their European cousins. As did Mittelberger, he felt that meat with every meal, butter and cheese on every piece of bread, and good, sweet water were the

[2] The comments in *Mittelberger's Journey* are almost always similar to Kalm's, and, in fact, in many places appear to be copied from him. Some may be found, for example, on pp. 107-108.

[3] *Kalm's Travels*, p. 211.

[4] Ibid., p. 56.

main factors.[5] Most interesting, perhaps, was the observation that Americans appeared to lose their teeth far earlier than in the Old World; women, especially, often had lost most of theirs by the time they were twenty. While Kalm suspected the tea they drank, today's observer would be more likely, perhaps, to suspect the sugar in it.

On disease and death: "the unanimous accounts of old people concerning the times of their childhood [state that] the inhabitants of these parts were at that time not subject to so many diseases as they are at present and people were seldom sick. All the old Swedes likewise agreed that their countrymen who first came to North America attained to a great age; and their children nearly to the same; but that their grandchildren and great grandchildren did not reach the age of their ancestors, and were not nearly so vigorous or healthy . . . it is almost an unheard-of thing that a person born in this country lives to be eighty or ninety years of age. . . . Those who are born in Europe attain a greater age than those who are born of European parents."[6] While the accuracy of such a comparison between life-span in Europe and the colonies is certainly open to question, it does have an interesting relationship to the life-expectancy figures that Greven found between the second and fourth generations of Andover residents. Peter Kalm's travels in the 1750s coincided with the maturity of Greven's fourth generation, which was the shortest lived of any group since the seventeenth-century immigration had taken place.[7] Kalm's conclusions seem to have a certain amount of validity when comparisons are made between successive generations of Americans rather than between contemporary Americans and Europeans.

Unfortunately, the extreme mobility of the Germantown population makes the generational approach advocated by Greven virtually impossible. In addition, the multi-religious

[5] Ibid., p. 56, and *Mittelberger's Journey*, pp. 65ff.
[6] *Kalm's Travels*, pp. 56, 194.
[7] Greven, *Four Generations*, pp. 193-194.

nature of the community provides church records that the Cambridge Group for the History of Population and Social Structure, which sets the standards for this kind of research, would undoubtedly find unsatisfactory.[8] Some of the problems include: the late establishment of the church records, so that only a span of fifty years can be studied for the eighteenth century; the entire lack of records for three of the five churches; a membership group in the churches that was regional and overlapped the actual Germantown community rather than being congruent with it; and last, but not least, probable persistent underregistration due to the fact that the largest of the churches initiated a fee—one shilling for baptismal entry, five shillings for adult burial, and two shillings six pence for child burial—around the mid-sixties.[9]

Despite these drawbacks, the thousands of births, marriages, and deaths recorded by families in the Germantown area during the last half of the eighteenth century present a challenge and an opportunity which cannot be evaded. The sample they provide does offer a fairly good cross section of the local population; rural and urban folk, comfortable and poor, various nationalities, different generations in regard to immigration. In addition, they meet some of the tests for probability used by statisticians in the field, for example, that of the ratio of male to female births.[10] By using a combination of aggregate statistics and a study of family groups wherever possible, many of the inadequacies can be overcome. When overall numbers are wanted, such as totals for age at marriage, age at death, and the like, the sheer size of the registers helps to reduce the amount of random error, while the general nature of the Germantown

[8] For the standards considered adequate by this group, see *EHD*, chapter 2, pp. 20-29; chapter 3, especially pp. 45-54.

[9] St.M.Rec., Minutes, vol. II, October 17, 1765.

[10] There were 2,603 boys baptized in Germantown compared to 2,367 girls for the same period, just over the generally accepted figures of 105-100.

material mitigates the chance of sampling bias.[11] Cross-checks are available through the tax lists, the census of 1790, the wills, and the genealogies to help the researcher decide whether a large gap in a family birth record is caused by a failure to register all the children or a period of infertility, miscarriage, or stillbirth. Various entries in the register may also provide material pertinent to unexpected factors. Thus the burial slip of a father may explain why a family is completed after only two or three children, and the records of confirmation may be evidence that a family is still present in the neighborhood although it no longer appears in the baptism register. Age at marriage, in fact, was never listed and can only be figured by reference to the burial or confirmation slips which do give age, or to a combination of the individual's own baptism slip and that of his first child, where the marriage slip itself is missing.

The marriage registers for Germantown are, in general, the least useful and most incomplete of all the demographic material. For one thing, a great number of the events listed do not refer to inhabitants of the community, nor even of the general region. Both St. Michael's and the Reformed Church appear to have been popular places for Philadelphia couples to marry in, either because they were near vacation homes or because a quick and quiet ceremony was required. Many of the names listed are those of the descendants of families that left the area in past decades but who returned to marry as a sentimental gesture. The standard information entered in the register was scanty; ages were not required, nor the name of the father, nor the occupation of the groom. Even residence is only given from time to time, and, most frustrating of all, marital status was frequently assumed to mean "at the time of the marriage" so that, of course, many widowers or widows were listed as "frei und laidig." It is usually only from other sources that the widow-

[11] For a discussion of these dual problems and sampling ideas in general, see Theodore Anderson and Morris Zelditch, Jr., *A Basic Course in Statistics*, 2nd ed., New York, 1968, Part III.

hood of a specific individual can be determined. Still, much of a demographic nature can be inferred about German-town marriages from the use of these 1,529 marriage slips, when combined with the other records.

One major way in which the marriage patterns of Ger-mantown appear to have differed from those in Europe was in respect to nuptuality: that is, the number of women, or men, who remained single throughout life.[12] For western Europe in the eighteenth century, this figure was found to be at least as high as 10 percent for women and up to 20 percent for males. Using the tax list of 1773 as a guide, it would seem at first as if these percentages would be borne out, for 19 percent of the taxables were single men. How-ever, following individuals through the century presents quite another picture. One year later (on the tax list of 1774), thirteen of those ninety-four single men had married, and thirty had moved out of the township, leaving fifty-one still single. By the tax list of 1780, another twenty-two, mostly younger sons, had gone, and fifteen more had married so that only nine of the original ninety-four were still single and living in the township. Four of these had married (three producing children), and another three had moved or died by the 1790 census. There were, then, within seventeen years, only two men who remained bachelors and stayed in the Germantown area. If the fifty-two who left and whose eventual status is unknown are put aside, it still leaves 95 percent of the known sample as having married, even if they left Germantown afterwards. As a matter of fact, only 3 percent of the households in 1790 are composed of a single man living alone. While this does not take into account young men still living at home or old men living with grown children, it probably does provide a rough index to those who never married at all.

The case for virtually universal nuptuality among women is much harder to make out and is almost entirely inferential.

[12] The information on Europe is found in Hajnal, "Marriage Pat-terns," *Population in History*, pp. 101-143.

It is based on the observation that each female who was buried was listed by next-of-kin or as a widow, if this was the case. In a file of 541 female burial slips, there are only 40 which do not list a woman as either a wife or a widow. This represents the maximum possible of never married within the sample since, while a woman who was married might not be listed as such, it is unlikely that one who was single would be given a fictitious husband. Careful examination of the individuals involved shows that several of the unassigned were widows whose husbands had died many years before, lowering the percentage still further. This impression is heightened by the fact that each church during the period specifically entered one woman as "a single person," indicating that this was a rare occurrence.[13] While there are several single daughters in their early twenties buried by their fathers, there are only 4 women over twenty-five so listed; 2 are twenty-seven, 1 is twenty-nine, and 1 is thirty. In only one case throughout the century was a single woman identified other than by her father: the single sister (she was entered by no name of her own) of Andreas Holtz (alias Wood) was buried on September 7, 1781, aged sixty.[14]

When it comes to the question of age at marriage, one is dealing with "one of the most sensitive registers of alterations in traditional patterns of familial and social behavior."[15] While the European pattern from 1740 to 1940 is regarded as one in which the mean age for women at marriage is generally above 24 and for men is about two years higher, both Greven and Lockridge have found a somewhat different story in New England. Men and women in colonial Dedham had an average age at marriage of 25 and 23 respectively, while Andover began its career with a strikingly

[13] St.M.Rec., Burial: Judith Eck, 72 years, 4 months, May 12, 1794; Ref.Ch.Rec., Burial: Catherina Eisenminger, 57 years, August 28, 1779.
[14] St.M.Rec., vol. II.
[15] Philip J. Greven, Jr., "Historical Demography and Colonial America: A Review Article," *WMQ*, 24 (1967), p. 447.

low age of 19 for women, rising slowly to around 21 in the early eighteenth century, and then abruptly to 24.5 in the third generation.[16] The Germantown picture appears to be a mixture of the Old and New World patterns and indicates how quickly a sociological institution like marriage may be affected by immediate conditions.

During the 1750s, while the town was receiving a heavy concentration of new immigrants, many of them recently from the Old World, the age at marriage tended to follow the European pattern rather closely, with a mean age for women of 25.0; for men, of 29.8. The relative stabilizing of the population, with families who were less mobile and a slower rate of growth (although the increase was still continual) during the sixties, seventies, and eighties, is reflected in the drop of the mean age of marriage for that thirty-year period to 22.2 for women and 25.8 for men. By the 1790s, it was possible for long-time residents to think of Germantown as becoming rather crowded, and there was a heavy influx of new inhabitants. In response to the changing conditions, the average age of marriage rose again to 25.5 for women and 27.1 for men. Although every effort was made to weed out remarriages so that the above figures would reflect age at first marriage, it was not always possible to do this. When there was no independent evidence that a person had previously been married, such as the existence of older children, he or she was assumed to be marrying for the first time, even when seemingly too old. There was enough indication that people occasionally did marry at a very late stage in life, so that it would have been slanting the data to cut these people out of the calculations. For this reason, however, the standard deviations are quite high, and it is useful to study the medians as well as the averages, so that some idea can be attained of the age by which at least half

---

[16] See the indexes of Lockridge, *A New England Town* and Greven, *Four Generations* for the sections that deal with age at marriage. See also Kenneth A. Lockridge, "The Population of Dedham, Massachusetts, 1636-1736," *EHR*, 20, (1966), pp. 318-344.

of the people in the sample were actually married. The results are summarized in table 16. The wide divergence from norms for females in the 1760s is an indication that too few cases could be determined to allow the application of statistical techniques.

TABLE 16

YEAR OF AGE AT MARRIAGE,
GERMANTOWN, 1750-1799

	Females				
	1750-1759	1760-1769	1770-1779	1780-1789	1790-1799
Mean age at marriage	25.0	22.5	22.2	22.0	25.5
Standard deviation	6.7	9.9	4.5	3.5	5.9
Median age at marriage	24.2	18.7	22.2	23.4	24.5
	Males				
	1750-1759	1760-1769	1770-1779	1780-1789	1790-1799
Mean age at marriage	29.8	27.2	24.7	25.5	27.1
Standard deviation	6.4	7.7	5.5	5.0	5.2
Median age at marriage	28.5	25.0	24.0	25.5	26.7

Almost one hundred years later, in 1890, the median age for men at marriage had changed very little, being 26.1, although that for females had already begun to show the drop that would take place in the twentieth century, registering 22.0 in 1890.[17] The rather consistently lower median age for marriage in eighteenth-century Germantown as

[17] Kirkpatrick, *The Family*, p. 139.

compared with mean age indicates that more people tended to marry before average age, but the few who waited remained single for quite a while.

In studying the actual cases in which age at marriage is known, certain other facts emerge. Throughout the entire period younger marriages tended to occur between the children of stable, well-established families, although the new family unit did not necessarily remain in Germantown. It may be that since land was not necessary for setting up a household in this craft- and industry-oriented society, there was not the same need to defer marriage until one had control of the family portion. A girl who waited too long, however, was likely to have to settle for a somewhat less appropriate match; Catherina Durr, of an old and comfortable Germantown family, reached the age of thirty without having found a husband and was finally married off to an immigrant laborer in 1797.[18] Family habit seems to have played some part in the age at which one married. For example, both of George Reiter's sons were married before they were twenty-five; Jacob Sorber's boys all waited until their thirties.[19]

In many cases, age at marriage was closely tied to another important demographic question. The degree of premarital intercourse that exists within a community is not easy to measure but has great influence on family structure in general. In eighteenth-century Germantown, those marriages where the ages of the partners deviated in some peculiar way from the general norms were almost always associated with premarital conception. Sometimes both partners were either far older than usual, or far younger—a groom who was nineteen with a bride of sixteen, for example. Another

[18] St.M.Rec., Marriage: vol. III, August 29, 1797. Tax records of the Durr family are available from 1773.

[19] St.M.Rec., The Reiter family, Baptism: vol. II, September 18, 1770; Marriage: February 26, 1792; Baptism: May 4, 1775; Marriage: vol. III, September 4, 1795. Ref.Ch.Rec., The Sorber family, Baptism: October 14, 1756; Marriage: April 3, 1791; Baptism: September 16, 1759; Marriage: September 11, 1792.

common kind of deviation was the one in which the bride was older than the groom, anywhere from one to six years. Premarital conception is one area in which the customs of the Old World seem to have carried over into the New. Rates were evidently much higher for Germany than they were for England,[20] and those for Germantown were considerably higher than they appear to have been in the earlier years of the New England towns; it is possible that an increased rate in this category is a general trend of the later eighteenth century.[21]

Close to 25 percent of first babies born to Germantown couples were born less than nine months after marriage for every decade from 1740 to 1800, with the exception of the seventies. This discrepancy may well be due to the fact that for the last three years of that decade the records are largely missing because of British occupation and the subsequent disorganization of the churches. It is doubly unfortunate, since this wartime situation is just the kind in which the greatest number of irregularities might be expected to occur. Oddly enough, the number of children born seven to eight months after marriage declined as a function of early births throughout the century while the number of four- to six-month children increased; in the 1790s, for example, the latter group accounted for four out of every five of the 25 percent of early births. A possible explanation for this might relate to greater prematurity rather than illegitimacy in the earlier years because of general conditions of health.

The high incidence of premarital conception in Germantown may also have been related to the attitude of the Lutheran Church toward betrothal as having true nuptial significance. One historian has maintained that late into the eighteenth century among Germans "the engaged lovers were held to be legally husband and wife [and] it was common for them to begin living together immediately after the

[20] Eversley, "Population," *Population in History*, pp. 51-52.
[21] See Greven, *Four Generations*, pp. 112-113, and Demos, "Families in Colonial Bristol," *WMQ* (1968), p. 56.

betrothal ceremony."[22] This may or may not have been true, but there are enough instances of parents who attempted to obscure the fact that their child was conceived premaritally to make it questionable. Although in general the church registers are plainly written, the cases among the marriage certificates of erasure, of crossing out, or of date changing almost always occur in connection with a marriage whose first child was born less than eight months after the dates of other marriages on that page. For example, in the records of St. Michael's Lutheran Church of Philadelphia, there is an entry for a couple named "Cress" of Germantown whose marriage is listed as having taken place in November 1749 but whose entry appears in the register between other marriages that all took place in November 1750. At the same time, St. Michael's of Germantown shows an incomplete baptism entry for the same couple in November-December 1750. Both entries were heavily crossed out and written over.[23] Other evasions included never baptizing the first child at all and having his first enrollment in the church take place at confirmation, allowing the first child to go unbaptized until the second was born and baptizing them both together, so that the relation between the birth date of the older child and the marriage date was no longer obvious, failing to hand in the birth date of the child being baptized during a period when full entries were the rule in the register and the baptism date itself was less than ten months after the wedding, and baptizing the oldest child in one church although all of the family's previous and subsequent vital events were registered in the other.

Actually, there must have been a good deal of toleration

22 George Howard, *A History of Matrimonial Institutions*, Chicago, 1904, vol. I, pp. 284-285.

23 This is not the same church as the Germantown one, although it was established at about the same time and was served for many years in the eighteenth century by the same pastor. St. Michael's of Philadelphia, Marriage Register: November 2, 1749, #88; St.M.Rec., Bapitsm: vol. I, November-December 1750.

for premarital conception.[24] After the 1750s, it was never mentioned as a cause of marriage by the minister's notes in the church records, although it appeared frequently before that time. Within a ten-year period, from 1784 to 1794, the Quakers disciplined six couples for the offense of fornication, a large number considering the size of the Meeting, but none was expelled and several are later found among the "weighty" members.[25] True illegitimacy was rare; out of over 5,000 baptismal certificates, only 44 (less than 1 percent) were issued to single mothers. In these cases the fathers were nearly always named. It might be supposed that far fewer illegitimate children would reach the church and that therefore the sample would be biased, but search of the court records only turns up seven Germantown bastardy suits in the course of the century. Social disapproval seems to have been reserved for those who ignored the conventional methods of handling these matters—one man who not only recognized a mistress and a bastard child while his wife was still living, but who wrote his will so that the legal wife held his property only in trust for life and then it descended to the bastard and mistress; and another who was careless enough to be declared the father of an illegitimate child by one woman in 1756 and then forced to marry another woman for fornication two and a half years later.[26]

Still, the majority of Germantown couples raised their families within the boundaries of a traditional marriage, producing their first child between twelve and fifteen

---

[24] This may have been more or less general in Pennsylvania. See *Mittelberger's Journey*, p. 93, "If a man gets a woman with child and he marries her, either before or after her confinement, he has expiated his guilt and is not punished by the authorities. But if he will not marry the woman . . . he must give her a sum of money. But there is no penalty on fornication."

[25] Women's Minutes, FrDR.

[26] Jacob Losh: Ref.Ch.Rec., Baptism: October 18, 1788; Burial: July 2, 1792; St.M.Rec., Burials: vol. II, November 24, 1792; WB W, #194, p. 314, December 1, 1792. For David Weidman, see St.M.Rec., Baptism: vol. I, November 6, 1756; Marriage: vol. I, July 27, 1759.

months after the wedding. The interval between marriage and birth of the first child has remained more or less constant from colonial times to the recent past, although the size of the completed family has, of course, varied widely.[27] Contraception has undoubtedly played a major role in changing patterns of family size, but for societies in which the topic was not discussed, this role is difficult to determine. Some demographers have postulated that in earlier centuries when the interval between the next-to-last and last child was a great deal longer than the intervals between the other births within a family, there was some form of birth control being practiced, while random intervals of twenty-three to twenty-six months between children with only a slight increase in spacing as the mother grew older, indicate a birth pattern based on natural rather than artificial factors.[28] In communities such as Andover, Massachusetts or Germantown, where the latter pattern held true, and where women tended to bear children throughout the entire course of their fertile years, the age at which they married made a predictable difference to family size. Greven found, for example, that when the average age at marriage rose by two years, the number of children in the family dropped by exactly one.[29] Yet age at marriage was still important in determining the eventual size of a family as late as the second half of the nineteenth century when contraception was quite generally used.[30]

The real difference in family size was determined by the

[27] Eversley, "Population," *Population in History*, p. 47, for earlier times; Kirkpatrick, *The Family*, p. 139, for figures from 1890 to 1950. The data for Germantown show that 58 percent of couples who had live children produced the first within a year of marriage, 72 percent within eighteen months, and 80 percent within two years.

[28] Hollingsworth, *Historical Demography*, p. 22, and Eversley, "Population," *Population in History*, especially section VIII, "Fertility in Marriage," pp. 46-52.

[29] Greven, *Four Generations*, p. 200.

[30] J. P. Monahan, *The Pattern of Age at Marriage in the United States*, Philadelphia, 1951, pp. 73-75.

age at which the last child was produced, and the changes in the course of the last two centuries are clearest here. Kalm had noted that women stopped having children earlier in the colonies than in Europe, but modern evidence, although scanty, would seem to dispute this. In areas of France and Belgium in the seventeenth and eighteenth centuries, women were found to have produced their last children when they were between 38 and 41 years old.[31] The Germantown figures are almost exactly the same: the average age of women at birth of their last child was 40.2. Just as significantly, the average age of the father at the time of the last birth in the family was 44.3. It is interesting to go beyond these averages into a more complete breakdown of the data: 10 percent of women had their last child when under 35 and only 0.7 percent were over 45, the youngest being 27 and the oldest 53; 50 percent were between the ages of 40 and 45. The truth of the thesis that conception continued as long as possible is illustrated by the ages of fathers at the birth of their last child. More of the men than the women who stopped having children before 35 are known to have died near the time of the last child. While 22 percent became fathers for the last time while still in their 30s, 41.4 percent were over 45, and almost half of these were over 50, three being in their 60s and one actually in his 70s. Since man frequently had second families by marrying younger women when their wives, who had passed the child-bearing age, died, the true limits of reproductive ability seem indicated. The significant difference in this respect between colonial times and more recent history is shown by the ages at birth of last child of 36.0 and 31.9 for men and women, respectively, in 1890, and 28.8 and 26.1 in 1950.[32] The longer years of childbearing in the earlier period not only had implications for the size of the family unit, but also for problems created by having children of such varying ages within

[31] P. Deprez, "The Demographic Development of Flanders in the Eighteenth Century," *Population in History*, p. 616.
[32] Kirkpatrick, *The Family*, p. 139.

a single family that their education, their relationship to their parents, and their inheritance were bound to vary significantly.

While the fertility rate for Germantown cannot be determined in births per thousand population, it is possible to sketch some rough ideas of gross fertility for the sample populations represented by the two principal churches.[33] If

TABLE 17

GROSS FERTILITY FOR GERMANTOWN CHURCHES, 1750-1799

	1750-59	1760-69	1770-79	1780-89	1790-99	Total
No. of marriages	416	299	272	235	225	1,447
No. of baptisms	1,031	817	863	741	1,103	4,555
Fertility rate	2.5	2.7	3.17	3.15	4.9	3.14

one works only with the 955 identifiable families who appear in the Germantown records from 1740 on, or the 890 who appear between 1750 and 1799, the rate is found to be 4.1, but this is still far lower than any estimates made of New England fertility and much more closely approximates the picture in Europe.[34] The rise in the rate, particularly the

[33] Although it would be satisfying to use the refinement of comparing births with marriages from half a decade earlier, as described by J. D. Chambers in "The Course of Population Change," *Population in History*, p. 333, the problems of the Germantown registers make it safer to use the same periods in order to minimize the effects of occasional sloppy record keeping.

[34] See the contrast between general American statistics and the European facts in Greven, *Four Generations*, p. 31 fn., where he not only states his own findings but those of other American historians who note fertility rates as high as 8 children per marriage, and contrasts them with findings as low as 2.45 and 2.61 in the English village of Clayworth. The figures presented by Louis Henry in "The Population of France in the Eighteenth Century," *Population in History*, p. 441, table 3, work out to between 4.2 and 4.6 for the period 1690-1763.

great jump in the nineties, may well be associated with the sales of small lots during that period and the consequent appearance of many young married couples.

In general, mobility plays an important part in the distortion of demographic data for any urban community. If a family does not remain in one location long enough to complete its span, the figures are apt to be distorted in the direction of smaller units. This is particularly true when the population figures are based on a single moment in time, such as a census list in a community where an unusual number of the people are young married couples (or old people). In Philadelphia, for example, Warner found an average of only 1.3 persons per household in the Middle Ward in 1774, although he noted that there were some families with five to seven children;[35] the likelihood is not that Philadelphians had exceptionally small families, but rather that those present at the time represented an unbalanced age group. Futhermore, since the children in a family were often as much as twenty years apart from the oldest to the youngest and the custom in craft centers favored the early departure of a child from his father's home, a large family might still be reduced to very few people actually living together.

For this reason the birth registers, despite their many defects, are a far better source of material on family size than the census lists. Most of the work that follows was done on the 890 families that could be identified as having registered their vital events, particularly the baptisms of their children, with reasonable faithfulness. In many cases, accuracy could be checked against wills or genealogies in family Bibles or unprinted manuscripts. When these families moved to Germantown after already having produced children, they occasionally had them rebaptized, although these earlier children are most apt to be found by reference to the confirmation slips.[36] Even more important for demographic accuracy,

[35] Warner, *Private City*, p. 17.
[36] For example, when the new pastor of the Reformed Church, Frederick Herman, arrived in Germantown in 1790, he entered all of

when one of the churches was somewhat disorganized and the regular functions were not being properly performed, people in this group registered their babies in the other church. The long gap in the Reformed Church records from 1779 to 1790 was therefore largely filled when the family slips were refiled alphabetically rather than by congregation. For example, to the two children of Johann Jacob and Catherina Matthaeus registered in the Reformed Church on August 16, 1775 and December 13, 1790, are added four others found in the records of St. Michael's—two in 1779, one in 1780, and another in 1782.[37] Thus, the presence of a large number of young families who had one or two children and then moved on is indicated by the fact that only 27 percent of the 267 families reporting two children can be shown to have remained in the area for more than three years and only 17 percent for over five years.

Even with all these qualifications, there is a statistically significant group of couples in colonial Germantown that had few, if any, children. Twenty-three percent of those who were married and left wills between 1700 and 1800 mention no children at all, 7 percent only one child, and another 12 percent name two children. While these wills do not include children who died early and undoubtedly leave out some who did exist but were in disfavor or had already received their inheritances, most of them represent the actual number of children at the time the will was written. Legal safety usually dictated that all prospective heirs be mentioned, if only to deny them a share, so that the will could not be broken by arguing that someone had been overlooked. The church records also reveal a number of

---

his previous children together with his new baby (Ref.Ch.Rec., Baptism: March 3, 1791). Defects are often noticed in strange ways; for example, William Tustin must have neglected to register one child, since the sixth child he had baptized was named "Septimus."

[37] St.M.Rec., Baptisms: vol. II, August 15, 1779; July 19, 1780; September 6, 1782.

completed families that never produced more than one or two children.[38]

Since there is little evidence to support the idea that birth control was widely practiced, the idea of genetic incompatibility, which led to involuntary failure to produce children, must be considered. This goes back to the concept of successful and unsuccessful families and would be worthy of some investigation. While beyond the scope of this discussion, there are a few indications, which emerge from the Germantown material, that infertility may well have been a fairly common problem rendered more or less invisible by the general growth of population during the eighteenth century. In the first place, the baptism records show that although it is possible to average out the span between births for the population at large, most families varied widely from the resultant figures with very regular, individual patterns of their own. For example, with a single exception, the first six children of Heinrich and Susannah Frölich were each exactly eighteen months apart,[39] while the Degers, Peter and Catherina, had a twenty-three- to twenty-five-month cycle, again with only one break, throughout the birth of nine children.[40] For others, the cycle seems to have been just as regular, but much longer—Peter and Judith Mayer, for example, only produced one child every four years over a twelve-year span.[41]

The two Landenberger families provide an excellent illustration of what this kind of difference in pattern could mean to a given marriage. In the case of Jacob, Jr. and

[38] The families of Jacob Schuster (Reformed Church) and Christofell [*sic*] Jacoby (St. Michael's) both provide examples.

[39] Ref.Ch.Rec., Baptisms: February 1770; August 1771; February 1773; January 1775; July 1776; January 1778.

[40] St.M.Rec., Baptisms: vol. I, March 1751; February 1753; March 1755; May 1759; vol. II., April 1768. Confirmations: vol. II, Easter 1773; Easter 1775. Ref.Ch.Rec., Baptisms: March 1763; March 1770.

[41] Ref.Ch.Rec., Baptisms: June 1755; March 1759; January 1764; January 1768.

Elisabetta, the period of fertility lasted from 1780 to 1799, during which time there were six children born, evenly spaced four years apart, with one three-year interval. On the other hand, in a space of only fourteen years from 1786 to 1800, Johannes and Anna Maria Landenberger produced thirteen children (including one set of twins), a new birth taking place in every year with the exceptions of 1790 (the year after the birth of the twins), 1793, and 1799.[42] Although three of their children died, there is still a great difference in the total number of live offspring produced by one family compared to another. In general, the results of research appear to show that these wide differences persisted from one Germantown family to another, making the size of family an individual and physical matter rather than the result of a culturally induced pattern. The danger of finding averages is obvious here, since it would tend to obscure the fact that there was really no standard type of family.

In another area, an interesting set of statistics survives that tends to support the theory that immigrants, for a variety of reasons, had fewer children than settled people.[43] The family trees of fourteen of the original Germantown settlers, including Pastorius, were inscribed in the records of the Abington Monthly Meeting during the nineteenth century.[44] These include children born before emigration, although probably not those who died before arrival in America. Of these Dutch and German Quaker families, two had two children, six had three children, three had five children, and one each had six, seven, and nine children. For

---

[42] The children of Jacob and Elisabetta Landenberger are registered in St.M.Rec., Baptisms: vol. II, November 17, 1781; December 28, 1787 (2 children); vol. III, September 26, 1804 (3 children). The children of Johannes and Anna Maria Landenberger are registered as follows: St.M.Rec., Baptisms: vol. II, April 8, 1787 (2 children); Ref.Ch.Rec., Baptisms: 1794 (3 children); August 7, 1791; August 26, 1792; August 17, 1794; July 9, 1795; Burials: July 6, 1796; September 5, 1797; St.M.Rec., Baptisms: vol. III, April 1, 1799; July 17, 1800.

[43] Potter, "Population in America," *Population in History*, p. 645.

[44] AbMMRec., pp. 17-20.

second-generation Germantown Quaker offspring, there are seventeen family charts.[45] As a group, these genealogies represent those who had either married into local English families or had become quickly assimilated into English culture with Anglicized surnames and given names. They also include a great many units that no longer lived in Germantown but had moved into that part of Philadelphia that later became Montgomery County. For these reasons their patterns cannot be thought to be representative of second-generation Germantowners, yet it should be noted that their family size was, in general, much larger than that of their parents or, indeed, of the general Germantown statistics as figured on the German churches. One family each had one, two, or three children; four had four children; two had five children; one had six; three had seven; two had eight; and one each had eleven and twelve. One of the families with seven children represented the offspring of two mothers. Strangely enough, if one cares to play the game of averages, this group produced exactly the same number of children per marriage (5.8) as Greven's first-decade Englishmen in Andover.[46]

The actual spread of family sizes for Germantown in the last half of the eighteenth century is illustrated in table 18. The totals are somewhat biased in favor of smaller families by the presence of many incompleted families from about 1787 on. Nevertheless, the pattern is clear: at no point did the median number of children per family rise above four, even in the completed decades, and the largest single percentage of households at any time produced no more than two children, at least before and during their period of residence in Germantown. The small percentage of families having over six children (never more than 20) is even more markedly in contrast with Greven's findings of 64-74 percent large families, when it is realized that he worked with

---

[45] Ibid., Baptisms: pp. 20-23; p. 31; p. 34; p. 37; p. 49; p. 56; p. 57; p. 72; p. 83; p. 90; p. 104.

[46] Greven, *Four Generations*, p. 23.

TABLE 18

Children Baptized per Family, Germantown Churches, 1750-1799

Children per Family	1750-59 Families		1760-69 Families		1770-79 Families		1780-89 Families		1790-99 Families		Totals Families	
	No.	%	No.	%	No.	%	No.	%	No.	%	No.	%
2	61	26.4	50	29.9	46	28.8	40	23.1	74	45.1	271	30.4
3	51	22.1	33	19.8	41	25.6	30	17.3	41	25.0	196	22.0
4	35	15.6	23	13.8	20	12.5	27	15.6	30	18.3	135	15.2
5	25	10.8	14	8.4	14	8.8	28	16.2	11	6.7	92	10.3
6	20	8.7	13	7.8	12	7.5	23	13.3	7	4.3	75	8.4
7	16	6.9	10	6.0	7	4.4	16	9.2	1	.6	50	5.6
8	11	4.8	7	4.2	7	4.4	8	4.6	–	–	33	3.7
9	4	1.7	8	4.8	6	3.8	–	–	–	–	18	2.0
10	5	2.2	1	.6	6	3.8	–	–	–	–	8	.9
11	2	.9	5	3.0	1	.6	–	–	–	–	7	.8
12 or more	1[a]	.4	3	1.8	–	–	1[b]	.6	–	–	5	.6
Total	231	100.5	167	100.1	160	100.2	173	99.9	164	100.0	890	99.9

NOTE: Families entered in decade when first child was born.
[a] Fourteen children.
[b] Thirteen children.

all families, while the Germantown figures only relate to those who had at least two children.[47]

The importance of individual patterns of fertility (or its opposite) to family size and structure in a precontraception society is even more apparent when the averages for intervals between births are broken down and studied more carefully. Both the Lutheran and Reformed churches accepted the Catholic doctrine in relation to the need for infant baptism, so that among faithful families those babies who died almost immediately appear in the baptism records, even though their burials may not have been recorded by the church. The baptism records, therefore, provide a better guide to the number of live births than the burial records do for infant mortality. This supposition is supported by the fact that, between 1750 and 1799, 70 percent of the babies registered were baptized within six months of their birth, one-third of these within the first month. Even more remarkable, at a time when infants were not likely to be taken out of the house except in cases of dire necessity, almost 5 percent of the registered children were brought to church when less than a week old, regardless of the season.[48] The logical corollary to this information is that when there is a large gap in the interval between baptisms in churchgoing families, it is not the result of failure to baptize children who died early, but rather an indication of a period of what might be called demographic crisis within the family itself.

This kind of crisis, whether due to temporary infertility, absence of the father, miscarriage, or still birth, was a regular feature of family birth patterns in Germantown between

[47] Ibid., p. 203. It is unfortunate that there is no way to chart the Germantown families and include those who had no children, or only a single offspring, but the reliability of records for very small families was too suspect to make them usable—that is, the possibility of mobility or apostasy was too likely in these cases.

[48] Baptism was almost always done at church. In those cases where the baby died at home almost immediately after birth, it was noted that it had been baptized at home, frequently by the midwife, "on account of great weakness, and died soon after."

271

1750 and 1799. A period of over five years between the baptism of children in a family occurred 11 percent of the time in observed samples of 2,625 intervals. In other respects the spacing of children appears to conform to statistical norms: in 1 percent of the cases, births were less than a year apart; 30 percent occurred one to two years apart; 38 percent were two to three years apart; 14 percent were spaced three to four years; and 6 percent four to five years. This last is a combination, most likely, of families with long but natural regular intervals and other groups where the length of time between children represents a true gap. While four years between children was the pattern for the Mayer family, it represented a definite break for Jacob and Maria Hegi, whose five intervals over a fourteen-year span were spaced as follows: twenty-six months; twenty-two months; twenty-six months; *four and a half years*; twenty-nine months.[49] There are no cases of marriages where there is a normal span of five years or more between births, so that all of these may be assumed to be times of crisis. Among marriages that produced children for a particularly long period —over twenty years—it is not uncommon to find two of these gaps. The family of Joseph and Catherina Bender serves as an example of this. Over a period of twenty-five years, they produced six girls and three boys, with intervals ranging from twelve to thirty-three months. There were two exceptions, however; a six-year gap between the first and second child, and a five-year gap between the seventh and eighth. This also appears to have been a relatively unsuccessful family in terms of survival, since five of the children died before the age of twenty-one.[50]

One reason that can definitely be pinpointed as causing

---

[49] Ref.Ch.Rec., Baptisms: May 19, 1753; November 2, 1755; June 2, 1758; October 12, 1764 (twins); May 24, 1767.

[50] Ref.Ch.Rec., Baptisms: October 1766; February 27, 1775; July 20, 1777; January 6, 1780; February 18, 1781; November 20, 1791. Burials: December 30, 1772; March 7, 1793; January 3, 1798; January 13, 1793; March 2, 1775.

deviation from the orderly progression of births within a successful family cycle is the death of the mother and the remarriage of the father. Conversely, a principal reason for an abbreviated birth span within a marriage is the death of the father. Although there is no way to measure accurately the precise amount of death and remarriage among couples of child-bearing age, the issue is so important in relation to the operation of the family, that it is worth sorting through what material is available to try to arrive at some understanding of the situation.[51] As has already been stated, the marital status of the parties to a wedding is only partially reported on the marriage certificates of the Germantown churches. A total of 13.5 percent (216) of the 1,529 slips makes note that one or both of the parties is widowed; in 82 cases it is the man who is remarrying, in 72 it is the woman, and in the remaining 62 both partners in the new marriage are listed as having been married before. The large number of cases where both parties to the marriage were widowed, indicates that widowers tended to marry widows almost as often as they wed young girls, which should not be unexpected in a society where there were enough men to go round, so that younger women were not obliged to take on the responsibilities of a half-grown family. Widows may have been dissuaded from marrying in many cases, however, by the inclusion in most wills of a clause stating that the widow forfeited her share of an estate if she remarried. Nor could she provide security for her children through remarriage since it was not the custom for stepfathers to assume responsibility for the children of a wife's

---

[51] The importance of this issue is mentioned by S. Peller, "Births and Deaths among Europe's Ruling Families Since 1500," *Population in History*, pp. 96-97. Although Peter Laslett shows a high incidence of remarriage in England in *The World We Have Lost*, New York, 1965, pp. 99-100, Greven and Demos both feel that the occurrence of around 40 percent remarriage for men is rather lower than expected in seventeenth- and eighteenth-century New England. See Greven, *Four Generations*, p. 29, p. 111; and Demos, *Little Commonwealth*, p. 67.

previous marriage. In only 4 percent of the Germantown wills written by married men are such children mentioned at all, a figure that can bear no relationship to the number of these men who must have had stepchildren.[52]

More can be gleaned from the baptism slips in relation to the remarriage of widowers and the place of the stepmother in the family. Although there are almost no figures available on the remarriage of mothers, that of fathers can be

TABLE 19

KNOWN LOSS OF A PARENT, GERMANTOWN, 1750-1799

	1750-59	1760-69	1770-79	1780-89	1790-99
No. of families	229	267	161	173	165
% losing a parent	23.0	20.0	17.0	15.0	7.5
No. of mothers who died	42	27	21	20	5
No. of fathers who died	12	7	9	6	7
No. of fathers remarried	37	23	16	17	4
Av. no. children first wife	2.9	2.7	2.1	2.6	1.4
Av. no. children second wife	2.9	2.2	2.8	2.3	2.2
Mean interval from children of one wife to those of next (in years)	4.5	4.3	4.2	4.4	2.0

[52] More often than not the bequest was merely a remembrance; e.g., £10 to Susannah Yakell, daughter of Mathew Inglis's wife by her first husband, to be given when the girl's young stepbrothers and stepsisters (one of whom was still unborn) should become of age and come into their share of the estate. WB H, #236, p. 482, February 24, 1747/8.

fairly well determined for the 890 Germantown families in the records of St. Michael's and the Reformed Church. There were only four instances of men who remarried twice; one in the sixties and three in the seventies, which appears, probably because of the war, to have been a risky time in general for family growth and stability. In the great majority of cases where a mother died during the fertile years, the father remarried and continued to produce children with a new wife. In over half of these, however, one of the wives is represented by a single child, and most often it is the first wife. The fairly even number of children produced per wife, as shown in table 19, relates to the overall situation rather than to conditions within individual families. Remarriage, estimated by the gap between the children of one wife and the next, was not as immediate as has often been thought; while there is one example of a baby born to a second wife just nine months after the death of the first wife, there is also a family in which twenty-one years elapses.

Although there is no way to document the thesis, one derives the impression that there was considerable drive to perpetuate the family. Remarriage was frequently associated with the death of sons within a motherless home, and virtually no widower whose wife left him childless remained unmarried. Those who never married again had from two to ten live children, at least one of whom was a boy. Wigard Miller was fifty-nine years old and had been a widower for many years when his only son, Enoch, died unmarried at the age of twenty-five. Miller married twenty-three-year-old Christina Hesser of Cresheim, a "spinster," and produced several more children, the last when he was seventy-one.[53]

The steady drop throughout the period, in the percentage

[53] St.M.Rec., Baptism: vol. I, February 15, 1747, for baptism of the oldest son; Marriage: vol. II, June 8, 1773; Baptisms: vol. II, June 14, 1776; October 2, 1778; March 30, 1788; Burial: vol. III, October 14, 1795. See also Roach, *Gen.Mag.* (1956), p. 123.

of families that lost a parent, as illustrated in table 19, parallels an increase in the life-span of the average Germantown citizen.[54] It is the first item in a series of statistics that point to the conclusion that Germantowners, in general, experienced growing health and longevity during the last half of the eighteenth century. The township had a great reputation as a healthful place to live; it remained basically free of yellow fever during the epidemics and was generally regarded as having good, pure water, high, well-drained land, and fresh, wholesome air. The Union School advertised as early as 1761 that "the Air is known, from long Experience, to be pure and healthy; often recommended by the best Physicians to Invalids."[55] Whether or not it was an advantage to the health of the people, Germantown always had more than its share of doctors.[56] Early in the century Christopher Witt had moved into the town, and had not only cast nativities and horoscopes and practiced medicine and the use of herbs, but had trained several other young men as well.[57] In 1773 there were three doctors listed in the area,

[54] The very large decline in the nineties, however, is probably also closely related to the fact that the sample, by its nature, represents a much younger group than those whose families began in the earlier decade. Obviously, the longer the span of births within a marriage the more likely it was that there was more than one wife. Thus, while 20 percent of marriages that produced children for ten years or more involves the loss of a parent, the figure rises abruptly to 42 percent for those spans of over fifteen years.

[55] *Pa.Gaz.*, March 5, 1761.

[56] See K. F. Helleiner, "The Vital Revolution Reconsidered," *Population in History*, pp. 83-86, on the fact that medicine and doctors had very little to do with the drop in mortality that occurred in the latter part of the eighteenth century. Also see Thomas McKeown and R. G. Brown, "Medical Evidence Related to English Population Changes in the Eighteenth Century," *Population in History*, pp. 285-307.

[57] See Edward Hocker, *A Doctor of Colonial Germantown: Christopher Witt, Physician, Mystic, and Seeker after the Truth*, Germantown History, vol. 2, #88, Germantown, 1948. Witt had a considerable reputation in his day as a naturalist, connected with Bartram and Peter Collinson. He was also something of a religious

and by 1793 there were seven, the largest representation of any profession within the township.[58]

As in the case of fertility, it is impossible to figure rates of mortality for the Germantown community, both since the total population at risk cannot be derived and because the records are not complete enough. It does seem, however, that the burial lists available deal more directly with the Germantowners themselves and less with the population of the surrounding region. In addition, more of the unchurched inhabitants are listed through the books of the two public cemeteries.[59] The total burials registered for the community number 2,199, of whom 1,015 were children under thirteen, and 1,095 were adults; the other 89 were adolescents between the ages of thirteen and twenty. Actual ages are available for 786 adults and 645 children whose deaths are filed in the records of St. Michael's or the Reformed Church. The general outline of mortality for the larger number is known because the burial grounds, while not giving ages, charged a different amount for children than for adults and also listed children between the ages of thirteen and twenty as "son" or "daughter" rather than merely as the "child" of a given householder.[60]

The least reliable statistic in the field of mortality for Germantown is that referring to infants, a condition that appears to be true of demographic material in general. As Hollingsworth states concerning England: "The under-enumeration of children dying in infancy . . . showed that large numbers of them were not mentioned before about 1770,

---

fanatic, having been a member of the strange, mystical Hermits of the Wissahickon.

[58] See table 10.

[59] Hood Cemetery Records and "Records of the Upper Burying Ground," *PMHB*, 8 and 9. In addition, there are some burials listed for the Germantown Meeting, 1747-1786, Collections of the Genealogical Society, HSP, although these are scanty and incomplete.

[60] See, for example, Hood Cemetery Records, January 29, 1775, Jacob Eckert's daughter and March 2, 1775, Johann Bender, child.

and the true infant mortality was much higher than it seemed."[61] In Germantown the burial records indicate that only about one in every three children who died was under twelve months, a demographically improbable figure, with most reliable studies indicating that during the eighteenth century almost twice as many infants died as children between the ages of one to twelve.[62] The causes of this failure to register infant death were undoubtedly common to communities in general; in Germantown, specifically, the cost of burial was apt to prove a deterrent, both in the churchyard and the public cemetery. One probable index to the decreasing trend in infant mortality during the second half of the century was the widening interval between birth and baptism. The importance of baptizing a live child in the

TABLE 20

INTERVAL BETWEEN BIRTH AND BAPTISM,
GERMANTOWN, 1740–1799

	1740-49 (%)	1750-59 (%)	1760-69 (%)	1770-79 (%)	1780-89 (%)	1790-99 (%)
0-31 days	53.5	38.5	23.0	20.0	10.5	11.5
1-6 months	36.0	46.5	55.0	54.5	47.5	41.0
7-12 months	7.0	7.0	11.0	11.5	15.0	17.0
Over 12 months	3.0	7.5	10.5	13.5	27.0	29.5

Lutheran or Reformed church has already been mentioned, as have the general figures for baptism within six months of birth for the entire period. When the material is analyzed further, the evidence grows for the premise that parents more regularly expected their children to survive past in-

[61] Hollingsworth, *Historical Demography*, p. 60.
[62] Peller, "Births and Deaths," *Population in History*, pp. 92-93.

fancy as the eighteenth century wore on. The only exception to the smooth progression toward later and later baptisms is the very slight increase in the one-month-and-under group in the 1790s; this may well reflect the yellow fever scare during that period and the fact that there is a slight numerical rise in the mortality of children for the decade. Where the burial figures are more complete, that is, among children from one to twelve years old, childhood mortality can definitely be seen to have been declining during the second half of the eighteenth century in Germantown. In the 1750s and 1760s, 53 percent of the total deaths of those over one year of age were of children under twelve. This percentage dropped in each successive decade: 45.5 percent of those buried in the seventies, 32 in the eighties, and 28.5 in the nineties were children between one and twelve.[63]

In general, the findings for Germantown would seem to bear out those for New England, that childhood death was far less a hazard than historical myth would indicate, although far more prevalent than in the twentieth century.[64] Gross child mortality rates for the Germantown churches (deaths divided by births and multiplied by 1,000) average out to 223 per 1,000 for the second half of the eighteenth century, with a high of 348 per 1,000 in the seventies, and an almost unbelievably low 96 per 1,000 for the fifties.[65] Meanwhile, the percentage of families who reported no child deaths at all rose from 65 to 76. The generally accepted belief that each family tended to lose several children can also be tested and rejected through use of the Germantown statistics. It was possible to run two separate checks for this topic—one by using the 309 church families who reported the death of at least one child, and another on the 143 non-

[63] These statistics are based on figures that exclude children who died before one year of age.

[64] See, for example, John Demos, "Notes on Life in Plymouth Colony," *WMQ*, 22 (1965), p. 271, and Greven, *Four Generations*, pp. 25-26; pp. 108-109; pp. 186-188; pp. 190-192.

[65] The greatest degree of underregistration of infant mortality appears to have taken place during this decade.

church-going families who buried children in the Lower
Burying Ground. The results for the church group showed
that 63 percent of those families reporting childhood deaths
lost only one child, 26 percent lost two, 8 percent lost three,
and only 3 percent reported the deaths of four or more children below the age of twelve. The statistics for the Lower
Burying Ground are, in every case, within two percentage
points of these results.[66]

More significantly, there is no particular evidence of large
numbers of childhood deaths caused by epidemic or contagious disease. In only a third of the cases where families
reported the death of more than one child, did the deaths
take place within six months of each other, and only 22 percent of the time did these deaths take place within a month.
Where the children did die within a short period of time,
it was usually the two or three closest in age to each other,
leading to the speculation that they might have been sharing a bed. Several of the instances of close death in a family
turn out to be very young twins, however, and it must be
remembered that their chances for survival, in terms of in-
herent strength, were less than that of single babies. There
are fifty-one cases where a family lost three or more children, but in only five of these is it clear that the cause must
have been some communicable disease. In one of these, all
the children (three) in the family up to that time were
buried within twenty-three days—one aged nine, one aged
six, and one who was two years old. Two more children,
who survived, were later born to the family.[67] Two of the
remaining examples of three children dying at one time be-

[66] Hood Cemetery families: burial of one child, 65 percent; two
children, 23 percent; three children, 8 percent; four or more children, 5 percent. The higher percentage for the largest category indicates a greater tendency for families to bury infants in the public
cemetery where they had a plot, than for church members to bury
infants in the churchyard.

[67] Leonhart and Anna Maria Wintergerst, St.M.Rec., Burials: vol. I,
September 24, 1756; September 22, 1756; October 15, 1756; Baptisms:
vol. I, March 1758; October 1774.

long in one family. William Tusten was unique in having
the kind of demographic record that has been considered
typical, perhaps because its very dreadfulness made a lasting
impression on people's minds. He and his wife had eleven
children between 1760 and 1775. The first three all died in
January 1764, and a pair died in February 1770. Seven
months later still another child was buried and three more
between 1784 and 1787, leaving only two survivors out of
the original eleven offspring.[68] The only family to lose more
children was that of John Nice, whose example indicates
that the difficulty must most often have been peculiar to the
individual family. Perhaps the problem was genetic, for
there are no signs of infection. Only once in the twenty-one-
year span during which eleven of his children died, did two
die close enough together to make it reasonable to suspect
contagious disease.[69]

Even when family deaths outside the sibling relationship
are considered, the evidence for contagious disease as an
important cause of mortality is exceedingly weak. In only
eleven instances beyond those mentioned above are members of a family who live together, such as husband and
wife, mother and child, widowed grandmother and grand-
child, father and child, or occasionally cousins, known to
have died within a month of each other. There are only
thirty-four additional examples, if the interval is stretched
to a year. Nor is there much indication of epidemic years
for the town in general. In only two years, 1774 and 1775,

[68] William Tustin (also spelled "Dosten"), Ref.Ch.Rec., Baptisms:
August 21, 1760; March 11, 1764; October 5, 1765; December 7, 1766;
May 12, 1768; February 19, 1770; May 24, 1772; September 8, 1776.
Burial: January 4, 1764. Hood Cemetery Records, February 19, 1770;
February 25, 1770; September 11, 1770; July 4, 1783; September 11,
1784; March 26, 1787.

[69] John Nice's children, Hood Cemetery Records: June 25, 1775;
October 19, 1775; August 6, 1776; August 11, 1777; October 13, 1778;
August 3, 1779; September 8, 1782; April 21, 1789; November 21, 1790;
August 13, 1793; November 28, 1796. Nice himself was buried April 3,
1794.

were there more than five multiple family deaths recorded for the whole population; in eight years there were no such occurrences registered at all. Philadelphians first used Germantown as a place from which to escape the yellow fever in 1793, and as one might suppose, there is a higher-than-usual number of families (five) who recorded more than one burial within a twelve-month span. On the other hand, the epidemics and flights to Germantown of 1797, 1798, and 1799 had only five such episodes altogether. In relation to seasonal variation, the pattern of deaths in the township does not follow the traditional one of preindustrial Europe or of the New England towns. These show the greatest months of mortality to be the cold, winter season of illness and semistarvation.[70] What pattern existed in Germantown was actually reversed, with the greatest percentage of deaths occurring between July and September. By and large, however, there was very little rise and fall in the death rate from one time of year to another, the only real difference being found in the deaths of very young children, perhaps as a result of "summer complaint." The unusually well-insulated stone houses and well-built cellars with their excellent facilities for food storage may have been largely responsible for the seeming ability of Germantowners to withstand winter health hazards.[71]

Those who survived to the age of twelve had about an 89 percent chance of living to be twenty-one; slightly over 90 percent for boys, slightly under 87 percent for girls. The greatest risk for boys in this age group appears to have been accidental—by drowning, by horse, by shooting, and one bizarre case of a young man who fell off a high swing.[72] The higher percentage of girls dying in this age group reflects the number of teen-age mothers and the possibility of

---

[70] See Lockridge, *A New England Town*, p. 69.

[71] Tinkcom, *Historic Germantown*, pp. 28-30.

[72] *Pennsylvania Packet*, July 15, 1784. Statistics are not available within this area, although the church registers frequently comment on the cause of death, particularly when it is accidental.

death in childbirth. There was also a higher percentage of female death in the 21–30-year bracket, probably for the same reason, but the insignificance of the difference—16 percent of the females as a whole compared to 13 percent of the males—indicates that the risks of childbirth have been much exaggerated. Figure 5 illustrates how closely the life expectancy of a woman of any given age paralleled that of a man in the same category—at least as closely as man to man in succeeding decades, for example.[73] The percentages here are figured on the specific group at risk in each category, that is, by eliminating from the calculations at each step all those who have died in the previous decade. The

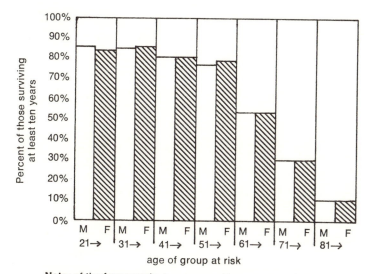

Note: of the four people, two men and two women, who survived beyond 91, none lived to be 100.

Figure 5. Ten Year Survival Expectation at Given Ages: Germantown, 1750-1799.

[73] Demos has demonstrated much the same thing for Plymouth in *Little Commonwealth*, p. 66, as has Greven for Andover, *Four Generations*, pp. 195-196.

chance of living at least another ten years if one lived to
fifty-one was almost as good as it was for a person who was
twenty-one. It was after sixty that the risks were greatly increased.

It is also useful to measure the percentage of adults surviving in each age category in relation to the whole group
whose ages at death are known, and to compare the results
of this measurement for the 1750s with those of the 1790s.
Figure 6 provides a graphic illustration of the way in which
the life expectancy of a 21-year-old increased in Germantown during the second half of the eighteenth century.

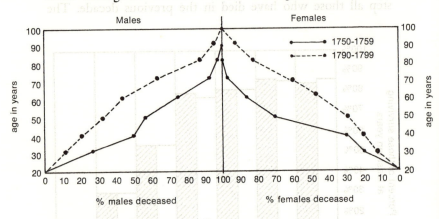

FIGURE 6. Life Expectancy, Germantown: 1750-1759; 1790-1799.

When considered in terms of average age at death for those
who had reached 21, there is a similarly dramatic change.
In the decade of the 1750s, the average age at death for an
adult male was 43.4 years. This, of course, reflects the tremendously large influx of young immigrants, which must
have fairly well swamped the older settlers during that
period and made a most peculiar age structure for the population at large. The steady picture of the next three decades
probably reflects more closely the average ages at which
adults died: the figure 55.8 years for men in the 1760s is a

twelve-point leap from the previous decade, but it remains stable for the next twenty years at 54.6 between 1770 and 1779, and 54.0 from 1780 to 1789. The lower average may well be related to the military occupation of Germantown by the British and the inroads made by the Revolution on the male population in the vicinity. Between 1790 and 1799 the upward trend for men was resumed, with an average age of death for adult males of 57.8 years.

The trend to higher average age among females was more consistent than that for men. From 45.7 years in the 1750s, it rose to 49.7 years in the sixties, remained almost stationary at 49.8 in the seventies, and then took a large leap to 55.7 years during the 1780s. This increase was no fluke, since it was repeated with another jump, this time of four years to 60.6 for the period from 1790 to 1799. In the long run, the steady gain among women caused them to outdistance the men. While females had predeceased males during the sixties and seventies, they crept ahead between 1780 and 1789 and were living almost a full three years longer by the end of the century.

Since there is no particular evidence that the overall structure of the population aged tremendously during this time—the number of widows remained proportional to the total population growth, for example—and there is even some indication that the new wave of immigration in the nineties was on the young side, the conclusion must be that Germantowners in general were living longer by the 1790-99 decade. Factors such as the rates of remarriage and later baptism appear to confirm these findings, making the mortality statistics the only demographic data in eighteenth-century Germantown to present such a consistent picture. Of course, this is the one area in which there was almost no conscious control, and any unconscious psychological factor would undoubtedly have produced group agreement that it was better to live longer. But life expectancy was almost completely tied to living conditions rather than medicine or health habits during this period, and the advantages of urban living in an uncrowded environment outweighed the disadvantages; impressionistic views of Germantown as a healthy place have validity.[74] Other demographic conclusions are more difficult to draw. There seems to have been general agreement among eighteenth-century Germantowners that the proper condition of adults, male or female, was the married state, since the choice was a conscious one and nuptuality was so high. In most other vital statistics for Germantown, the individual differences often seem more important than the common denominators. Age at marriage varied widely; each family went its own way in relation to the number and spacing of its children, leaving no clue as to whether or not this was involuntary. Neither the clear patterns of European peasants nor those of New England yeomen emerged, but rather a mixture reflecting a mixed population of new arrivals and established settlers, of individual families with no community traditions to predispose them to a uniform pattern of life within their own walls.

[74] See McKeown and Brown, "Medical Evidence," *Population in History*, pp. 285-307.

CHAPTER 8

All in the Family

THE sociological concept of stability of populations has long confused the surface permanence of the face of a community with family continuity beneath. For this reason Peter Laslett and John Harrison were surprised to find that the seventeenth-century English towns of Clayworth and Cogenhoe had both a high rate of mobility and a tendency to nuclear family quite contrary to the traditional picture of English rural life.[1] Williams reported in his modern study of Ashworthy that village life was not necessarily "conservative" as most sociologists regarded it, but that continual dynamic change was actually taking place, often obscured by the use of large-scale investigations based on statistical material and general surveys. His novel results were obtained by concentrating on detailed inquiries into specific cases.[2]

The reason for the confusion is not hard to find: it is a question of point of view. If the observer concentrates on a community at large, as historians have done for so many years, he may find that a family named "Smith" has remained on the same farm for several centuries. He may even note that most of the surnames in the area have had a long history of continuity, leading to the conclusion that the communal village was a place of close-knit permanent families—and from the vantage point of the community in general, he is right. But what was going on within those families? If the custom of the country was primogeniture, or, in fact, any kind of impartible inheritance, and tracts of land were not so large that they would support ever larger and

---

[1] Peter Laslett and John Harrison, "Clayworth and Cogenhoe," in *Historical Essays, 1660-1750, Presented to David Ogg,* H. E. Bell and R. L. Ollard, eds., London, 1963, pp. 166-168.

[2] Williams, *Ashworthy,* introduction, especially p. xx.

larger family clans, it is obvious that the family itself must have undergone continual stress and change, as those members who would not inherit were forced to migrate. Surely, too, in the days before easy, long-distance communication, family bonds stretched across even relatively short distances were bound to weaken and snap, particularly among the majority of illiterate or semiliterate people.[3] Moreover, while extended families, defined as households occupied by more than a husband and wife and their direct offspring, may have existed, they were not usually static or permanent arrangements. Rather, they covered the period from the marriage of the "heir apparent" and the birth of his children to the death of his old parents and the departure of his siblings. This continual tendency toward nuclear rearrangement was even more apparent where the youngest, rather than the oldest, son inherited the homeplace or where children were apt to receive their portions before the parent died. In any case, one can hardly seek the causes for the breakup of the family and the loss of community-wide social norms in the migration of Old World villagers to the unstructured new continent. Even the word that describes this condition, "anomie," is sixteenth-century European in origin, rather than being a new coinage to describe the American experience.[4]

In New England, for the first few generations at least, it would seem that a more closely connected family system was developing. It was not an extended family in the pure sense of kin under a single roof, but in the more useful definition of living close enough together to be continually involved in each other's lives.[5] Nuclear families arrived and provided for their children within their own townships, clos-

[3] For the suggestion that modern families may actually be more successful at maintaining communications on extended family lines, see Eugene Litwak, "Geography, Mobility, and Extended Family Cohesion," *American Sociological Review*, 25 (1960), pp. 385-394.

[4] See Robert K. Merton, "Social Structure and Anomie: Revisions and Extensions," in *The Family*, p. 231 fn.

[5] Greven, *Four Generations*, pp. 15-16, pp. 138-139.

ing the gates to newcomers, so that the places of those families that died off could be taken by the increasing progeny of the remaining groups. In clinging to close family relationships, the New Englanders were bolstered by puritan doctrine which stressed the sanctity and basic importance of the family and which assumed, in fact, that the state was made up of families rather than individuals.[6]

It is perfectly possible, however, that the developments in New England were atypical of the American colonies, especially since the homogeneity of the early settlers there and their conscious efforts at community were uncharacteristic. Certainly the Germantown experience was completely different. A quick survey of just how different may be made by comparing the number of families bearing the same surname in Germantown with those who did so in a New England town of approximately the same size. In 1755 the town of Chatham, Massachusetts had been in existence for about 100 years and contained 155 ratables.[7] While Germantown at about the same time (1766) was only 78 years old, it had 211 listed families. Chatham's 155 families bore only 34 surnames: 6 of these names appeared only once, but 7 families had more than 6 branches; leading the list there were 20 Nickersons, 19 Eldredges, 15 Smiths, and 10 Godfrees: there was, in summary, an average of 4.56 families for every surname. In Germantown, on the other hand, there were 143 different last names among the 211 ratables: 99 of these appeared only once, and none belonged to more than 6 families; the average number of households per given name was only 1.47. By the time Germantown

---

[6] Edmund Morgan, *The Puritan Family: Religion and Domestic Relations in the Seventeenth-Century New England*, 1944: rev. ed. New York, 1966, pp. 133-134, pp. 143-144.

[7] The Rate Bill for Chatham, 1755, was destroyed by fire in 1919. A copy appears in William C. Smith, *A History of Chatham, Massachusetts: Formerly the Constablewick or Village of Monomoit*, 1947: rpt. Chatham, Mass., 1971, pp. 316-319. The Germantown figures are derived from the 1766 List of Property holders and the *U.S. Census*, 1790.

had reached 100 years of settlement, the population had more than doubled, and the number of kinship groups had, of course, risen sharply, but the average per name had only increased to 1.7. The potential for individual isolation was enormous in these conditions; by the end of the century its effects were being felt in the most personal ways. Conrad Werner, for example, was a widower with a mentally defective daughter. His fears for her maintenance after his death could not be resolved by any appeal to extended kinship relationships. The best he could manage was to leave all of his estate to a neighbor in exchange for a promise that the girl would be cared for. If the neighbor should move away or predecease the child, Werner's only recourse was to urge that the neighbor's heirs, although unknown to him, would take over the responsibility along with the property.[8]

Actually, in the beginning Germantown was made up of a very closely connected kinship group. All the original Crefelders appear to have been related to each other in some way or another; one of the three OpdenGraff brothers was a son-in-law of van Bebber; the Streepers brothers were cousins of the OpdenGraffs, and Kunders and Arets were married to Streepers' sisters; in addition, one of the Streepers was married to the sister of Renier Tyson. In a more distant connection, Lucken, Tunes, and Keurlis were also related, and a twelfth member of the group, Jan Sieman, was married to a Lucken.[9] There was no patriarchal head of the group, however. Most of the arrivals were quite young; the only member of an older, unifying generation who accompanied them was the elderly widowed mother of the OpdenGraffs; she died shortly after her arrival in Pennsylvania. The quick admixture of immigrants from other places and early removals by the original settlers combined to prevent the formation of any further patterns of extended family relationships.

[8] Conrad Werner, WB X, #465, p. 680, January 9, 1798.
[9] Pennypacker, *Pa.Ger.*, IX, p. 56.

It may well be that the system of redemptioners, as it developed, also worked at weakening the expectation of family unity even among kin who themselves did not arrive under those conditions. Although many of the horror stories of the separation of mother and child, husband and wife, brother and sister may be discounted, the fact remains that enough of them were true to create a psychological climate in which such family dispersements were believed to be the general rule.[10] The tendency of German immigrants to come in sibling groups—young brothers with or without newly acquired brides—may be noted on Rupp's list of immigrants and shows particularly among the newly arrived families in the Germantown records of the fifties. It was along these sibling lines that the family then tended to split. Within a few years, one of the immigrant brothers would have moved on to settle in Skippack, perhaps, or Towamensin, while the other remained fixed in a trade in Germantown. Often, brothers and sisters split immediately upon arrival, with only one coming to Germantown, each of the others heading for a separate establishment in a more rural location.[11] Even if parents accompanied their grown children to America, there seems to have been little to prevent early division into separate nuclear units. Thus, the three sons of Garret Dewees arrived in Germantown with him in the late seventeenth century, but within ten years only one son still remained in the township, the others having moved, one to the area of the three lower counties, one to what later became Montgomery County.[12] This principle of splitting the family at the sibling level continued to operate throughout the century as illustrated by the Hoger-

[10] For a brief history of the redemptioners' trade in Pennsylvania, from the emotional point of view, see Diffenderffer, *Pa.Ger.*, X.

[11] See, for example, the twelve adult children of David Jäckel, Schwenkfelders who came to Pennsylvania together in 1734, but scattered on arrival. *Schwenkfelder Genealogy*, p. 468.

[12] Harriet LaMunyan, *The Dewees Family: Genealogical Data, Biographical Facts and Historical Information*, Norristown, Pa., 1905, GHS.

moed family. Although the father left his Germantown land
in 1760 to all six of his children equally, the sisters quickly
sold out and moved away. By 1773 the three brothers were
living in separate parts of town, and by 1780 two of them
had left town permanently.[13]

The constant reassertion of the nuclear pattern was not
only true of families of poor or moderate means, where
most of the children were obliged to seek their own livings
in less expensive areas than Germantown, but also of the
wealthiest, best established families in the township. Two of
the most prominent names in town were united in 1723,
when George Bringhurst married Anna Ashmead.[14] In 1734
George owned substantial property in Germantown, and
over the course of their marriage the couple produced ten
children: the first, seven and a half months after the wedding; the last, twenty-one years later. Of the six girls, only
two lived long enough to be married, and only one, who
did not live in Germantown, had children of her own; so
no descendants of the female line remained in town. All four
of the boys began their adult lives in the township, but the
youngest, who was only seven when his father died, was
never able to accumulate any property, and by 1798 he had
moved away from Germantown.[15] Two of his six children
could be traced in Philadelphia and Montgomery County;
the others disappeared from the family records entirely.
The three second-generation sons who lived out their lives
in Germantown produced twenty-five children among
them, eleven girls and fourteen boys. Only five of these
third generation offspring became Germantown residents,
and only three of them had children. By the fourth generation (mostly born in the nineteenth century), there were
still only five descendants of George and Anna who lived

[13] Matthias Adam Hogermoed, WB L, #319, p. 504, August 23,
1760. Also 1773, 1780 tax lists.

[14] The following information comes mainly from the *Bringhurst
Genealogy.*

[15] 1773, 1774, 1780, 1791 tax lists, 1798 Direct Tax, *U.S. Census*, 1790.

in the township, out of a possible several dozen. In addition, what had happened to those who had moved away was largely unknown to the family genealogist, indicating how quickly members of the kinship group tended to lose touch with each other, even when education and money would have been more than sufficient to maintain contact through letters and visits.[16]

There are many bits of evidence pointing to the fact that even those branches of a family that remained physically close often had weak kinship ties. One of the most important areas in which this showed up was in relation to religion. Although a large minority of families had loyalties that kept them all within the same church, there were more kinship groups where, on the adult sibling level, religious preference was expressed through different institutions; the Engle family, for example, had branches in literally every church and meetinghouse in the township, a condition that was bound to weaken the ties of blood. Although the church as an institution played much less of a part in the lives of people than it did in more homogeneous communities, the vital moments of life were still celebrated within its walls; perhaps most important, relatives of different religious denominations could not stand as sponsor or godparent to a new baby. As early as the mid-eighteenth century, Mittelberger had remarked that, contrary to the customs in Germany: "Many parents act as sponsors for their own children because they have no faith or confidence in other people on this important point."[17] The Germantown church records show that this kind of nuclear independence continued to grow throughout the period: actually, in the fifties, the

---

[16] The evidence on lack of continued kinship relationship is largely negative for Germantown and is a topic that would bear greater investigation. The traditional view, repeated by Lemon (*Best Poor Man's Country*, pp. 115-116) without any proof, is that somehow Pennsylvania families kept in close touch after dispersion. This may well be an area in which a hard, new look would result in some useful revision.

[17] *Mittelberger's Journey*, p. 69.

time at which Mittelberger wrote, only 15 percent of Germantown parents stood in for their own children; by the 1790s, the percentage had risen to over 57.[18] When other relatives did stand in as sponsors, it was more frequently grandparents than any other relation, such as aunt or uncle or cousin.

At the other end of life's cycle, there was no great tendency for families to be buried together. Mothers and their small children frequently appeared close-by in the same cemetery, husbands were usually, though not always, buried next to their wives, but large family plots or private burying grounds were rare. This was not merely a result of membership in different churches leading to burial in sectarian plots; those families who used the public nonsectarian facilities also tended to bury near the end of town in which they lived, rather than near the plots of other kin. There was one interesting exception to the general lack of family solidarity in regard to burial customs. This was the case of those young married women who died before producing any live children of their own. They were frequently listed in the death records by their fathers, rather than by their husbands, and buried with their blood relatives rather than with their new conjugal family.

Finally, lack of extended family closeness is seen in the failure to make use of kinship terms in describing those to whom one was, in fact, related. There is ample proof that most of the more permanent families in Germantown became through the decades more and more intricately entwined in networks of interrelated marriage. Yet, designations of relationship are almost never used, except in referring to parents, grandparents, children, and, infrequently, to uncles, nieces, nephews, and first cousins. While the lack of elaborate kinship vocabulary is generally part of the structure of the English language and indicates a definite attitude toward extended family throughout western cul-

[18] Based on St.M.Rec., Baptism: vols. I-III; Ref.Ch.Rec., Baptisms: all the sponsor lists.

ture,[19] the New England family man of the seventeenth and eighteenth century not only acted in close concert with his distant relatives, he addressed them in recognizable terms of family connection.[20] The Germantown researcher discovers only by luck that the sponsor of a baby was a cousin or a stepsister, or that a young married man was renting a piece of property from his brother-in-law rather than from a stranger. There is no evidence that family ties encouraged joint participation in local organizations or joint action in specific causes, such as the petition to make Germantown the capital or a subscription for the yellow fever poor. By the time the spelling of a particular surname varied from one branch of a family to another, and the descendants were living in different parts of the township, following different occupations, and far separated in terms of accumulated wealth, it is dangerous to think of them in any sociological sense as still being "kin."

One place in which the weakness of kinship ties shows most clearly is in the choice of executors for wills. The position of executor was no mere sinecure in the eighteenth century. It carried with it not only the responsibility of settling the estate properly, but often that of managing the money, selling real estate, providing day-to-day guidance for a widow or young orphan children, and, even more personally, seeing that the children got "good and sufficient schooling," were brought up in the right church, and were put out to appropriate trades or businesses.[21] In 277 wills left by Germantown men between 1700 and 1800, the largest single category of executors, 223, were designated "friend" or "friend and neighbor." Executors chosen from among nuclear family members included 131 wives, 51 eldest sons and 55 younger sons, 17 daughters and 37 sons-in-law; there

[19] Talcott Parsons, "The Social Structure of the Family," *The Family*, pp. 173-175.
[20] Morgan, *Puritan Family*, pp. 150-160.
[21] See, for example, Jacob Gensell, shopkeeper, WB N, #31, p. 69, November 10, 1763.

was a sprinkling of stepsons, grandsons, mothers, stepfathers, and fathers-in-law. On a collateral line there were 23 brothers, 16 brothers-in-law, 1 sister, and 11 nephews. Beyond this, there were only 4 executors who were designated "kinsman." Probably because of the necessity of continual supervision of the young family, a local resident, even if he was not a blood relative, was preferable to a brother who lived twenty miles up-county. When the wife was chosen as one executor, a well-known member of the community was usually picked as the other to assist her in legal matters, members of the Dunkard and Mennonite sects most often choosing coreligionists.[22] Poorer people so frequently designated as "friend and neighbor" some influential member of the town who must have been chosen because of his reputation rather than some actual relationship that, after mid-century, these men began occasionally to renounce the job.[23]

One result of the indifference to and ignorance of all but the most rudimentary ties of kinship was a failure to form any specific marriage patterns within eighteenth-century Germantown. None of the special taboos that usually flourish in communal societies regarding appropriate or forbidden mates seem to have existed. Cousins married cousins, widows married the brothers of their deceased husbands, and even stepbrothers and stepsisters are known to have married.[24] Pragmatism and propinquity seem largely to have

[22] Examples include: Jacob Swenck, WB L, #124, p. 204, January 10, 1759, who asked his "friend" Charles Widderholt to assist his wife in handling a very complicated estate and Peter Shilbert, WB G, #154, p. 196, April 29, 1745, who asked his "Brethren" in the church, Theobald Endt and Henry Slingluff to take care of his affairs and oversee his wife.

[23] The first example noticed was in the probate of the will of Johannes Herbert, WB I, #108, p. 174, October 7, 1749.

[24] The continual intermarriages among the Ashmeads and the Bringhursts are one example; the marriage relations of the Nice family another. Among one set of siblings in this family, there was a sister who married two brothers (serially), and another who married a cousin of the same name (*Schwenkfelder Genealogy*, pp. 146ff.). Two years after Elizabeth Streeper (widow) married George Kastner

governed the choices. Once again, religion was not generally a prime consideration. The Hortter and Rex families were not only members of different churches, but moderately to very active in their respective institutions. Still, this did not hinder intermarriage among their children, particularly since these matches were especially suitable in terms of approximate wealth and social standing. In situations such as this, there was no clear-cut rule on which church the new family unit chose. Sometimes the children were baptized in the mother's old church, yet in other similar cases the babies entered the father's church, and in still a third type half of the children were baptized in St. Michael's, half in the Reformed Church.[25]

On the other hand, among the sectarian Quakers, Schwenkfelders, and Dunkards, religious affiliation was important enough to become a basic factor in the choice of a marriage partner. Members of the sects seem to have maintained much closer contact with those who moved away, and these relationships were often used to help find appropriate spouses for Germantown young people. As late as thirty years after migration, Melchior Schultz wrote home to Germany in 1767, enclosing a map with the homesteads of all the Schwenkfelders still living in Pennsylvania and explaining how the members of the group kept in touch by dividing the area into two districts, the central point of each within an hour's ride of all members of the sect.[26] The Quakers strictly forbade marriage outside the Meeting, and

---

(widower), her grown son, William, married his stepfather's grown daughter, Magdalena; Roach, *Gen.Mag.* (1956), p. 87.

[25] Jacob Hortter, Jr. and Anna Rex, St.M.Rec., Marriage: vol. III, December 10, 1797; Burial: vol. III, September 29, 1800. Frantz Bockius and Susannah Müller, St.M.Rec., Marriage: vol. II, January 23, 1776; Ref.Ch.Rec., Baptisms: June 29, 1777; July 26, 1778; n.d., 1796; May 1799. Isaac Budemann and Magdalena Happel, St.M.Rec., Baptism: vol. I, dom ii, p.t., 1760; Burial: vol. II, June 30, 1767; Confirmation: 1784; Ref.Ch.Rec., Baptisms: July 22, 1770; July 26, 1772; April 9, 1775.

[26] *Schwenkfelder Genealogy*, p. 84.

it was one of the rare causes of disownment for eighteenth-century Germantown members. This necessity of finding Quaker partners even if one had to go to the English community to do it, helps to account, no doubt, for the early anglicization of the Crefeld settlers.

Although there is very little hard evidence to support it, it would seem, particularly in the later part of the century, that diverging life-styles within the township, as well as solidifying class lines, were playing an increasing role in the choice of a marriage partner. The families near Market Square, the Bensells and Ashmeads, the Delaplaines and Wisters, formed connections with wealthy Philadelphians or county gentry of English descent, rather than with local people of the next rank, however substantial. There was also some tendency for this assimilated local population to intermarry with the Quaker mill-owners' families, such as the Robesons and the Livezeys, either by joining the Meeting or marrying members who had fallen away.[27] It is significant, perhaps, that the only case of fornication entered in the records of the Germantown Meeting that did not result in marriage was one in which the girl in question was the maid of the boy's father. Although she was pregnant, he merely denied the charges, and no further action was taken.[28]

During the 1750s, the pastor at St. Michael's kept rather more complete marriage records than was the rule at other times or in other churches, and though there are only about eight years of these entries, they offer some interesting insights into mid-century marriage patterns.[29] The heavy immigration from Germany that took place during the period is reflected in over 20 percent of the 206 marriages recorded during the decade, which listed at least one of the partners as an immigrant; of these, about half were between two

[27] Some of the Ashmeads, for example, had actually been Quakers themselves at one time.

[28] Men's Minutes, 12^d 2mo 1760.

[29] St.M.Rec., Marriage: vol. I, 1751-58, inclusive.

immigrants; in most of the rest it was the groom who was the newcomer. One possible explanation of this is that a male immigrant was more likely to have been working alongside the head of the household, perhaps as a trainee, so that his future status seemed closer to that of the family, while the female was more likely to be merely "a servant." Marriages among servants accounted for 10 percent of the total, and in half of these cases both parties were in service and married with permission of the master or masters involved, often because of pregnancy. When only one partner was actually considered to be a servant, it was almost always a female who married a local resident, either an apprentice or the son of the house in which she worked. Only twice did male servants marry the daughter of the house. On the other hand, there are several cases in which apprentices married the bosses' daughters, and this was not a bad way for an able boy to get ahead. Cornelius Weygandt, for example, a young immigrant, not only learned the trade of turner as an apprentice to John Bechtel and married one of the daughters of the family, but also received an important piece of land and a house near the center of Germantown for a nominal sum and "the love and affection [Bechtel] bore them."[30]

Finally, marriages between apprentices and the girls of the family indicate that familiarity was likely to breed something far more promising than contempt. Although there is no evidence that marriages were arranged in Germantown with an eye to uniting properties, and a great deal of data that points in the opposite direction (i.e. that landholders thought in terms of breaking up their holdings for cash profits), a large number of marriages among the children of neighbors are also recorded. That personal choice played an important part may be inferred from the sizable amount of premarital conception that took place. Still, it must be remembered that even when both parties to a marriage were of long established, solid Germantown back-

[30] Keyser, *Germantown*, p. 233.

ground, the twentieth-century sociological principle that states that "in America, marrying is marrying out rather than marrying in,"[31] seems to have held true, and many of these new families left town to form nuclear units of their own elsewhere. The constant stream of new people through Germantown and its position of centrality within a larger area provide a clue to the opposite side of the coin, in which Germantowners so often found it easy to meet and marry people from out of the township. This also appears to have been largely a matter of individual choice, although the link through which the couple met can often be traced to a business or religious connection of the father's.[32] Parents were often not even consulted on the choice of a partner: Anthony Henckle, for one, tried to overcome this in his will by tying the amount of his daughter's wedding portion to whether or not the girl sought and obtained her mother's consent.[33]

Henckle's problem was particularly thorny, since it touched on an area far more sensitive than merely acquiring parental consent for marriage. Demographic study of Germantown has shown that the age at which a man completed his family (45 percent over 45 years: 20 percent over 50 years) overlapped the age at which he died (from a low of 43 years in the 1750s, to a high of 57 years in the 1790s). This resulted in a situation in which the mother was often left to bring up the children, or at least the younger ones, not always an easy task in a society in which women had very few civil rights and little underlying respect. Fathers frequently attempted to pass their authority on to their surviving wives, and many wills specifically stated,

[31] Karl N. Llewellyn, "Education and the Family: Certain Unsolved Problems," *The Family*, p. 279.

[32] Examples of this might be the daughter of William Dewees, who married her father's erstwhile partner in the Wissahickon Mill, Henry Antes; and the daughter of Henry Rittenhouse, who married Dielman Kolb, a religious associate of her father and grandfather.

[33] Anthony Henckle, WB I, #233, p. 362, February 22, 1750/1.

as did that of Henrich Acker, that all the children must
subject themselves to their mother until they were of age,
while she, if she wished, might bind them out to service or
require them to earn their own living.[34] Another man went
further, not only giving his wife sole right to choose the
trades to which the boys were to be apprenticed, but also
giving her complete control over the disposition of his
property (which was considerable), including the ability
to cut off the sons with a shilling, if they attempted to con-
test her authority.[35] Those children who did not wish to remain under the mother's control might use apprenticeship
as a means of escape: "Those of my children who are under
age and willing to learn trades may be put out but those not
willing are to obey their mother until they come of age."[36]
The Nice family seemed to have particular difficulties with
unruly sons. In 1719 John Nice left equal shares of his
property to all his children, but the eldest son, Matthias,
was to receive his "only if he mends his ways." Otherwise,
the young man was to be cut off with half a crown; the
executors, not including the mother, were to be the judges.
Sixty-three years later, his grandson, in leaving *his* property,
gave his son, Charles, immediate possession of the homeplace, but under the care and inspection of the executors
until he turned twenty-one. If he misbehaved before then,
they were empowered to dispose of the estate. Charles's
mother was named one of the executors,[37] an interesting
comment on the changing position of women.

Other issues related to rearing the young arose from the
likelihood that a parent would die during the minority of
children. A man who was left a widower with young children virtually always remarried, and women did so most of
the time. The census records of 1790 show several house-

[34] Henrich Acker, WB K, #13, p. 20, August 11, 1752.
[35] John Ashmead, WB I, #184, p. 294, August 18, 1750.
[36] John George Cressman, WB O, #183, p. 238, June 13, 1768.
[37] John Nice, WB D, #164, p. 138, October 29, 1719; William Nice,
WB S, #106, p. 104, April 16, 1782.

holds containing small children, where there are no men, and the women are regarded as family head, but there are no listings at all that include either groups of men or men and young children without at least one woman. It was evidently possible for a mother to play a role that accepted a son, even a very young one, as the surrogate head of the family, but impossible for fathers and daughters to assume similar roles. In all of the wills in which there are minor children, there are also wives, although it is frequently obvious that the wife is not the mother of the children. The emphasis on the disposition of the property in the event of the wife's remarriage indicates that this was a common and anticipated circumstance. The stepmother problem had two aspects: one was that the older children of the husband should allow the second wife proper enjoyment of her rights, which often included use of a single room and kitchen privileges in the family dwelling "without molestation"; the other was that the stepmother and a future husband she might marry would not abuse or neglect the children. This was solved through stipulations that if the wife remarried, the children might come into their property right away, or be guaranteed the use of income on invested principal, or collect rent from the new husband to be used for their education and maintenance. Since a stepfather was in no way obligated to provide for the children of his new wife, whether natural or acquired, and, in fact, since he almost never did so, it was particularly necessary that these arrangements be carefully made. On the personal side, it might be provided that a teenager be allowed to choose his own guardian or, in one case, if the wife remarried and the children "suffer," the executors might remove them from the stepmother and bind them out to trades.[38]

---

[38] Examples of some of these situations may be found in Henrich Cress, WB T, #296, p. 514, July 14, 1787; Stephen Riegler, WB U, #173, p. 431, January 23, 1790. For an unusual case of a stepfather's generosity, see Joseph Woollin, WB F, #128, p. 139, November 20, 1739. These were, however, his wife's biological children and had been very young when he married into the family.

Each of these situations was apparently handled individually, but the solutions were all, in fact, related to the larger questions of patriarchalism and changing patterns of family influence and control of its members. Bernard Bailyn provided the framework for this discussion in 1960, with the publication of his enormously influential and creative study on the wider meaning of the term "education."[39] His argument stressed the way in which the American experience of constant confrontation with the unknown and the unexpected required an education preparing one for a life of mobility and rapid change, rather than of stability and tradition. For these purposes the old extended and patriarchal family of the communal society was no longer the best vehicle for socialization of the young; what was needed in education was not transmission of the ways of the past but training in creativity and flexibility. Thus, the family declined as a primary institution of education throughout the seventeenth and eighteenth centuries in New England, despite laws that attempted to bolster its wavering strength. Of course, a child internalizes what *is* rather than what is told him. No amount of preaching the sanctity of the family or of reenforcing it with external legalities, can overcome daily observations of its diminishing power and usefulness as a social tool.[40]

The only question that might be raised in relation to Bailyn's analysis is whether the very traditional, stable, patriarchal family he sees as the starting point of western social development, ever really existed, even in Europe, even before the seventeenth century. Given the results of recent studies of the mobility and nuclear form of rural families in England before the eighteenth century, it is probable that the earlier "ideal" state of the extended family has been

[39] Bernard Bailyn, *Education in the Forming of American Society: Needs and Opportunities for Study*, Chapel Hill, N.C., 1960.

[40] For the modern sociological and psychological supports for this observation, see Merton, "Social Structure," *The Family*, pp. 255-256.

much exaggerated.[41] Certainly the distinctly mobile history of the families that settled in Germantown during the eighteenth century points to a breakdown going on among European kinship groups coincidently with the American experience, if not preceding it. And unless one is prepared to alter the traditional meaning of "patriarchal" considerably, it is hard to see how "families which were nuclear in structure and highly mobile geographically, would, or could, have been patriarchal in character."[42]

The community did, of course, still consider parents responsible for the actions of their children. There are several cases in the early Court Book of the Germantown corporation in which fathers were hauled before the court to pay the costs of a son's misdemeanors: "[A complaint is noted against] Abraham OpdenGraff's son, Jacob, for having taken a horse out of [the sheriff's] custody. The said Jacob answers that he brought the horse thither again. The Court fines him one-half crown to be paid within fourteen days besides what his father is to pay the sheriff according to the law of this corporation."[43] Even when a son was fully grown, the rules of the Germantown Meeting required that his father appear to place a request for a marriage certificate, whenever it was possible. Where the father was not available, another male relative might be called upon to deal with an unruly youngster, such as Israel Roberts who was "stubborn in continuing to frequent Taverns and drinking strong liquors to excess and now also has been fighting."[44] Yet the belief in the preeminence of the family was such that there was evidently some hesitancy on the part of the Meeting to interfere too vigorously in family life. Isaac

[41] Laslett and Harrison, "Clayworth and Cogenhoe," *Historical Essays*, or see, for example, E. E. Rich, "The Population of Elizabethan England," *EHR*, II (1950), pp. 247-265.

[42] Greven, *Four Generations*, p. 99 fn.

[43] Records of the Court of Record, 20ᵈ 11ᵐᵒ 1701.

[44] Men's Minutes, 15ᵈ 9ᵐᵒ 1762; 23ᵈ 10ᵐᵒ 1776.

Deavs was twice rebuked for abusing his aged mother and kicking and beating his sister until they were forced to flee the house in the middle of the night, and then of using ill language to his uncle, but nothing was actually done to deter him.[45]

If the family was to fulfill its responsibilities, however, it needed help, and in every period of rapid social change since the Italian Renaissance that help has been available in the form of some kind of etiquette book, providing a guide for the training of individuals on the way up. This aid was available to Germantown parents for the first time in 1764, with the publication of *Christopher Dock's One Hundred Necessary Rules of Conduct for Children* which appeared in Christopher Saur's *Geistliches Magazien*, and supplied a brief outline of the basic social skills needed by an American child.[46] Except for a good deal of pious admonition to "remember God and meditate upon Him,"[47] Dock, a well-known and popular German schoolmaster of the time, offered intensely practical advice on everything from table manners to stretching in church. The work included a section of rules of behavior for a child in the house of its parents, for behavior in school, on the street, in meeting or church, and in a variety of miscellaneous circumstances. The sections concerning church and school are least innovative, containing mainly conventional ideas for keeping awake during the sermon, removing one's hat at the mention of the name of Jesus, and being obedient to one's teacher and kind to one's fellow students. The material on behavior in the streets is more interesting; it gives an idea of the sorts of things that a country child needed to know to act properly in a town, and, by so doing, painted a rather

---

[45] Ibid., 23^d 12mo 1785; 23^d 5mo 1788.

[46] The following discussion is based on a translation of *Dock's Rules* by Samuel Pennypacker, *Pa.Ger.*, X (1899), pp. 87-97.

[47] Ibid. In part I, see, for example, rules 1-4; 6; 18-19; 21-22; 50. In part II, 51-53. In part III, 66. In part IV, 77.

Brueghel-like picture of street behavior in Germantown, the town of which Dock was probably writing, since it was the one in which he had taught. Among other things, one was expected to refrain from eating in the street, urinating in public, splashing in mud puddles, throwing snowballs, hitching rides on wagons or sleds, and watching the "mountebanks" and "wanton dances" at the annual fair. Advice for the home was even more basic and intimate. The child was instructed in the subtleties of grooming from combing the hair and brushing the teeth to the proper method of spitting and blowing the nose. He was reminded above all to show respect to his elders and to obey his parents, and if there was any difference between the rules in the book and the ways followed in his own home, the child should, of course, respect "what is customary."[48]

The family as the site of more formal training, either academic or manual, was also becoming less important in eighteenth-century Germantown than tradition would lead one to believe. The emphasis New Englanders placed on the need for some kind of formal community-organized education was not unique in the American colonies, nor, indeed, in western society in general. Immigrants arriving in the New World from Europe at the end of the seventeenth and throughout the eighteenth centuries, were coming from a background in which such divergent personalities as Louis XIV of France and Frederick II of Prussia had recognized a need for compulsory state education on the primary level.[49] One of the undebated continuing tasks of the short-lived Germantown corporation had been the operation of the local school. The superiority of an outside agency for dealing with the formal training of youngsters was admitted by the large number of families who supported these institutions in eighteenth-century Germantown, and

[48] Ibid., part I, 48.
[49] Bailyn, *Education*, pp. 26-27, for New England; Anderson, *Europe in the Eighteenth Century*, pp. 284-287, on primary and secondary education in Europe.

who handed over not only their sons to the day school, but their servants and apprentices to the night school and their daughters to the local elementary school.[50]

Following the pattern of many seventeenth-century New Englanders and Virginians,[51] Germantowners set aside specific sums of money or the interest therefrom in their wills to be used for the children's schooling. While the kind of education was most often left to the discretion of the executors, to "be so kind as to assist in a religious and decent and reputable education of my children," the legator was occasionally more definite in what he meant. Thus Henry Cress instructed his executors to keep his two youngest sons at school until they could read and write intelligibly and pay for their "cloathing, meat, drink, washing and lodging as long as they want" to continue their studies, up to the age of twenty-one. His daughter was to be "kept in necessaries" and taught to read and write until she was eighteen.[52]

Since the correlation between job and class has always been close,[53] it might be expected that fathers would have attempted in the new situation to assure the status of their sons by making sure they were trained to follow the occupation that had maintained the family position to that point. Yet, as Bailyn points out, by Benjamin Franklin's time "the automatic transfer of occupational and social role from generation to generation . . . had . . . been so generally dis-

[50] There are several references to a night school in various eighteenth-century documents. The most complete is that in the Minutes of the Union School, October 4, 1762, which stated that the trustees, at the request of the inhabitants, had decided to open a night school for the winter. It was run by the English usher of the Union School, from six to nine o'clock each evening and cost ten shillings per quarter, plus two shillings, six pence for firewood; the pupils were to find their own candles.

[51] Bailyn, *Education*, p. 28.

[52] Christian Lehman, WB Q, #168, p. 201, September 16, 1775; Henry Cress, WB T, #296, p. 514, July 14, 1787.

[53] See Jones, *Towns*, pp. 121-124.

rupted that the exception was becoming the rule."[54] Whatever documentation remains for Germantown bears out the
truth of this statement. Examination of fathers and sons
who appeared on township tax lists, or whose occupations
are given in their wills, shows very little tendency for traditional family patterns to develop. Some of the best established families in certain crafts did maintain themselves
through, perhaps, one son. There is usually a Bringhurst
coachmaker, an Engle tanner, and a Keyser cordwainer to
be found in the records. Yet, by the third generation there
are also Keysers, for example, who are masons, house carpenters, yeomen, and just plain laborers.[55] More frequently,
a son followed some craft that was allied to that of his father,
although not identical to it. Thus the son of a tanner might
become a currier, or that of a chairmaker, a chair trimmer.[56]
The son occasionally raised his status by a change in title,
although the job was actually much the same; Charles
Bensell styled himself "doctor," while actually fulfilling
much the same function for the town as had his father, who
had been known as an "apothecary." In some instances
family continuity in a trade or occupation was maintained
through the daughter's husband who had been an apprentice
in the family business.[57] For the most part, however, fathers do not appear to have trained their sons to follow in
their footsteps; the second generation of most skilled-craft
families appears on the tax lists as "yeoman" or "laborer."

[54] Bailyn, *Education*, p. 36.
[55] For various occupations of the Keyser family, see the Will
Books, especially: Dirck Keyser, WB K, #245, p. 375, February 3,
1756; Dirck, Jr., WB D, #70, p. 54, June, n.d.; Peter, WB D, #325,
p. 405, October 16, 1724; Andrew, WB Q, #200, p. 236, January 8,
1776; Jacob, WB P, #369, p. 528, February 16, 1774; Mathew, WB
O, #34, p. 43, November 5, 1766; Jacob, WB T, #224, p. 381, September 13, 1786; Jacob, WB S, #7, p. 9, September 1, 1781.
[56] Baltus and Matthias Reser, 1773 tax list; William and John
Bringhurst, 1780 tax list.
[57] Morris Leeds, "Genealogical Data in Regard to Leeds Family,"
typescript, 1947, private collection, shows that Tunes Kunders left
his dyeing business to his son-in-law, Griffith Jones.

This factor is undoubtedly related to the departure of Germantown sons for larger pieces of property further up-country, which could be farmed, and leads to the somewhat novel conclusion that socialization within the Germantown family considered as a unit tended to rustication rather than urbanization. From the point of view of the town and the American trend toward city building, the character of Germantown as a growing craft and industrial center was supported by constant new accretions from the outside rather than by the creation of a traditional, inherited class system.

More evidence in this direction can be offered in relation to the softening of the apprentice system and weak parental control over the choice of an occupation in an open market. Morgan, in *The Puritan Family*, laid stress on the individual nature of career choice in seventeenth-century New England, without examining the implications of this pattern in the breakdown of the patriarchal family structure.[58] The Germantown wills make this connection quite clear, however. Only 21 of the 116 men who mentioned minor children specified that they were to be put out to trades. Of those who did, almost all left the choice of a career up to the child himself, and many put it on the basis that the child would be put out, not only to what he wished, but only *if* he wished.[59] In fact, the only definite stipulation that was made was that of one man who ordered that his children might be bound out if they wished, but *not* as servants.[60] A few men left their own tools of the trade to their sons, particularly those whose sons were already grown and were practicing the father's craft; however, most included the tools with the rest of the personal estate, which was to be sold, and the cash proceeds to be divided among the heirs. Some men tried to influence the future directions of their families; one offered a nephew £20 with which to purchase

[58] Morgan, *Puritan Family*, pp. 68-78.
[59] John Paul, WB S, #328, p. 455, November 13, 1783, for example.
[60] George Karst, WB O, #13, p. 18, September 1, 1766.

tools if he would agree to set up in a trade, and another gave his son a stocking loom and frame for his own at the age of twenty-one and an equal share of the estate with his brothers and sisters, if he stayed with his mother and helped to run the business for at least two years after he came of age. If he insisted on going off on his own, he was to have only the tools.[61] Finally, Jacob Surber rather plaintively requested that the best of his tools be saved from sale if there were any of his sons who "wants to use them."[62]

By far the most common expectation of Germantown fathers was that their children would live at home until they were of age, whether or not he was there to supervise them. For this reason, most of the wills directed that the wife, who was usually one of the executors when there were young children involved, should have the right to sell whatever she wished to obtain the cash necessary for keeping the family together. When the youngest child reached twenty-one, or occasionally if the wife remarried before that time, the estate was to be broken up, and each child was to receive his share. This implies, of course, that very few children were shipped off to be apprentices in the homes of others. There is little proof and much doubt that the apprentice system was ever well developed anywhere in the American colonies.[63] Outside of a few instances of apprentice indentures which were validated before the early Court of Record, some listings of runaway apprentices in the eighteenth-century newspapers, and several indentures before the mayor of Philadelphia between 1771 and 1773, the Germantown public records are silent on the subject.[64] The mayor's Indenture Book, however, by its very omissions, is a partial indication of how little apprenticeship must have been part

---

[61] George Reiff, WB L, #160, p. 252, April 25, 1759; Jacob Rebold, WB L, #328, p. 519, September 13, 1767.

[62] Jacob Surber, WB O, #124, p. 164, October 13, 1767.

[63] Bailyn, *Education*, pp. 29-32.

[64] For example, Records of the Court of Record, 14^d 4mo 1692; 8^d 6mo 1693; 9^d 10mo 1701. *Pa.Berichte*, June 19, 1761. *Germantowner Zeitung*, May 31, 1785.

of the Germantown picture. Of over 9,000 indentures that were listed for Philadelphia city and county during this two-year period, only 31 related to Germantown in any way, and of these, 21 had to do with servants rather than apprentices. Only 4 Germantown boys were assigned as apprentices, 1 of these to his own uncle, and in only 6 instances did men from the township arrange to act as masters for boys from other places. The record kept of indentures by the guardians of the poor for Philadelphia between 1751 and 1797 appears to contain but 1 Germantown master and 2 children.[65] Of course, there must have been many private arrangements made as well, but the system could hardly have been very effective. In some cases where it is known that a boy did serve as an apprentice, he frequently followed another trade in his mature life, as did George Bringhurst who, although assigned to Aret Klinckin to learn the trade of weaving, became instead a saddle maker.[66] In the majority of cases a boy was raised at home, and usually, at least for the older boys in a family, by his father. If he learned a trade, it was probably by working days for a neighbor, returning home in the evening. There are, in fact, several examples on the tax lists of sons of one family whose occupations closely parallel those of other families in adjoining houses.[67]

The maintenance of close nuclear ties during the minority of Germantown children did not necessarily engender a close relationship with those children as they matured.

[65] Book of Record of Indentures Before the Mayor of Philadelphia, Oct. 3, 1771–Oct. 5, 1773, Phila.Arch. Volume 2 of the original is missing, but there is a copy of the whole work in *Pa.Ger.*, XVI (1905). "Memorandum Book," The Record of the Guardians of the Poor, manuscript, is also in the Phila.Arch.

[66] *Bringhurst Genealogy.*

[67] 1789 tax list. For example, George Hesser worked as a skin dresser for John Gorgas who lived nearby, rather than working in the inn, which he eventually inherited from his uncle. Peter Fraley made chaises for his neighbor, John Bringhurst, rather than working as a carpenter for his father.

Greven found, in the early generations in Andover, a tendency for married sons to settle close to their fathers, frequently remaining dependent on them.[68] This pattern did not develop in Germantown. There were only 13 cases during the last thirty years of the century in which a grown son, married or single, lived either with, or next door to, his parents for as long as ten years. Joint living apparently was thought of as a temporary condition rather than a permanent way of life.[69] On the other hand, as second-generation and newly arrived parents became less likely to own other land in the outlying parts of Pennsylvania, there was a jump in the percentage of married sons who lived temporarily on their father's property. In 1773, 26 of the 461 ratables had been sons who lived in the parental home or in a tenement on the same land: 19 of these were single, 6 were married, and 4 were living with widowed mothers who still controlled the property. By 1791, on a base of 530 taxpayers, there were 57 men (25 single, 32 married) who lived with their parents. In addition, there were 3 pair of married brothers, 1 pair of single brothers, and 2 pair of one each who were sharing properties. Thus, while the number of taxpayers had increased by only 14 percent, the number of extended family units had jumped by more than 135 percent, the biggest gain coming in the category of dependent married sons. When a family did remain in close contact over a long period, there is usually some documentary evidence of a uniquely cooperative extended pattern: brothers Jeremiah and John Balthesar Traut made a joint will, the Schuster family lived side by side and shared a cow.[70]

---

[68] Greven, "Family Structure," *WMQ*, p. 253, and *Four Generations*, p. 98. In the former work, he calls this pattern a "modified extended family," a term he later abandons.

[69] The statistics in this section are compiled through study of the 1773, 1780, and 1791 tax lists and the 1798 Direct Tax. Some use was also made of the *U.S. Census*, 1790.

[70] Jeremiah and John Balthesar Traut, WB I, #171, p. 775, June 21, 1750. For the Schusters, see 1780 tax list, John and Jacob. There are

Nowhere is the distinction between a rural community based on land value and a craft society based on a money economy more clearly marked than in the area of independence for the grown son. The Germantown pattern more regularly fostered autonomy. In New England, whether or not one accepts the thesis that fathers tended to hold on to their sons by means of control over the land, there was no freedom for the next generation until some property division was made, and this nearly always meant land in the hometown, probably from the home farm.[71] But in the Germantownship, for every married son who continued to live with or near his parents, there were many, many more who did not. Some merely moved out of the house and down the street, renting property on the strength of their earnings, if they had not come into land or inherited money. Of fifty men who were renting houses in Germantown in 1798 and who had other members of their families who owned available property there, thirty-five were nevertheless renting from nonrelatives. There is much evidence in the wills of Germantown fathers to show that sons who came of age and daughters who married were given what was thought to be their fair share of the father's worth, in cash, and sent out on their own, long before the father died. The will might also stipulate that after the younger children were made equal by a cash sum, then those who had already

---

several other examples on the same list, as well as on the 1791 tax list. The Knorrs, for example, each had a cow, but shared a horse.

[71] Demos, *A Little Commonwealth*, tends to disagree with Greven that a patriarchal society was maintained by fathers who held on to their land. He feels that whether the land was legally deeded or merely turned over informally, "for most people a real and decisive measure of economic independence came rather early in their adult lives," pp. 162-170. Greven, however, states that this independence did not come to any marked degree before the fourth generation, *Four Generations*, especially chapter 8, pp. 222-258. Lockridge sees the situation in Dedham as an essentially peasant problem, the son "would stay in the village, for his father's death held out the promise of land," *A New England Town*, pp. 74-75.

received their start might share in the residue, if any. Just as frequently, however, a long departed child was merely recognized by the gift of one to five shillings as "already having had his full share."[72] Occasionally, grown children, known from other sources to be living at the time of the legator's death, are not even mentioned in the will, indicating that they were no longer considered the father's responsibility. With families as spread out by age as the demographic figures show them to have been, a money economy provided a much more sensible way for the eldest to become independent. Since it was usually directed that the homeplace was to be kept together and the money of the estate used to support the family until the youngest child was twenty-one (or until the mother died, whichever came last), it might have been too late, practically speaking, for the older siblings to start families of their own, by the time they acquired their inheritances.

There was also some precedent, although not as much, for setting a child up on his own property before the father died. This was usually done only by the older families, who possessed a great deal of land in the up-county "German purchase" which had been part of the original Penn grant, or by wealthy men who owned several lots and houses within the Germantownship itself. Very rarely, the son was allowed to live on property he would one day inherit, but without any rights to the place until the father died. In his will George Riter finally made over to his son, John, "the thirty-five acre plantation in the Germantownship where he already lives," and to Michael, a younger son, "the one hundred acre plantation in Marlboro township, Montgomery County, where he already lives."[73] Those who could afford it, however, were more likely to provide their sons with legal title to their separate establishments, often as a

---

[72] J. Theobald Endt, WB O, #130, p. 171, November 17, 1767.
[73] George Riter, WB X, #103, p. 150.

wedding present.[74] There were instances, too, in which fathers sold their land to their sons or sons-in-law, and this was regarded as the equivalent of having given them a share in the estate. Thus, John Gumre's son, John, was provided for in full "having already bought from his father the plantation where he lives in Roxborough," while son, David, was to receive £25 and the family home for the price of £150, paid to the estate at £10 per year. The money was to be used to support the widow and the younger children.[75] Often the purchase price in these cases was far less than the true value of the property; one father sold to his daughter and her husband a house and lot worth £205 for £5 and the "love and affection I bear them."[76]

The infrequency with which property was passed on while the father was still alive appears to have been due less to a desire to enact the heavy-handed patriarch than to a disinclination to cast oneself in the role of King Lear. Even relatively poor parents set their children up with as much as they could manage to spare when the child was ready to go on his own, but rarely at the expense of their own comfortable old age. The problem of the aged and their support was a particularly painful one in a newly emerging associational society where family links had weakened but community accountability was not yet established. Sociologists have frequently blamed urbanization and modern technology for "gravely interfering with the efficient functioning of the family as the unit responsible for the economic

---

[74] For example, see the will of John Luckens, WB G, #130, p. 157, January 24, 1744/5, who mentioned a previous gift of 300 acres above North Wales where "his son now lives," or John Johnson, WB X, #33, p. 45, March 17, 1794, whose son had received 50 acres and a house on Main Street in Upper Germantown. This had not been so quickly given; the house had been built as a wedding present in 1768, but the deed was not transferred until 1787. Deeds in Brief, "6306 Germantown Ave."

[75] John Gumre, WB F, #68, p. 70, May 24, 1738.

[76] Miller property, Deeds in Brief, "7413 Germantown Ave."

welfare of its members, and notably in regard to the support of the aged."[77] But the roots of the problem go right back to eighteenth-century towns like Germantown—to the beginnings of nonagricultural communities and the proliferation of mobile, nuclear families. The understanding of the responsibilities of the community did not extend, even in the flawed and hard-hearted manner of the nineteenth century, to an obligation to provide for the poor and elderly, terms that were close to synonymous, since a society with an endemic labor shortage could always find a useful place for young, able-bodied persons without family support. In its original charter, the government of Germantown had offered such aid as a possibility, though not an obligation: "Poor and old people, under our jurisdiction, who cannot longer support themselves by the labor of their hands, and indigent widows and orphans may make themselves known to the General Court, by which they shall be helped as far as possible."[78] Yet, ninety years later, the poorhouse of Germantown listed only ten old women and two old men as residents.[79]

The family, on the other hand, was often too thoroughly scattered, too busy with its own affairs, to pay much attention to its parents. Certainly, the position of the elderly in a traditional environment as the transmitters of accumulated wisdom was not applicable to the new situation where, as Bailyn put it, "To none was there available reliable lore or reserves of knowledge and experience . . . parents no less than children faced the world afresh. In terms of mere effectiveness . . . the young . . . stood often at advantage . . . they thereby gained a strange, anomalous authority difficult to accommodate within the ancient structure of family life."[80] There are many indications in the German-

---

[77] Eveline M. Burns, "Personal Interaction and Growth in Family Life," *The Family in a Democratic Society: Anniversary Papers of the Community Service Society of New York*, New York, 1949, p. 15.

[78] "Laws," *Pa.Ger.*, IX, p. 328.

[79] *U.S. Census*, 1790.   [80] Bailyn, *Education*, pp. 22-23.

town records that parents and children completely lost touch with each other under these conditions: Lawrence Sweitzer, for example, in his will called himself "antient and weak" and left a small amount to his sons "if they were still living," which he did not know.[81] Even when the children's whereabouts were known, if they were located at a great distance, the aging parents might be stranded by a lack of any kin near enough to help out. In 1742 John Bernhard Keppler was forced to sell his large, valuable, and beloved "plantation" in Sommerhausen for this very reason: "The cause of selling this Plantation is the owner's being unable (through Old Age) to look after it, his children being settled from him."[82]

Perhaps most important of all for the light it throws on family relationships is the evidence of lack of filial interest, even among those who lived in close proximity to their parents. There are numerous examples of successful sons living right in Germantown, whose parents could be determined from the tax lists to be living in the most marginal of circumstances. In 1773, to cite one illustration, Conrad Wolf, a laborer, was worth £6, the lowest valuation on the tax scale. He was, nevertheless, providing a home for his son, Christopher, a butcher, who was married and assessed at £6, the same as his father. By 1780 the situation had changed considerably. Christopher had become a substantial citizen; he had moved to Upper Germantown, owned a house and three acres of land, and kept a servant and a cow; he was assessed in the top 20 percent of the township's taxpayers. His father, on the other hand, was now sixty-nine years old and could probably no longer work full time as a laborer; he was renting a tiny house on one-half acre in the "poorhouse" section of town and was one of the few people in Germantown rated so poor that he paid no tax at all.[83]

[81] Lawrence Sweitzer, WB Q, #238, p. 285, May 8, 1776.

[82] *Pa.Gaz.*, April 22, 1742.

[83] 1773, 1780 tax lists; St.M.Rec., Baptism: vol. I, October 29, 1750; Burial: vol. II, March 14, 1788. Also WB X, #349, p. 524, December

Other signs of weak family responsibility, emotional if not physical, are more subtle, but they exist. There was the son who kept track of every penny he spent on his mother during her last illness and charged the estate with it: "Peter Ax for keeping [his mother] for nine weeks before death." There was another son who charged for six years' service to his father, who had become disabled, and there was a family of daughters who hired "a woman to sit up with the corpse" of their mother rather than do it themselves.[84]

Small wonder that the individual came to think first of providing for himself and his wife in old age, without placing much reliance on the tender, loving care of his children! When such concern was forthcoming, it was usually rewarded in some special way: Ulrich Basler left all of his "small estate or effects" to his youngest daughter, Mary, and her husband, since "they well deserve the same for their kindness and respect to me in my advanced age and weakness." The other children were cut off with five shillings. In addition, "having brought up the son of [his own son, Joseph] to nearly ten years and received no consideration from said Joseph, he [the grandson] is to serve Mary until seventeen years in place of board."[85] If there were no children to whom one might turn, then it was perhaps possible to strike a bargain with a collateral relative. This was how Abraham Paul provided "social security" for himself and his wife. He agreed to leave his entire estate, real and personal, to his nephew and namesake in return for the services of the younger man who was to live with him on the planta-

---

22, 1796. By the time the son died in 1796, he was status conscious enough to style himself a "victualler" rather than a butcher.

[84] Information of this nature can be found in the final estate accounts, which occasionally accompany the inventory and the original copy of the will on file in the City Hall Registry of Wills, Philadelphia. Those cited are indexed as follows: John Frederick Ax, Accounts, 1766, #155; George Dannehower, Accounts, 1795, #128; Christiana Hause, Accounts, 1758, #59.

[85] Ulrich Basler, WB Q, #268, p. 317, July 20, 1776.

tion, working the land and furnishing the elder Pauls with meat, drink, clothes, and all other necessaries for a comfortable life, and also providing care and attendance when either of the old people became sick or infirm.[86] Where none of the relatives was willing or able to care for the elderly, they might all be cut out of the will in favor of some neighbor who was more obliging.[87]

The primary way in which a man protected himself against the exigencies of old age, however, was by hanging on to what he had. A small cash payment, either loan or outright gift, to send a son on his separate way, some furniture and perhaps a few pounds to set up a newly married daughter in housekeeping—these were, in fact, shrewd insurance by which a father guaranteed to himself the use of his own property without having to support dependent children. Those children who stayed at home, living with the parents, or on the property, and following the father's career, often fared worse than those who took their stake and became independent, either in Germantown or elsewhere. Sons whose trades required greater skill than that of the father often outstripped the older generation on the tax lists, as had Christopher Wolf. But sons who either followed the same trade, or who were classed merely as "laborers" or "yeomen" never appear to have achieved complete independence until after the old man's death. Peter Dedier was a stocking weaver working with his father, John. He lived at home as a single man paying only a head tax until he married and moved out in 1774. Six years later, he was renting a small property near his father, and although he already had four children, his father kept a tight rein on the purse strings, being worth, in 1780, more than four times as much as the son. It was not until 1789 that Peter finally came into possession of the family homestead

[86] Abraham Paul, WB T, #302, p. 523, August 8, 1787.
[87] See, for example Christoph Streyszka, WB E, #294, p. 218, February 7, 1732/3, or Nicholas Schandey, WB M, #242, p. 429, December 1, 1762.

and then with the requirement that he pay his stepmother £15 a year out of the estate, allowing her a room, a set of stairs, use of the kitchen and "necessaries," and a decent amount of furniture and cooking equipment. Meanwhile, his brother who had left home as soon as he came of age, was long in possession of a thirty-five-acre plantation in Bristol township, to which there were no strings attached. By 1798, four years after his stepmother had died, nine years after the death of his father, and twenty-five years after his own marriage, Peter Dedier was finally independent and moderately prosperous.[88] His case was fairly representative of the small minority of sons who chose to follow an older, more traditional pattern in a new and individualistically oriented society.

The arrangements by which John Dedier protected his wife were typical of the provisions made for older widows in eighteenth-century Germantown, although the average widow might have to rent the rest of the house to strangers while keeping a room for herself, or rent a room in the home of a neighbor, since the children so frequently moved away, leaving her behind. The twenty-six women listed as living alone and head of house at the time of the 1790 census testify to this situation, for when they lived with a son or other relative, they were counted as part of that family. The relatively lonely position of elderly women is also highlighted by the fact that when they had discretionary property and drew up wills of their own, widows chose "friends and neighbors" as executors twice as frequently as they chose sons and daughters.

[88] This family history is a compilation, as are many of the others, of the tax record, the census, the church (in this case, Reformed) baptism, marriage, and burial records, wills (WB U, #104, p. 245, March 21, 1789), and inventories (1789, #104). Where a substantial number of these sources produce material, it is possible to put together a fairly adequate picture of family life. As in other cases, it is important to recognize the name through its many spellings. "Dedier" appears in various places as "de Dieu," "Dittier," and "Deteir" as well as the spelling that has been accepted here.

The husband had to face a dilemma when trying both to protect his wife in her old age and to make sure his children got their inheritance in time to give them a youthful start. It was probably for this reason, rather than for any attempt to keep the wife faithful to the grave, that most legators stipulated that the widow, if she remarried, lost all but her original dower rights in the estate. Once she had a new husband, he could be expected to provide for her future and the inheritance could be used at once for the benefit of the children. Further proof of this lies in the fact that when there were no children the wife almost always received the whole estate outright (barring small bequests to charity or to siblings and their offspring), without any restriction on her right to remarry.[89]

For the widow who had children and remained unmarried, the husband had several choices: he could allow her the full control of the property, including the homestead as long as she lived, usually excepting some sort of money payment to each child when it arrived at age; he could allow her full use and control of the property until the youngest child reached maturity (variously considered to be between fourteen and twenty-one years) at which time all real and personal property would be disposed of, the money divided equally between wife and children, the wife receiving a share equal to that of one (or sometimes two) of the children; or the children could receive equal shares of the estate in cash, while the wife retained the right of house privileges, as did Susannah Dedier, plus some income in cash and goods to be paid yearly by the children. Where the heirs desired to sell the house, they were obligated to provide their mother with a comfortable room elsewhere during her life, though, interestingly enough, there was little idea that she should live with them. The use of houseroom as the widow's share was most frequently chosen when the wife was also the biological mother of

[89] John George Bogert, WB L, #88, p. 151, September 9, 1758; Jacob Hinn, WB N, #70, p. 134, May 19, 1764.

the family. When she was the stepmother, she was more often given the cash settlement, which allowed her greater independence from her grown stepchildren.[90]

These basic patterns of inheritance are not dissimilar to those followed in English rural villages today.[91] But there were almost as many actual methods for disposing of one's property after death to the next generation, as there were eighteenth-century Germantown property holders.[92] The most common division of property was also the simplest: the executors were to hold a public sale of everything and then divide the resulting cash equally among all the children, but a trend to individualism in the settling of family matters had taken precedence over any customary kind of division based on traditional ways. Some, to be sure, followed the old German custom of leaving the homestead to the youngest, rather than the oldest, child.[93] Given the long age span between the oldest and youngest and the weak and nuclear form of family relationship that existed in eighteenth-century Germantown, there was a good deal of logic to the choice. Whether the father was still living or not, the oldest children were likely to be long established elsewhere by the time the youngest child came of age, so that in a sense he was the only one left to provide for. It is interesting that the Germantowners who were not German by ancestry or who had been most completely Anglicized less

[90] Examples of one of these types may be found in just about any Germantown will where a man leaves both a wife and children. For the various types, see: Jacob Engle, WB Y, #119, p. 139, February 26, 1799; Adam Haas, WB S, #55, p. 55, January 5, 1782; George Karst, WB O, #13, p. 18, September 1, 1766; Dennis Streeper, WB N, #295, p. 547, July 25, 1766.

[91] Williams, *Ashworthy*, p. 86, p. 95.

[92] Lemon notes that for rural Pennsylvanians, individual conditions rather than custom, or even law, tended to guide decisions on division of property. *Best Poor Man's Country*, pp. 91-92.

[93] Heinrich Boehmen, *Martin Luther: Road to Reformation*, John W. Doberstein and Theodore G. Tappert, trans., 1946: rpt. New York, 1960, pp. 3-4 describes this form of inheritance as it had existed in parts of Germany since the Middle Ages.

frequently chose this method of transmission of property, no matter how sensible it appears to the outsider.[94]

Since the land itself was not charged with any particular emotional overtones, one finds very little antagonism among Germantown families over the matter of the division of the estate. Out of 103 cases that reached the Common Pleas Court of Philadelphia during the second half of the eighteenth century, and in which the sheriff and a jury had to be called to divide a piece of land over which a family could not agree, only 4 involved Germantown.[95] In a nonagricultural community, the question of impartible inheritance was irrelevant to the main issue of a fair share for each of the heirs. In fact, a piece of town property that was divided and had improvements in the form of buildings, wells, and the like added to the newly created lots, gained in total value, despite the smaller size of each holding. Rationality, therefore, usually governed the apportionment of the property. Where a father had left his land to be sold and the money equally divided, the family frequently divided the land instead, deciding among themselves what made a fair share; each was then free to sell or stay, as he saw fit. In one case, the parent could not decide what would make an equitable division of his property and left each of his three sons a one-third interest in each of his three lots. After he died, the brothers wasted no time in deciding for themselves, and each bought the others out of one of the lots for five shillings; a reasonable solution only arrived at by men who saw land as an economic, rather than a psychic, asset.[96]

---

[94] For contrast, see Garret Rittenhausen (WB G, #10, p. 33, February 19, 1742/3) who left land outside the town to his older son and the homestead to his younger son, who was also to make cash payments to the elder; and Thomas Roberts (WB K, #285, p. 450, August 24, 1756) whose home went to the eldest son, the youngest receiving a house and lot in Philadelphia.

[95] Prothonetary of the Court of Common Pleas, Partition Deeds 1740–1869, mss, Phila.Arch.

[96] Deeds in Brief, "Vernon Park, 5708 Germantown Avenue," February 21, 1740/1: Peter Shoemaker, Sr., to three sons Isaac, Peter, and John. April 25, 1741; Peter, Jr. and John to Isaac.

Where one sibling really wanted to stay in Germantown while the others planned on moving, there appears to have been little difficulty about releasing shares to the stay-at-home. This was often a daughter, married to a Germantown man who had been renting property, and who thus was enabled to acquire land of his own.[97]

A fair share was not necessarily an equal share, but the conventions governing the meaning of "fair" seem to have been accepted by everyone. For many, of course, it meant exactly equal, without any distinction as to sex or particular condition of an individual child. There were, however, some intensely personal exceptions: an extra £100 to John Bringhurst's son, Isaac, "being lame"; a special gift of money to Anna DelaPlaine's son-in-law, Joseph Ferree, in "consideration of his care and kindness"; an extra £15 to George Moyer's son, John, to "make him equal with the rest of his brothers."[98] There were also a few more general exceptions to the principle of share and share alike. In keeping with the extra portion awarded to the eldest son of those who died intestate, many legators showed some slight favoritism to their first-born male heir.[99] It was hardly ever a full double share, often being as simple as John Roop's bequest to his oldest son, Cornelius, of "£12 over the others."[100] In the earlier part of the century, girls frequently received less than their brothers, the dowry decided upon at marriage usually being considered their full share, no matter how successful the father was in later years. In keeping with Bailyn's thesis that the status of women tended to rise in colonial America, daughters were more and more

[97] See, for example, Deeds in Brief, "5450 Germantown Ave., Thomas Armat House," April 6, 1784; March 29, 1792.

[98] John Bringhurst, WB X, #152, p. 221, April 4, 1795; Anna Dela-Plaine, WB W, #40, p. 79, March 8, 1791; George Moyer, WB W, #142, p. 238, April 9, 1792.

[99] For a description of the workings of the Pennsylvania intestate rules in the eighteenth century, see J. G. Rosengarten, *Pa.Ger.*, XIII, p. 75.

[100] John Roop, WB W, #99, p. 176, November 2, 1791.

placed on equal terms with sons as the century progressed.[101] On the other hand, the girl's portion was far more frequently left to her in trust, giving her the right only to the interest, while her brother received his share outright. While this was occasionally an effort to keep her money out of her husband's hands, it more often appears that she was thought of as needing the help of the executors in managing an estate. In addition, the idea that women might own real property with the rights of transfer and sole control was slow to develop. A woman who had such property to leave in a will of her own sometimes felt it necessary to defend that right, as did Rebecca Keyser who asserted that her estate was left her by her mother and she was therefore "fully empowered" by "instruments of writing" to dispose of same.[102] It was only at the very end of the century that a man might, like Philip Conrad, leave all his property, real and personal, "including my house and lot dwelling" outright to his widow, while in only one case did a man whose money had originally come from his wife, leave it back to her when he died: "since all residue of my estate came by means of my wife, I give it back to will as she chooses among her children or grandchildren."[103] Even in this last case, the husband's wishes are implicit, for the wife, Ann, is not to give the money to the poor or a favorite servant or friend, merely to divide it according to *her* own desires among *his* designated heirs.

There is one other area of inheritance of enough general importance to be discussed here. A glance at the demographic statistics on mortality (figure 6) shows that one of

[101] Bailyn, *Education*, p. 25. For earlier and later examples, see Aret Klincken, WB C, #57, p. 71, February 20, 1707/8; and Jacob Bowman, WB X, #473, p. 689, January 22, 1798. It is also interesting to compare the variation in custom from one generation to another within a single family. For this, see Deeds in Brief, "Wyck, 6026 Germantown Ave."

[102] Rebecca Keyser, WB U, #19, p. 65, February 23, 1788.

[103] Philip Conrad, WB Y, #199, p. 235, November 9, 1799; John Wynn, WB T, #297, p. 517, July 16, 1787.

every five people who lived to maturity would die by the age of forty. This meant that an elderly man who had several children, themselves married and with families of their own, was bound to have lost at least one of them by the time he himself died. Decisions were, therefore, required on provisions to be made for the offspring of deceased children. The most common legacy was that they should share in the single equal portion that would have been the parent's lot, were that parent still alive. For grandchildren whose parents were still alive, a wealthy legator sometimes left cash bequests of several pounds at age, or small gifts of affection to a favorite youngster: "to Susannah Nice, youngest daughter of my daughter, Susannah Nice, six silver teaspoons."[104]

In the final analysis, signs of special favor or warm kinship ties are rare among the Germantown records and only serve to highlight the fragile and transient meaning of "all in the family." The quickly changing nature of life and opportunities in an open-ended New World community favored the individual who was free of old ties, responsibilities, and prejudices. The family structure best adapted to training and nurturing people for this way of life was the smallest possible unit, the nuclear group, which really operated under a kind of utilitarian contract limited to that moment during which the parties involved might benefit from the relationship. The parallel between this sort of family and an associational society is obvious: the rights and obligations were conscious and revocable, not internalized and eternal. Each family was free to develop its own mores and customs, setting itself apart from other units and cutting itself off from the support of a common pool of tradition. The loss of stability and security was balanced by the ability of the individual to move freely into the new society unhampered by the demands of a large, tightly structured family or kinship group.

[104] Susannah Nice, WB X, #71, p. 98, August 16, 1795.

CONCLUSION

In 1683 a small group of men from Holland met in a cave that served as the Philadelphia home of Francis Daniel Pastorius to draw lots for their right to land and a voice in the building of a new little city in Penn's woods. Nearly 120 years later, in the handsome brick City Hall just a few blocks away from the old Delaware River caves, a group of wealthy owners of much of that same Germantown land opened the books on a subscription offering, which turned the main road of the town into a turnpike and the town itself into a suburban backwater. The physical changes that had taken place on the now-valuable property of the Germantownship were, of course, tremendous. A hilly forest of tall trees and tangled undergrowth bisected by a narrow, crooked Indian trail had been transformed into a bustling, prosperous community of homes and gardens, workshops and stores, schools and churches. The trail had become an important road, still exposing the traveler to choking dust or impassable mud at times, but wider, straighter, and lined with fruit trees, taverns, and inns. Pastorius had intended that Germantown should become a city, and in many ways it had. Land was measured by perches rather than acres, and valued for its commercial location rather than its arability. The majority of the inhabitants lived on less than an acre of land, and all but 15 percent of them earned their living in trade or manufacture. Work was frequently divorced from the home; numerous workshops and stores jostled for position with the rows of narrow houses that bordered the Main Road in the most built-up part of town. The population was a polyglot one, made up of a bewildering array of nationalities and religions. Even in terms of absolute numbers, for its day, the place was considerable, as it possessed the fourth largest population of any Pennsylvania community outside of Philadelphia.[1]

[1] According to Lemon's data for other communities (*Best Poor*

Yet the fact is that eighteenth-century Germantown was described by many contemporaries as a village—a thriving village to be sure, but a village just the same. Others, perhaps less used to visiting Philadelphia, or with less experience of big cities in general, perceived that there was something here that was too separated from rural tradition to be merely a village; these made use of the word "town." This lack of recognition persisted over the course of time as the population grew, houses sprang up, and public buildings—church, market, and school—were built and enlarged. If anything, contemporary attitude became less inclined to endow Germantown with urban attributes. Contemplation of this state of affairs is sobering to the historian, with his adding machine and formulas for measuring change. He must realize that no matter how much the quantifiable data change, the atmosphere of a community may remain the same, and it is this atmosphere that will have more effect on the inhabitants than a long series of statistics that indicates that their town is getting more urban by the minute (or decade). Nor, of course, did the people of that time have any access to, or interest in, mathematical statements of the way in which their community was changing; the era of self-conscious involvement in one's own sociological or psychological inner workings was still far in the future.

There must have been some essential way in which life did not change in quality the way that it did in quantity; some way by which things were not really very different at all, although the Mennonite meetinghouse was now built of stone, and a tenement housed several workmen where once the Bringhurst family had raised its vegetables for the table. Lemon found that this continuity of a mode of living existed in rural Pennsylvania despite "marked alteration of the surface of the land," backed by an ever-present belief in individual material success, and a desire to preserve free-

---

Man's Country, figure 36, p. 136), and the *U.S. Census*, 1790, only Lancaster, York, and Reading were larger.

dom and privacy, rather than to build community.[2] The whole theme of Warner's *Private City* revolves around much the same discovery, applied to the burgeoning metropolis of Philadelphia. These concepts are not easy to apply to Germantown: the material is so spotty in the beginning that the individual settler stubbornly resists resurrection, and the records are most frustratingly missing just when the greatest physical changes are taking place. Yet this very gap has its own negative evidence to offer. If the character of the settlement, or of the people who inhabited it changed drastically as Germantown grew, there should be some kind of a marked "before" and "after" appearance to the picture of economic, institutional, and family life on either side of the chasm. But there isn't. Social goals and methods of community life change little; the latter show an increasing tendency to become associational rather than informal, but this is more an acceleration than a change of direction. A pattern of individualism and pragmatism as opposed to one of communalism and tradition is common to both sides of the data gap, adding the evidence of a "half-way" situation to the same side of the Pennsylvania scale as that already weighted by Warner and Lemon in their work on the large city and the rural county.

If this pervasive pattern has validity, one must seriously consider that the opportunistic individualist is not really "American" as has so often been thought, but is, in fact, a European transplant—perhaps not a true example of European society in general (it would take a great deal of research to test that thesis), but at least of those who made the decision to migrate to the New World. Certainly the immigrant who came to Germantown in the eighteenth century had acquired the habit of self-reliance by the time he arrived. He was already an individualist, basically oriented toward solving his own problems in his own way, rather than by reference to the ways of tradition. Had he been a strong traditionalist, it is unlikely that he would have

[2] *Best Poor Man's Country*, pp. 218-219.

embarked on such an adventure in the first place. Both Lemon and Warner come to the same conclusion in relation to the material that they handle. While talking of the reasons for the development of family farms rather than the creation of rural villages in colonial Pennsylvania, Lemon notes that "the fundamental force leading to dispersion was the rise of individualism over peasant values in western Europe," while Warner considers that privatism, which is his own category of individualism, is common to the development of urban areas in many nations besides America.[3] The opportunistic individual, therefore, is probably not an American type in the sense that he developed in the western hemisphere in response to the wilderness situation, but rather a European type in the sense that he was an individual who was willing, even anxious, to emigrate to a strange, but promising new environment.

The outward manifestation of the individualist of the seventeenth and eighteenth centuries was his willingness to move. Whether he perceived mobility as negative or positive—a method of getting away from religious persecution or a way to achieve a better economic position in life—is less significant than the fact that he considered moving and facing the incalculable challenges of the unknown to be a superior way of life to accepting the limitations of familiar, traditional paths. Again, this was neither new nor unique to the American immigrant, nor, in fact, to the mobile European who moved across mountains and rivers rather than across the ocean. The medieval cities of Europe were, after all, peopled by those who saw no future in landed servitude but who were willing to take their chances on not being found for a "year and a day" and acquiring the right to chart their own futures. The lesson once learned, however, was unlikely to be forgotten; moving away was a possible, even a desirable, solution to social, economic, or personal problems. In the end, perhaps, mobility became a way of

[3] Ibid., p. 108; Warner, *Private City*, p. 4.

life, an end in itself, rather than the means to a better tomorrow.

Casting off traditional patterns of behavior and thought, particularly those that invested the land with mystical connotations, combined with the moral justification of the profit motive, which was supplied by the Protestant ethic, made it just as possible for a first-generation seventeenth-century immigrant to act out of rationalized economic self-interest, as it was for his Americanized descendant, seven generations later. It is unnecessary to quarrel over whether the lure of the New World was symbolic or concrete: Pastorius was perfectly comfortable collecting rents for the Frankfort Company and amassing a considerable fortune to pass on to his sons, while at the same time explaining that he had come to Pennsylvania because of a strong "desire in my Soul . . . to lead a quiet, godly & honest life in a howling wilderness."[4] The use of land as an economic tool, easily converted into cash when the time came to move on and "make something of oneself," was common to all German-towners of every period and every nationality, to about the same degree. There is no statistical correlation through time or by background between traditionalism and first-generation action in relation to land transfer either by deed or by will. Continual dispersion of holdings took place among the majority, with a slight exception in the middle decades of a tendency to centralize and increase land ownership among a tiny minority of long-term residents. From what can be gleaned from the wills, there was never any generally held idea that children would prefer the homestead over a cash settlement as a patrimony. That properties broke down further and more rapidly toward the end of the eighteenth century, was a function of increased population pressure and land value rather than a change in its emotional value for its owners.

The same tendency toward dispersion, which was notice-

[4] Pastorius, "The Beehive," p. 223.

able in the way that families dealt with their property in colonial Germantown, runs through a great variety of other measures that can be applied to the study of family life in general. The overriding observation on dispersion as a core factor is that family development was nuclear in form from the very beginning of settlement, when the immigrants tended to arrive as individuals or nuclear families rather than in large extended groups. Even where the latter was the case, scattering soon took place, as each family head sought to go wherever he was most likely to better himself. There are no clear-cut indications that traditional family patterns ever developed, and many to illustrate the way in which each household handled its own business to provide itself with the best pragmatic solutions for specific situations. Kin were rarely chosen to stand sponsor for infants, to look after orphaned children, or to assist a widow in executing her husband's will. Since it was common to marry out of the church, families drifted away from each other in relation to religious practice, and even burial did not seem to bring relatives together in a collective plot, or even in the same cemetery.

The other force in addition to mobility that intensified the isolated quality of the Germantown individual was the heterogeneity of the region into which he moved. This was a condition faced most critically by those who came to the middle colonies, and it added an extra dimension to the difficulty of developing community life or of joining one already in existence. Unlike a European wanderer who left the countryside for a town or city in some other part of his homeland, or an Englishman who came to New England to build a new life, the immigrant to Pennsylvania did not find a new home that had any relation at all to his old one. For the community he joined in the New World was not an entity with any common bond of accepted beliefs into which he might be absorbed, but a collection of individuals, much like himself in their individualism, but unlike in every other respect—in language, in religion, in background. It is obvious that the raw material for a communal society was not present, but the Pennsylvania inhabitant was not terribly interested in a carefully worked out associational form of government either. In Germantown, since he had brought no ready-made institutions with him, he shaped his community through pragmatic solutions to everyday problems within a framework of the government provided by the English proprietor. When that framework was changed from a relatively independent borough to an almost powerless township, there was no great objection raised. County records throughout the century refer to problems in getting Germantowners to fill offices or sit on juries, similar to those noted by the original borough government. Much of the newspaper space dealing with politics in Germantown was taken up with men who had somehow gotten onto the ballot and were asking to be taken off again. Perhaps one of the main reasons why Germantown never appeared to assume urban status in the eyes of contemporary observers was the total disinclination of its inhabitants to engage in the building of institutional symbols. Those civic chores that could only be cared for by the local community were handled either in the scattershot method of voluntary association, as used in rural Pennsylvania, or in the committee fashion that had become the pattern for Philadelphia.[5] Those areas most apt to relate to an urban environment, such as the Library Company or the fire company, were dealt with by the Philadelphia method; those required anywhere, such as schools or cemeteries, were controlled by the more rural association of "the Inhabitants of Germantown." Rules and regulations, indicative of associational methods of doing things were often necessary, even in these rather informal institutions, since the actual individual members were constantly changing.

Heterogeneity also played the greatest part in shaping the institution of the church, since the many different re-

[5] Lemon, *Best Poor Man's Country*, pp. 115-116; Warner, *Private City*, p. 10.

ligions in Germantown from the time of its founding made the principle of dispersion once again the operative factor. Although religious persecution was on the wane in Europe after 1680, and many of those who came to Germantown came from an area in which toleration was fairly well established, the degree to which the various denominations and sects managed to get along is probably particularly related to the conditions of Pennsylvania, of which Germantown was a kind of miniature reproduction. As there was very little areal or social segregation among the members of differing congregations or, for that matter, between those who were religious and those who were unchurched, it was necessary to adapt to the idea that one's own beliefs were not "the only way to heaven," and that traditions too deeply held or acted upon were bound to create difficulties in adjusting to life. Proof of this lay in the fact that those religious disputes that disturbed the peace of the community took place between members of the same denominations, where doctrinal issues were unavoidable, rather than among those of different churches. Nor did this change throughout the century, from the time of the Keithian troubles of the Quakers in the 1690s, through the exodus of many of the Moravians, the organizational disputes of the Lutherans, and the financial difficulties of the Reformed Church after the Revolution. What emerged was the lesson that one could use the church for the utilitarian needs of life, without being dogmatic or rigid about structure or philosophy, and that this shallow, even superficial attitude toward religion would minimize the potential for friction and make life more pleasant for everyone. Intergroup cooperation was therefore high, and extended to the sharing of facilities, as well as to contributions for denominational projects.

An attitude of tolerance or, more probably, apathy toward differences marked the one area in which centrality, rather than dispersion, was an active feature in the sociology of Germantown. The pragmatic approach to life, which sought individual economic betterment as a primary goal, dictated that it was much easier to pursue one's interests if one could communicate directly with others. People in rural areas where living was more segregated by nationality were less likely to require a common language, but urban centers, particularly Philadelphia, almost demanded English as a passport to success. The street signs may have been bilingual, but this was more for the convenience of new arrivals or occasional country visitors than for top-level local businessmen. Germantown manufacturers and merchants not only had to contend with Philadelphia in terms of sales and orders, but also in relation to legal business conducted on the county level at the downtown courthouse. Even the small craftsman or tradesman, whose orientation might be entirely centered in Germantown, could hardly succeed without the patronage of the resident summer people, most of whom were completely English in culture and descent. But acculturation was not entirely limited to language facility. It was not easy to follow even those personal old traditions of family life that had been brought along when wife and husband were from different backgrounds, religions, and nationalities, and while intermarriage as a force for acculturation was illustrated most clearly by the Quakers, it operated among the rest of the population as well. Lemon found very little difference in the behavior of members of one national group and another,[6] and the Germantown material corroborates that finding, both in respect to life-style and to the acquisition and use of property. Constantly arriving strangers, both direct from Europe and from other parts of the colonies, kept the township from settling down into some kind of common cultural pattern composed of elements borrowed from all of its inhabitants, because the mix was continually changing. If community and family culture was not a mosaic, since individuals shared and communicated freely, it was also not a melting pot since no "American" style ever emerged.

One final way in which dispersion operated in German-

---

[6] Lemon, *Best Poor Man's Country*; see, for example, pp. 13-18.

town throughout the decades of its independence, was in the constant emergence of divergent measures of class and economic success. There were any number of distinctions, which tended to become more marked and stratified as the century progressed: all gradations from rich to poor became easier to identify; wealthy Philadelphians whose residence in Germantown was merely a second home were readily distinguishable from local citizens, however cultured, well educated, or prosperous; there were those who were self-employed or master craftsmen, and those who were laborers or apprentices; there were immigrants and long-term residents, owners, and renters; literate and illiterate; those who were community minded and those who never participated. As in the case of acculturation, however, the constant accretion of new individuals and the loss of old ones, prevented the social situation from hardening, and kept Germantown a place where a new individual arriving without a great load of traditional baggage on his back could seize the social and economic opportunities offered and make something of them. Since the European who arrived in the New World was most commonly this sort of individual, he was able to fit in almost immediately and required very little in the way of "Americanization."

Yet there is undoubtedly a significant variation between the American experience and European society, and the course of development in Germantown provides a clue to its nature. The Old World community could incorporate a great number of mobile individualists as a kind of leavening to an overall structure of tradition and stability, while New World communities were composed almost entirely of these rootless inhabitants. Many families did come to settle down and establish themselves in traditional ways, even coming to transmit political power from one generation to another and setting a kind of stamp on the life of the society. But the proportions were reversed from those of Europe—it was the stable families who were the exceptions and the transients who made up the base of the community. It made

Conclusion

little difference whether the constantly shifting bulk of the population were fourth-generation Americans or new arrivals just off the boat from England, Germany, or Scotland. They represented a diffuse element in the community, which could not be assimilated into an integrated whole, and they created a society whose primary orientation was to the principle of dispersion rather than centrality.

BIBLIOGRAPHICAL NOTE
ON THE SOURCES

THERE are many advantages to working on the history of a community that has always enjoyed a certain historical importance. Much of the basic spadework has been done; the archives have been scoured for references, letters and other private materials have been collected, tombstone inscriptions have been transcribed, and maps and drawings of the area have been assembled. In the case of Germantown, there is the additional bonus of an excellent bibliography of the printed sources and suggestions concerning the unprinted ones in Harry Tinkcom, Margaret Tinkcom, and Grant Simon, *Historic Germantown* (Philadelphia, 1955). While the older, antiquarian secondary works such as Namaan Keyser's *History of Old Germantown* (Germantown, 1907), Marion Dexter Learned's *Life of Francis Daniel Pastorius* (Philadelphia, 1908), or John MacFarlane's *History of Early Chestnut Hill* (Philadelphia, 1927) must be used with great caution and their interpretations generally re-evaluated, they often fill in gaps where original material is no longer available, or indicate directions that might otherwise have been overlooked. They also have copied or described most of the material from the early printed sources such as the *Pennsylvania Archives* and the *Pennsylvania Magazine of History and Biography* (*PMHB*): a check of several volumes of each of these works failed to turn up a single reference to Germantown, however remote, that was not already listed by one or another of the secondary sources.

Much Germantown material may also be found in the more general works on the Pennsylvania Germans or on Germans in colonial America. The *Proceedings and Addresses of the Pennsylvania German Society*, which began in 1890 (*Pa.Ger.*), contain an enormous amount of useful material, particularly in their early volumes (before 1900).

Their contributions fall into two categories: translations of colonial German books and documents such as Samuel Pennypacker's English version of *Christopher Dock's One Hundred Rules*, Pa.Ger. X (1899), and secondary works such as the "Settlement of Germantown, Pennsylvania and the Beginning of German Immigration to North America," *Pa.Ger.* IX (1898), by the same author. This article, which is actually book length, was part of a series entitled *Pennsylvania: The German Influence in its Settlement and Development; A Narrative and Critical History*, which ran in the Society's publications for many years. Most of the secondary works on Germantown history, or on German history in general, first appeared in this form, often, like Keyser, later being independently published as well. In these later editions, the works are usually exactly the same, except for pagination, so that there is no reason to consult both versions, and the only problem is a certain amount of bibliographical confusion.

The more general writings on various aspects of German-American history can also be extremely valuable for the local historian, if he keeps it firmly in his mind that he is *not* writing about the Pennsylvania Germans in general, but about Germantown in particular. Perhaps one of the causes of continual misinterpretation of colonial Germantown has been a transference of information about the Pennsylvania "Dutch," such as that which appears in James O. Knauss's *Social Conditions Among the Pennsylvania Germans in the Eighteenth Century* (Lancaster, 1922) from the rural setting in which it took place to the urban village of the German-township. On the other hand, primary sources like *Peter Kalm's Travels in North America, The English Version of 1770*, Adolph Benson, ed. (New York, 1937), secondary books like Frank Diffenderffer's "German Immigration into the Port of Philadelphia, 1700-1775," *Pa.Ger.* IX (1898) and X (1899), and Daniel Rupp's *Collection of Upwards of Thirty Thousand Names of German, Swiss, Dutch, French and Other Immigrants in Pennsylvania From 1727 to 1776*

(Philadelphia, 1876), are indispensable. The histories of the various German churches or sects usually have chapters on Germantown as the earliest of the German settlements and supply information not readily available elsewhere: examples are listed throughout the footnotes and include such voluminous works as the *Genealogical Record of the Schwenkfelder Families* (New York, 1923), which runs to over 1,000 closely printed pages; the old, but excellent Theodore Schmauk's *History of the Lutheran Church in Pennsylvania, 1638-1820* (Philadelphia, 1903); and Daniel Cassel's inaccurate, but necessary *History of the Mennonites* (Philadelphia, 1888).

Secondary information specifically related to Germantown, both published and in typescript form, is plentiful at the local Historical Society. There are a number of family scrapbooks, such as one for the Johnson family, and another for the Haineses, which supply interesting material, and a remarkably complete set of family genealogies for most of those families who played any major part in the history of the area. Among the most useful, containing additional material such as deeds, indentures, wills, and inventories, along with the more usual family trees and panegyric narrative, are unpublished histories of the Luckens family and the Leeds family (the latter is in the possession of Mrs. Harris Cooperman and not at the GHS), and published works on the Gorgas, Wistar, Livezey, Tyson, and Bringhurst families. Perhaps most vital of all is Charles Jenkins's amazing typewritten collection of "Newspaper Items Relating to Germantown: Historical and Genealogical" (1934), which includes all the articles from over eighteen Pennsylvania newspapers and journals, including translations of those that appeared in Saur's *Pennsylvanische Berichte*, that had anything to do with Germantown at all, whether by way of advertising or news item. It would have been impossible to have done the analysis of many areas in this book, particularly in the field of real estate, without the assistance of this magnificent collection. There are also in the possession of the Germantown Historical Society a number of pamphlets relating to the history of local institutions, such as S.A. Ziegenfuss, *A Brief and Succinct History of Saint Michael's Evangelical Lutheran Church of Germantown, Pennsylvania, 1730-1905* (Philadelphia, 1905), or the unprinted "History of the Union School" by Harold Gillingham, one of its former headmasters.

Other local libraries have occasional material of importance. The Friends' Free Library in Germantown owns one of twenty-five privately printed copies of Julius Sachse's very useful translation of *Letters Relating to the Settlement of Germantown in Pennsylvania, 1683-4* (1903). A meticulously handwritten, two-volume history of St. Michael's by one of its nineteenth-century ministers is stored in the Lutheran Seminary Library in Mount Airy: J. W. Richards, "A Historical Sketch of the Evangelical-Lutheran Church of St. Michael's, Germantown, Pa." (1845). This library also has an excellent collection of German materials, including the full series of the *Pa.Ger.*, and most of the important works relating to German churches, within and without Germantown.

The documentary materials required for quantitative histories have not been generally collected or used by local historians or historical societies. These fall into two major groups: governmental and institutional. The public papers include the tax lists, the court records, and the estate papers of individuals probated through the county. The tax lists for Germantown that still exist are generally found together with the lists for Philadelphia County in a variety of places. The earliest, that of 1693, is reprinted in the *PMHB*, 8 (1884); the Constables' Returns of 1734 are available in the *Publications of the Genealogical Society*, 1895; the 1798 Direct Tax is on microfilm of the National Archives and may be seen at the Federal Record Depository, in Germantown. A detailed tax list for Philadelphia County, 1767, may be found in manuscript in the rare book room of the Van Pelt Library, University of Pennsylvania. Others, covering a random number of years, from 1767 on, are stored in the original, in the Philadelphia City Archives. Those for the earlier years, such as the tax list of 1773, cover only the names, valuations, and assessments of the taxpayers; beginning around 1780, the ledgers are more complete, including descriptive material on real estate, luxury items, livestock, and the approximate worth of a man's occupation. From all the lists it is possible to derive nuptiality, since single men always paid a head tax. Further information may be obtained by consulting the clear and concise *Descriptive Inventory of the Archives of the City and County of Philadelphia* (Philadelphia, 1970) by John Daly, Archival Examiner.

This inventory also provides a guide to the Court Records that are available for the county. Many of these are still filed with the courts themselves and are not accessible to the researcher, but the archives department has on hand the Docket of the Quarter Sessions Court for petty criminal cases, road petitions and viewers' reports, appointments of township constables, highway supervisors, overseers of the poor, tavern and peddler's licenses, from 1753 to 1838; there are some gaps, most notably from 1780 to 1790. The Docket for the Court of Oyer and Terminer and General Gaol Delivery is also available for some of this period on microfilm. These records generally list the charge, the jurors, the witnesses, and the findings. The Records of the Court of Common Pleas are much less satisfactory. While the Appearance Docket exists beginning in 1762, it only gives the names of the parties and is almost impossible to use for historical purposes. Of more use are the records, also under the auspices of the Prothonetary of the Court of Common Pleas, of Partition of Property Deeds, 1740-1869 and Sheriffs' Deeds of Sale, 1736-1905. Miscellaneous items of interest, such as the County Commissioner's Minutes, may be found by reference to the *Inventory*.

One other essential body of public Germantown information, which is part of the county records, is the collection of wills, inventories, and accounts. They are unfortunately not in the archives, but are part of the current Department of Wills at Philadelphia City Hall. The originals are not readily available for researchers although it is occasionally possible to see some of those that are in better shape, at the arbitrary discretion of their custodian. The Will Books, which are more or less open to the public, are also in the basement of City Hall Annex and are complete and relatively accurate copies of the originals. Books A to X deal with eighteenth-century Philadelphia County and are arranged chronologically. This means that when searching for wills from a particular township, it is necessary to read each one to determine the home location of the testator, which, however, is almost always mentioned on the form at some point. There are no copies of the inventories and accounts, many of which are almost crumbled away, and even more of which are just missing, even when listed in the index. Unless one is very lucky and finds the guardian of the gate in a particularly good mood, it may well be impossible to see those that are still in existence.

The records of Germantown's government are involved with the period of charter before 1707. There are four documents, all available at the Historical Society of Pennsylvania, in the manuscript department. The first is the Grund und Lager Buch, a typescript of which is also on file at the Philadelphia Archives. This contains Pastorius's original plan for the division of the township. The second is the Raths-Buch der Germantownischen Gemeinde or General Court Book of the Corporation of Germantown, which includes the rules, regulations, and ordinances passed in regular session, along with the consideration of road petitions, election returns and, other housekeeping chores handled later on a county-wide basis by the County Commissioners and the Court of Quarter Sessions. This book is available only in the original manuscript copy, which is in very bad condition and almost unreadable in places. It is in German and Dutch. Third is the Records of the Court of Record of

Germantown, which no longer exists in the original. The HSP has a nineteenth-century copy, which appears to be complete, although in one case dealing with an accusation of fornication, the words "being naughty" are used, an undoubted bowdlerization of the original (2^d 3mo 1704). There is an abridgment of this material in the *Collections of the Historical Society of Pennsylvania*, I, pp. 243-258, which has frequently been taken by local historians as a translation of the Raths-Buch, which, in fact, it is not. It may be because a single page of the original Court of Record Book has been pasted into the manuscript of the Raths-Buch. Lastly there is the Gesetz Buch. Reference is made to the existence of this document in the Raths-Buch on 26^d 12mo 1701/2, and it is in the HSP among the Pastorius Papers, I. It is this material that is translated by Pennypacker in "Laws, Ordinances and Statutes . . . ," *Pa.Ger.* IX (1898). Excerpts also appear in Edward Hocker, *Germantown, 1683-1933* (Germantown, 1933), pp. 37-39, reported to come from "a manuscript by Francis Daniel Pastorius which came to light on the Pacific Coast in the later years of the nineteenth century."

The records of Germantown's eighteenth-century religious organization are more scattered. The Lutheran records have for the most part not been translated, but are stored in the safe of St. Michael's Lutheran Church in Germantown, under poor conditions, where they are rapidly moldering away. They include three volumes of the Church Register for vital events, continuous from 1746, with scattered baptisms before that date, Treasurer's Accounts and Minutes of the Elders beginning in 1766, and a miscellaneous collection of deeds, contributor lists, and the like. The Reformed Church on Market Square was merged with the Presbyterians in the mid-nineteenth century, and its records are in the Presbyterian Historical Society, Philadelphia. They are well kept, and, in addition to the Register for vital events, which begins in 1753, there are complete Minutes of the Consistory including the election of deacons and trustees and various miscellaneous lists of contributors. The Treasurer's Accounts are continuous from 1751. All of the above is qualified by the fact that the Church was disorganized and kept no books from 1780 to 1790. The complete set of records was translated, including notation of page numbers, by William J. Hinke, during the 1930s, and bound typescripts are filed with the originals. The Records of the Germantown Friends' Meeting are both scanty and scattered. There were no minutes kept before 1756, although the Meeting began in 1683, and no records of vital events, except for a few listed with the Abington Monthly Meeting Records, Swarthmore microfilm. This includes some nineteenth-century copies of family trees of the original settlers, a few dozen marriage certificates, and one short collection of burial records, 1747-1783, which give no information outside of the name of the deceased. The Minutes of the Men's Preparative Meeting of Germantown are in good condition, and all three volumes are stored in the Friends' Department of Records at 4th and Arch streets in Philadelphia. Since they frequently allude to the fact that "collecting the accounts of Births and Burials is too much neglected" (24^d 1mo 1759), it is probable that nothing more was ever recorded. There is a slim volume of Minutes of the Women's Preparative Meeting of Germantown, beginning in 1794. There are two Account Books of the Germantown Meeting. The first goes from 1731 to 1738, including lists of contributors during that period and forming almost the only information on the membership; it is in the collection of the Genealogical Society at HSP. The other begins in 1738, continues into the nineteenth century, and is at the Friends' Department of Records.

The records of the other institutions are also scattered. Those of the Upper Burying Ground have been printed in the *PMHB*, 8 (1884) and 9 (1885), and those of the Hood Cemetery and the Concord School may also be seen at the HSP. The original Minute Book of the Union School is at Germantown Academy at Fort Washington, Pennsylvania.

No trace was found of the Mennonite or Brethren records—no one at those churches had any idea of their location, and it seems that they probably have been lost or disappeared into private collections of papers outside of the area. There are also many miscellaneous documents and manuscripts relating to Germantown history which are noted and located in the footnotes. One might refer once again to the collection of 85 Deeds in Brief pertaining to Germantown properties, which are in the files of the Philadelphia Historical Commission, Philadelphia City Hall Annex.

As far as the ideological and theoretical bases of this paper are concerned, sources are completely covered in the footnotes. *An Introduction to English Historical Demography*, E. A. Wrigley, ed. (London, 1966) and *Population in History: Essays in Historical Demography*, D. V. Glass and D.E.C. Eversley, eds. (London, 1965), might be mentioned again as essential starting points for general concepts and methodology. For general reading on urbanology, the bibliography in Louis Mumford, *The City in History* (New York, 1961), is the best place to begin. Excellent bibliographies for the materials of sociological history appear in Philip Greven, Jr., *Four Generations* (Ithaca, N.Y., 1970) and Kenneth Lockridge, *A New England Town, The First Hundred Years* (New York, 1970). These only go to point up how little work has been done outside the New England area and how important it is that others follow up with studies of towns in other regions. As I hope I have proved, a lack of well-kept town records may make the work difficult but not impossible or without value to a further understanding of the nature of colonial community life.

Library of Congress Cataloging in Publication Data

Wolf, Stephanie Grauman.
  Urban village.

  Bibliography: p.
  Includes index.
    1. Germantown, Pa.—Social conditions.   2. Family—
Pennsylvania—Germantown.   3. Urbanization—Penn-
sylvania—Germantown.   4. Community organization.
I. Title.
HN80.G46W6   301.36′1′0974811   76-3025
  ISBN 0-691-04632-8